Shakespeare & the Uses of Comedy

J.A. Bryant, Jr.

Shakespeare & the Uses of Comedy

THE UNIVERSITY PRESS OF KENTUCKY

Copyright © 1986 by The University Press of Kentucky

Scholarly publisher for the Commonwealth,
serving Bellarmine College, Berea College, Centre
College of Kentucky, Eastern Kentucky University,
The Filson Club, Georgetown College, Kentucky
Historical Society, Kentucky State University,
Morehead State University, Murray State University,
Northern Kentucky University, Transylvania University,
University of Kentucky, University of Louisville,
and Western Kentucky University.

Editorial and Sales Offices: Lexington, Kentucky 40506-0024

Library of Congress Cataloging-in-Publication Data

Bryant, J. A. (Joseph Allen), 1919-

Shakespeare and the uses of comedy.

Bibliography; p.
Includes index.
1. Shakespeare, William, 1564-1616—Comedies.
I. Title.
PR2981.B75   1987   822.3'3   86-7770
ISBN 0-8131-1595-7

For Allen, Virginia,
and Garnett

Contents

Acknowledgments

It is a pleasure to acknowledge some of the support I have received during the course of this study. I am grateful first of all to the University of Kentucky for leaves of absence and to the staff of its Margaret I. King Library for generous assistance more times than they will remember. I am grateful, too, for the encouragement and support of my colleagues, especially John Clubbe, John Cawelti, Jerome Meckier, Armando Prats, and Robert Hemenway. I want also to thank George Core for both support and forbearance over the years and for permission to reprint substantial portions of my essay entitled *"The Merchant of Venice* and the Common Flaw," which appeared in the *Sewanee Review*, 81 (Summer 1973), and was copyrighted by the University of the South in that same year. Substantial portions of chapter 8 are reprinted by permission of the Modern Language Association of America from my article "Falstaff and the Renewal of Windsor," which appeared in *PMLA*, 89 (1974). The Houghton Mifflin Company has graciously given me permission to take quotations from *The Riverside Shakespeare*, ed. G. Blakemore Evans (1974).

1

Shakespeare's Exploration of the Human Comedy

The subject of this book is Shakespeare's exploration of the human situation through the mode of dramatic comedy. It is a book with many predecessors and almost as many creditors, most of whom will be acknowledged as their contributions appear. Several comprehensive works have proved valuable throughout, however, and deserve to be acknowledged at the outset. These include the volumes of E.K. Chambers on Shakespeare and the Elizabethan dramatists, still vastly useful after more than half a century, the source studies of Geoffrey Bullough, Muriel C. Bradbrook's *The Growth and Structure of Elizabethan Comedy*, Leo Salingar's *Shakespeare and the Traditions of Comedy*, L.C. Knights's *Explorations*, Francis Fergusson's *The Idea of a Theater*, and the books and essays of Northrop Frye. Yet even among such well-established contributions as these, presuppositions about the nature of comedy vary, and that variation increases rapidly as one goes farther afield. For this reason it may be wise to set down at the beginning some of the presuppositions that have determined the shape and direction of the present undertaking, especially those having to do with the nature of comedy and poetry.

This book proceeds on two major assumptions: first, that most art is a manifestation of humanity's perennial quest for meaning and therefore constitutes an exploration of the known world or some aspect of it; second, that comedy is at once the primal and the most comprehensive form of literary art. As critics from Aristotle's time to the present have attested, comedy as we know it in the West took its being either directly or indirectly from some of the primitive forms of religion, particularly Greek religion, which gave an intelligible shape to humankind's perception of the recurring process of birth, maturation, death, and renewal.[1] Our forms of tragedy ultimately derive from this same indeterminate matrix, as does the dithyramb; but all the forms we now call comic retain something of the recognizable sweep of their ancient source in that they too celebrate the renewal of the race in its perpetual displacement of the decadent and dying with a vigorous if callow youth.

Shakespeare, of course, began his work with the literary examples that were immediately at hand—a couple of Roman comedies in a school textbook, some fragments of Greek romance transmitted through Gower, a handful of prose tales—but being the kind of artist he was, from the beginning he used his materials as devices for exploration rather than as mere models or molds, supplying all of them, of whatever derivation, with freshly observed characters and events and letting matter and form participate, as it were, in a mutual reshaping process. This is why his plays, even the earliest ones, are unlike any produced by his contemporaries. He never lost sight of the human situation—or, more likely, he never thought for long to look at anything else. Thus his comedies exhibit a series of transformations of the conventional or stereotyped views of almost all the basic human relationships—between married people, between parents and children, between lovers, siblings, friends, enemies, and strangers. The comedies are also revitalizations of those relationships; for as readers and viewers for almost four hundred years have testified, Shakespeare's plays continue to be as immediately convincing as they are illuminating. Moreover, they continue to stand as extensions of reality as well as representations of it, and consequently they invite exploration in their own right. Alexander Pope wrote that to study Homer is to study nature. He might with equal justice have written the same of Shakespeare.

The present study consists of chapters on each of the comedies through *Twelfth Night* (ten in all), one chapter dealing with the so-called dark comedies, one on the last plays, and one each on *Troilus and Cressida* and *The Tempest* as representatives of those two special groups. All seventeen of these plays, however, with the possible exception of *Pericles*, which has been left out of consideration, can with justice be called comedies; for at or near the center of each of them is the action that has distinguished comedy since the Renaissance, the mating game of the young, which from Shakespeare's time to ours has played a determining role in the perpetuation of the human race. This action has long served as the main trunk of our social tree, and all those special branches that from time to time have given warmth, character, and enhanced meaning to individual mating actions—the discovery of love, the recognition of the role of sacrifice in human intercourse, the acceptance of the inevitability of death, and the generation of charity—are best thought of as subsidiary actions. In Shakespeare, of course, these subsidiary actions often turn out to be more arresting than the central one; but the main trunk is always there and, except in two of the comedies, always dominant at the end, where the assurance of social continuity is expected to justify any licentiousness that has developed in the course of the so-called comic business.

Taking the comedies in at least approximate chronological order may tempt one to generalize about what some have called Shakespeare's philosophy, but prudence demands a measure of caution in this regard. Shakespeare was not a philosopher, and there is no evidence that he ever thought systematically about the nature of human beings, society, or the cosmos. It is more likely that writing was the means by which he did most of his thinking, letting his reflections take the form of dramatic fictions which ostensibly did nothing more than present in lively fashion the commonplaces beloved of those minds he was expected to address. Today we see that many of those fictions, seemingly innocent enough when proffered as entertainment, embodied ideas which, had they been recognizable at the time, might have brought him ridicule, censure, or worse; and sometimes, as in his now widely recognized anticipations of the work of Freud and Jung, he achieved insights which would not be articulated fully until the present century. One can only wonder how fully he himself grasped the implications of what he had set down on paper, apparently with great casualness—and wonder, too, how much remains that we ourselves do not yet fully see.

An older historical scholarship made much of the conformity of Shakespeare's thinking with conventional notions of order, citing sometimes such passages as Ulysses' speech in the third scene of *Troilus and Cressida*; but to judge by the general import of that play and the evidence of others, including *King Lear* and *The Tempest*, Shakespeare might have found at least interesting, if not congenial, Henri Bergson's notions of being as duration rather than as static order and of organic life in all its forms as the product of pluridimensional creative evolution,[2] to say nothing of Alfred North Whitehead's vision of a universe that is one, continuous, and characterized by process.[3] He might also have recognized a fair characterization of his own accomplishment in Susanne Langer's description of comedy as "the pure sense of life . . . developed in countless different ways . . . always new, infinitely complex, therefore infinitely variable in its possible expressions"; and he would certainly have understood her characterization of the essential structure of comedy as "the basic biological pattern which all living things share, the fund of conditioned and conditioning organic processes that produces the life rhythm."[4] What the view of Shakespeare the sixteenth-century man was about any of these matters we can most likely never know. What is important is that he wrote plays which repeatedly encourage us to see life as a process, infinitely variable (to borrow Langer's phrase) but marked by recurrences which in their rough regularity constitute a rhythm, and that somewhere early in his career he must have come to see comedy as the exploration of that rhythm by the creation of analogous representations of it in the relatively imprecise medium of language.

This is not to suggest that Shakespeare's conscious motive

when he sat down to write a comedy was exploration. Undoubtedly his conscious motive was to support himself and his growing family at Stratford, and he probably considered himself lucky to be able to turn out salable manuscripts competitive with those being produced by the talented young men around him, most of whom had had the advantage of university training. If he had been asked by some impertinent reporter—assuming the unlikely possibility that such a thing could have existed at the time—about his reasons for writing, as legend has it William Faulkner was once asked, he surely would have given young Faulkner's answer—namely, to make money. Being human, Shakespeare must have coveted the approval of his colleagues in the theater, but probably of no one else. Certainly neither he nor they plied their faintly disreputable trade in hope of fame or preferment. For most of them, working in the theater was a means of survival. For Shakespeare, however, survival cannot have been absolutely everything, though it is unlikely he could have seen with any clarity something that we, four hundred years later, consider obvious: that his mind and talent were of that rare order which makes the adjective *creative* more than a metaphorical compliment. Even at the beginning of his career (or what appears to us to have been the beginning), the composition of plays was for Shakespeare a species of *making*—poetry in its original and noblest sense, one of those activities wherein the finite human mind may seek to lay hold on reality. It involved an examination of effective actuality, the world about him in space and time; an examination of comparable parts of the vast realm of possibility, whether generated by his own imagination or that of others; and his participation in the resultant new implementation and redirection of process.

At the outset he could not have seen that the world he was creating in his comedies was uniquely "Shakespearean" and that it was real—alive, we commonly say today—in ways that the dramatic worlds of his contemporaries were not. At the end, one suspects, he saw the truth well enough to have understood Matthew Arnold's phrases about him: "Self-schooled, self-scanned, self-honored, self-secure." Even in his later years, however, the native humility that is said to have been Shakespeare's during his career in London probably would have prevented comprehension of the astonishing laurel that Arnold accorded him early in that poem with the phrase, "outtopping knowledge." This placed him above all his contemporaries, perhaps above all of Arnold's contemporaries as well, and set him, as Arnold clearly knew, in a pantheon with the likes of Homer, Dante, and perhaps Goethe. We sometimes call this bardolatry, yet it is that rare transcendence of common knowledge, our own as well as his—the lore, the systems, and the symbols—that makes Shakespeare perennially fascinating; and it characterizes to some degree everything he wrote, the earliest comedies as well as the mature histories and the most impressive of his tragedies. He began with what he and all his contemporaries knew, or could easily discover for themselves, and expanded that fund of knowledge into visions of authenticity that we are still unable to assess completely.

It should be clear by now that several views of comedy are not relevant to a study of this kind. Three of these should be mentioned here briefly, if only to sharpen the focus on what we are supposed to be looking at. One of the most prevalent, at least outside academic circles, is the view that the primary function of comedy is to produce laughter. No one, of course, denies that laughter does accompany most comedy; for laughter, if Bergson is right, is the natural response to any rigidity that impedes or presumes to impede the life process which true comedy celebrates.[5] That is, we laugh at the absurdity of the unassimilable person or element when it appears, and we laugh (presumably with relief) when it is defeated or discredited. Being creatures of habit, however, we laugh also at fossil rigidities that have little or no bearing on the comic action at hand—the so-called comic conventions, stereotypes, pre-established signals for indulging in the relaxation that laughter can produce. Shakespeare wrote a modicum of this basically unfunny kind of laughter-producing business into his early plays; but his mature practice suggests that he came to think less of it, and his comment in *Hamlet* on actors who would introduce improvised business of their own is well known. In any case, producing laughter is at best an incidental aspect of the serious comic writer's activity.

A distantly related view holds that comedy is a genre, the members of which are identifiable by the possession of a sufficient number of discrete details, usually conventions of plot, character, and language, that custom has established as its distinguishing characteristics. Persons holding this view tend to think of comedy as a distinct substance, or concatenation of substances, very different from simple history and at the opposite pole from tragedy; thus the study of individual comedies frequently becomes, with them, a series of exercises in literary taxonomy. Thinking of this sort is usually at work whenever we find such characters as Launcelot Gobbo, Shylock, Falstaff, or even Iago being interpreted primarily according to their presumed derivation from some established set of conventions, such as those of the *commedia dell'arte*, the folk play, or Roman comedy. Thinking of this sort has prevailed when we hear that the drunken porter was placed in *Macbeth* for comic relief or that *Romeo and Juliet* is essentially a comedy with a tragic ending. In the latter two examples the notion of substance has been applied to tragedy, which many Elizabethans, following medieval precedent, defined as any work that concludes in death, usually the untimely death of a person in high place and more often than not a death in some degree unwarranted. The notion of substance can become downright mischievous whenever the genre-minded critic is working with something like *Troilus and Cressida* (witness editors' disagreement about the proper classification for that play), which has most of the details one associates with comedy but which ends in frustration or death for several of the principals. In recent decades it has forced admirers of Shakespeare's last comedies to invent new classifications altogether, the most recent being that of tragicomedy, which requires us to assume, after the manner of John Fletcher, that the work at hand involves a mixture of substances. One should also note that the middle comedies have long been subjected to similar desperate reclassifications—the terms "dark comedies" and "problem comedies" are still fairly common—and some critics dealing with these plays have invoked special criteria by which to judge and evaluate them. The view adopted in this study is that all these plays, middle and late, are best seen simply as explorations of human actions, some of them perhaps new to drama but all containing intimations of the same universal rhythm that characterizes those other literary productions we unhesitatingly call comedy.

A third view of comedy not strictly relevant to this study is one which, like the foregoing, affects our thinking about all forms of drama. This view, widely held nowadays, maintains that a play is not fully realized until it is acted. A clear statement of this belief appears on the first page of J.L. Styan's influential *The Dramatic Experience: A Guide to the Reading of Plays:*

A play is not like a novel or a poem. This is a truism that need[s] to be repeated. Because the playwright must put his ideas for his play into so many words on paper, it is all too easy to read them as if they work like those in other books. A composer of music writes a notation for the sounds in his mind, but the fullness of the music is heard only in performance; so it is with the drama. Once one is in the habit of reading a play as if it were, say, a story that is all dialogue, or a poem that is broken up for speaking, then habits of thinking, useful for discussing a novel or a poem, can be applied wrongly to drama.[6]

To begin with, Styan's analogy shows an unfortunate misunderstanding of music, or at least of music comparable in stature to Shakespeare's plays; most musicians know that the "fullness" of that kind of music is at best only approximated in performance. The ultimate fullness, one imagines, occurs in the mind of the composer and begins to suffer reduction the minute it is limited to a set of symbols on paper. Any performance of those symbols can only reduce the music further. Admittedly, a good performance will realize more than most nonprofessionals are likely to get otherwise, and that is one justification for the performance of a Mozart quartet or a Beethovan sonata. A dozen performances, all different but all legitimately derived from the score, can of course give us much more. Nevertheless, the closest approach to the fullness of the music that the composer conceived will most likely occur in the quiet study of a trained and perceptive reader who may hear in his or her mind something like the complex, multivalent composition that a Mozart or a Beethoven was hearing as he first set it down.

In reading Shakespeare's plays we are dealing with the work of a genius who, according to Ben Jonson, was praised by his actors for never blotting a line. Even allowing for exaggeration, that report should tell us that Shakespeare—lie Mozart, who is said to have written in the same way—was not merely turning out scripts for a theatrical performance. The theater is undoubtedly the best place to realize the fullness of a great many plays. It can be an excellent place to realize some of the fullness of any play, including Shakespeare's, given directors and actors who are trained, intelligent, and talented readers; but it is by no means the best place to exhaust the meaning of a play that can legitimately be called a dramatic poem. The full experience of any poetry worth remembering will be solitary, not communal. So it is with the dramatic poetry of Shakespeare, regardless of the fact that his dramatic poems came to the world first as theatrical performances. We hear behind Hamlet's "And let those that play your clowns speak no more than is set down for them" (III.ii.38-40)[7] an aesthetically sensitive author's pained awareness of what it means to hand over an intricately wrought contrivance to minds that may only partially comprehend it, and, in any case, may in the heat of a performance be only too ready to sacrifice complexity of insight for the immediate effects that gesture and a skilled voice can achieve.

This is not to denigrate the many contributions that have resulted from two decades of scholarly focus on the Shakespearean play in a theatrical situation. We who tend to be closet readers are well served by reminders that the circumstances of Shakespeare's plays, no less than those of the plays of his contemporaries, included a company of trained actors, a sophisticated stage, and a receptive audience. Nevertheless, the present study proceeds on an equally valid premise that Shakespeare differed from most of his contemporaries in that the plays he wrote were private accomplishments as well as public ones. That is, the compositions he produced for his fellow actors were inevitably dramatic poems as well as scripts for theatrical performance. Today they continue to exist in both of these modes; they function in both, and they manifest their superiority in both. Their greatness, however, lies where the greatness of literary art has always lain: in the efficacy of the artist's exploratory assault upon reality and in the images of coherence, however tenuous these may be, that the artist discovers in the composition of his or her poem, story, or play. Admittedly, the artist's productions are symbols in words, and words—more than the matter of any other medium—are uncertain and unstable. No one can have known that better than Shakespeare, or known better than he that what he produced was at best a set of dreams. Yet Shakespeare's dreams are persuasive things and make us one with Caliban, who whispers to the two uncomprehending fools: "The clouds methought would open and show riches / Ready to drop upon me, that, when I waked, / I cried to dream again" (III.ii.141-43). The path to full enjoyment of such riches as these is a long one of patient scrutiny and sustained attention; and our objective at the end is to see the text standing free of serial bondage, revealed once more as the whole which its author, who had had the genius to conceive it whole, *sub specie aeternitatis*, could set down without blot or correction.

The decision to focus on comedy in this study is a matter of simple preference and perhaps needs no explanation. One consideration that influenced it, however, was a recognition of the remarkable way in which Shakespeare in all his comedies managed to express a concern about the unequal treatment of the sexes throughout most of historical time. In that concern he was almost without peer in his own day and, for that matter, with the possible exception of Euripides, almost without peer in the long course of Western literature.[8] Shakespeare's concern manifested itself early in his public career and mounted steadily as his career advanced. The signs of it are clear even in the adaptation of Plautus that he shaped into *The Comedy of Errors*, and it took a major leap forward with the denouement of *Love's Labor's Lost*. Thereafter, in such plays as *A Midsummer Night's Dream, The Taming of the Shrew,* and, most notably, *Much Ado about Nothing,* Shakespeare portrayed with increasing harshness the injustice done to women in fashionable society. Moreover, in his numerous presentations of the woman disguised as a male (*The Two Gentlemen of Verona, The Merchant of Venice, As You Like It, Twelfth Night,* and *Cymbeline*) sometimes accounted for as a happy accident of a theater with only boys in it to play the women's parts, he developed concomitantly an androgynous figure, unique in Elizabethan literature, that was not appreciated until our present century. In the three problem plays, *Troilus and Cressida, All's Well That Ends Well,* and *Measure for Measure,* the failure of men to understand and appreciate women's potential became a subject of Shakespeare's major concern; and by the time he reached what was to be his last phase, he was writing plays that required for their full understanding a recognition of woman as being on equal terms with man.

Another consideration in choosing comedy as a subject was the tendency, still noticeable in certain quarters, to think of comedy as a form as somehow less noble and certainly less significant than tragedy. It is true that from as far back as we have any record comedy has stood in contrast to tragedy as one of the two principal modes of dramatic poetry; and we have Plato's word for it (in the *Symposium*) that Socrates once argued that these two contrasted modes are products of a single impulse. Nevertheless, Aristotle's treatise on tragedy survived; his treatise on comedy did not. Consequently the critical tradition has found it easy to do what it might have done in any case: treat comedy as an inferior mode. The assumption behind this study, however, is that, like woman and man, comedy and tragedy are complementary aspects of a single order of being. Except for their respective decadent forms, melodrama and farce, both dramatic modes result from a poet's confrontation with the order of the universe and differ principally in the point of view the poet chooses to give us. In tragedy the poet focuses on a protagonist's recognition of his or her own expendability in the eternality of process and tempts audiences to see themselves as perishable entities in the same perpetual flux. (One hopes that Aristotle was right about the catharsis that follows their initial pity and terrifying enlightenment.) In comedy, by contrast, the poet concentrates on a happier protagonist's temporarily fortunate participation in the same process and invites us to share in the joy of his or her success. Although the threat of inevitable death remains, comedy normally does not dwell on that, but rather invites our ridicule of any person or thing that has attempted to resist the flow, including those members of the community—parents, magistrates, rival suitors, spiritual mentors—who because of age, position, wealth, or even virtue have claimed immunity to time's ravages.

Yet there is an irony in such laughter which audiences have not always perceived. Shakespeare reminds us, at least once in every comedy and sometimes even explicitly, that golden lads and girls are no more immune to process than are their elders. Thus, in submitting to the charm of Shakespeare's comedies we inescapably find ourselves looking forward subconsciously to the dissolution that in the tragedies we thought we had confronted but, after the death of the protagonist, managed to escape. The world of Shakespeare's tragedies is, after all, at several removes from our own. It is like ours, certainly, but greater and more terrible; and ultimately it is different. The world of his comedies, however, even when set on a seacoast in Bohemia or in the middle of the sea, is always our own. We rejoice in its survival, as we rejoice in the discomfiture of its challengers; but in the end we see that the world itself also must dissolve—towers, palaces, the great globe and all the beautiful people who inherit it—and leave not a rack behind. This final consequence of Shakespeare's confrontation with reality through comedy, hard as it may seem initially, communicates a comfortable resignation even as it unsettles, and tempts the viewer or reader to look again—or as Caliban puts it, to dream again. Thus the present study is simply another look at the perennially mysterious world of comedy that

Shakespeare created, seemingly with the back of his hand, when his audiences probably had asked no more than that he amuse them for the space of a sunny afternoon. One suspects that even for Shakespeare, backward glances, if he ever indulged in them, produced more than a few surprises.

2

The Comedy of Errors

Most students of *The Comedy of Errors* agree in calling the play an early one—some say Shakespeare's earliest play, or at least his earliest comedy. Clearly the basic plot comes from Plautus's *Menaechmi*, a play that Shakespeare may well have read not long before, at the Stratford Grammar School; and to this he added a frame story from the popular tale of Apollonius of Tyre. Older criticism of the play, however, often soured on the fact that Shakespeare, whether young or not, developed it mainly from farce and kept it farcical. Schlegel, more generous than most, called it "the best of all possible *Menaechmi*."[1] Coleridge pronounced it "remarkable as being the only specimen of *poetical farce* in our language" but declined nevertheless to call the play a comedy and observed that "farce dares add the two Dromios."[2] Hazlitt simply disliked it.[3] Even those modern critics who have inclined to be approving have praised "romantic" elements that Shakespeare either added or developed from hints that he discovered in Plautus. This was the burden of H.B. Charlton's criticism[4] and more recently that of Harold Brooks;[5] and John Arthos in an engaging essay has written of the additions (comments on hierarchy, humanity, providential care, and a sense of the mysterious) by which Shakespeare highlighted what Arthos considers to be the essentially romantic spirit of Plautus's achievement.[6]

On the other side of the same coin, the most notable attempt to demonstrate the importance of farcical elements in *The Comedy of Errors* has been that of Bertrand Evans, who, considering laughter to be the aim of comedy, found the excellence of this play to consist in its "creation, maintenance, and exploitation of the gaps that separate the participants' awareness and ours."[7] Thus in Evans's exposition of *The Comedy of Errors* such things as the multiplication of crossed purposes and doubled Dromios become the cardinal virtues of a simple but remarkable play. Harry Levin's brief introduction to the Signet edition of the play is a much more comprehensive account of the variety of things that can interest a reader of Shakespeare's earliest comedy; nevertheless, it repeats Coleridge's quip about farce daring to add the two Dromios and thereby adds additional weight to an unwary reader's tendency to assume that Shakespeare by such strategies was seeking to enhance a "knockabout farce."[8]

We really do not know how Shakespeare intended his play to be received (if indeed he ever thought about the matter); but fairness, to say nothing of our own pleasure, would seem to require that we avoid limiting our responses to it. We can best regard the business of doubling the Dromios, as more than one commentator has suggested, as the necessary consequence of adding to the story the part of the *Amphitruo* plot that appears in Act III, scene i. In Plautus's version, as in the numerous treatments that have come out since Plautus's time, something like the following takes place: Jupiter and Mercury disguise themselves respectively as Amphitryon and his servant Sosia and shut master and servant out of their own house; subsequently Jupiter invades Amphitryon's bed to sire Hercules on Amphitryon's wife Alcmene. The real question to ask, therefore, is not why Shakespeare doubled the Dromios but why he added this particular device from the *Amphitruo*, especially since he was not free, Elizabethan taste in marital comedy being what it was, to pursue the matter to its traditional adulterous length.[9] One also needs to ask why Shakespeare may have wanted to add a frame plot involving a near death for the father of the twins. Answering either question involves a reference to the traditional pattern and function of comedy, both of which require the displacement of the *senex* or parent, and a general recognition of the lovers as a pair whose mating can restore the stability of the social order.

The special problems here are, first, that the old man is not obstinate. (Egeon would certainly encourage the marriage of his sons if he could only find them) and, second, that the lovers cannot really come together until the doubleness of the males reveals itself to permit their accommodation to the two females—the first of these a woman already married, who must provide the hope of succession in Ephesus; and the second, a younger sister who needs to be mated to the still unrecognized twin from Syracuse and moved westward to that city to insure stability there also. The impediment to social readjustment in *The Comedy of Errors* is thus a set of accidental circumstances, or Chance if one prefers, rather than a conscious desire on the part of someone to frustrate the designs of nature and the needs of society. Evans has rightly called *The Comedy of Errors* a play without a "practiser," that is, a play without someone for better or for worse to manipulate the action.[10] What makes this play go remains a mystery to the end; and but for the fact that several of the principals recognize that and refuse to believe that the events are all a matter of mere chance, one might be tempted to give up and declare the whole thing farce. Part of the appeal of the play, however, lies in its power to tempt us to believe that something unseen and unnamed has here made all things work together for good.

Any farce will permit such a view of things, but most farces do not suggest it and none ever requires it. For example, when Plautus's twin Menaechmi see strange happenings in Epidamnus, they think madness and send for a doctor. In Shakespeare's version, their counterparts at first think of witchcraft. Thus Dromio of Syracuse reports that when Nell, the fat kitchen wench, demonstrated intimate knowledge of his birthmark, mole, and wart, "I, amaz'd, ran from her as a witch" (III.ii.144); and his master observes:

> There's none but witches do inhabit here,
> And therefore 'tis high time that I were hence.
> She that doth call me husband, even my soul
> Doth for a wife abhor. But her fair sister,
> Possess'd with such a gentle sovereign grace,
> Of such enchanting presence and discourse.
> Hath almost made me traitor to myself;

But, lest myself be guilty to self-wrong,
I'll stop mine ears against the mermaid's song.
[III.ii.156-64]

Adriana and the Courtezan suspect madness in Antipholus, of course, but it is a conjurer they go after rather than a physician; and this like the other references to demons and witches we might dismiss as accidental differences between the aberrations of a pagan world and those of a Christian one, were it not for things that we in our special awareness see and the characters in the play do not.

An excellent example comes in the first act when a friendly merchant of Ephesus returns to Antipholus of Syracuse the thousand marks that he had given the merchant for safekeeping and Antipholus immediately hands the sum to Dromio to "bear it to the Centaur, where we host" (I.ii.9). Such a free and easy handling of so large an amount is characteristic of the youthful traveler certainly, but one thousand marks happens to be precisely the amount for want of which Antipholus's father, Egeon, at that moment stands condemned to die before the sun sets. Moreover, the merchant tells Antipholus that a fellow Syracusan has been arrested in Ephesus that very day and will die if he cannot find money to pay the forfeit; but Antipholus is not concerned about life and death, even of a fellow Syracusan; and besides, he has no reason to think his father anywhere but safe at home. He is the only traveler in his mind's eye, and his own needs are the only needs that concern him:

I to the world am like a drop of water,
That in the ocean seeks another drop,
Who, falling there to find his fellow forth
(Unseen, inquisitive), confounds himself.
So I, to find a mother and a brother,
In quest of them (unhappy), ah, lose myself.
[I.ii.35-40]

We, however, see the callous Antipholus as standing side by side with brother Death, who seems almost certain to lay claim to his father by day's end regardless of whom or what else the young man may find in Ephesus. The irony of his situation is that a simple act of charity, a single gesture of selfless concern for the fellow citizen that the Syracusan merchant has told him of (I.ii.3-7), would bring him to the rescue of his parent; but Antipholus has not yet grown to the point of selfless charity, and he will not even begin to do so until the general epiphany that comes at the end of the play. If we think further along this line, we can see the irony compounding itself: had Antipholus indeed moved in charity and therefore discovered the presence of his father, he might also have forestalled that epiphany in Act V, where not just two people are reunited and made happy, but everybody. Fate, fortune, chance, or providence—who can say? The ultimate mover of this complex Shakespearean machine remains a mystery, as it should remain; but mover there must be. Appropriately, it is the Abbess who, with a metahphor that would have been startling for a virgin religious but that is nevertheless quite suitable for the religious who has also known motherhood, invites all the participants and all the audience to see a meaningful pattern in the day's events:

> Thirty-three years have I but gone in travail
> Of you, my sons, and till this present hour
> My heavy burthen [ne'er] delivered.
> The Duke, my husband, and my children both,
> And you the calendars of their nativity,
> Go to a gossips' feast, and go with me—
> After so long grief, such nativity!
>
> [V.i.401-07]

Thus Shakespeare has found even in the shape, movement, and accidents of a "knockabout farce" at least a suggestion of an orderly and purposeful universe. It is no wonder that in his exploration of Plautus's *Menaechmi* he also found a few real people there.

To begin with, behind the mask of the shrewish wife of Menaechmus I he found Adriana, still a devoted wife, understandably impatient with things that upset the household routine but eager to go to almost any length to please her spouse, old enough to be capable of jealousy and conceivably of shrewishness too but not yet confirmed in either. As Shake-speare presents her, she is still able to recall fondly the close-ness she once enjoyed with her husband and to plead with him that it not be allowed to end altogether:

> The time was once, when thou unurg'd wouldst vow
> That never words were music to thine ear.
> That never object pleasing in thine eye,
> That never touch well welcome to thy hand,
> That never meat sweet-savor'd in thy taste,
> Unless I spake, or look'd, or touch'd, or carv'd to thee.
> How comes it now, my husband, O, how comes it,
> That thou art then estranged from thyself?
> Thyself I call it, being strange to me,
> That, undividable incorporate,
> Am better than thy dear self's better part.
> Ah, do not tear away thyself from me;
> For know, my love, as easy mayst thou fall
> A drop of water in the breaking gulf,
> And take unmingled thence that drop again,
> Without addition or diminishing,
> As take from me thyself and not me too.
>   [II.ii.113-29]

One should note here Adriana's use of the waterdrop metaphor that Antipholus of Syracuse had used only moments before—and note, too, the ethical superiority of her version of it. One can only wonder whether Antipholus himself takes note of it, for at this point he is meeting Adriana for the first time and stands dumbfounded at her importunateness:

> Come, I will fasten on this sleeve of thine:
> Thou art an elm, my husband, I a vine,
> Whose weakness, married to thy [stronger] state,
> Makes me with thy strength to communicate:
> If aught possess thee from me, it is dross,
> Usurping ivy, brier, or idle moss,
> Who, all for want of pruning, with intrusion
> Infect thy sap, and live on thy confusion.
>   [II.ii.173-80]

When Antipholus does not disabuse her, she proceeds with him to the upper room, joyous in the belief that her husband is once more beside her:

> Come, come, no longer will I be a fool,
> To put the finger in the eye and weep,
> Whilst man and master laughs my woes to scorn.
> Come, sir, to dinner. Dromio, keep the gate.
> Husband, I'll dine above with you to-day,
> And shrive you of a thousand idle pranks.
>
> [II.ii.203-8]

Later, when her sister Luciana dutifully reports what she innocently takes to have been a husband's attempt at infidelity in his own house, Adriana, hurt and angered, delivers a condemnation that dissolves midway in her more potent love for the man:

> *Adr.* My tongue, though not my heart, shall have his will.
> He is deformed, crooked, old, and sere,
> Ill-fac'd, worse bodied, shapeless every where;
> Vicious, ungentle, foolish, blunt, unkind,
> Stigmatical in making, worse in mind.
> *Luc.* Who would be jealous then of such a one?
> No evil lost is wail'd when it is gone.
> *Adr.* Ah, but I think him better than I say,
> And yet would herein others' eyes were worse:
> Far from her nest the lapwing cries away;
> My heart prays for him, though my tongue do curse.
>
> [IV.ii.18-28]

It is this generous aspect of Adriana's character, displayed throughout the whole course of the play, that weakens our inclination to see her as an anglicized version of Plautus's shrew and gives credence to Luciana's defense of her when the Abbess scolds in Act V. "She never reprehended him but mildly," says Luciana, "When he demean'd himself rough, rude, and wildly" (V.i.87-88); and we believe her.

Rough, rude, and wild though he may be, Antipholus of Ephesus is himself not without redeeming aspects. He has affection for his wife, he does promise her a chain in order to demonstrate that affection, and he conscientiously tries to make good on that promise. Moreover, it really is a business matter that makes him late on the fateful day of the play, not another woman, as Adriana fears. Thus when his attempt at husbandly compliance is frustrated by the locked door—and that, to his further embarrassment, in full view of the merchant, Balthazar—he impetuously decides to dine (for the first time, he protests) with a pretty, witty, and wild young thing of the streets. Here we find our impulse to laughter diminished by a sense of regret that an error of which both are innocent has caused the good will and intentions of two basically decent people to go pathetically wrong. Had they been otherwise than decent and attractive, we might have found ourselves in a moment of farce, which asks that the participants be depersonalized or at least unsympathetic. As it is, we are involved once again in a situation similar to the one that put old Egeon, who is both innocent of wrongdoing and appealing in his concern for his sons, almost within range of the boys' voices and yet in jeopardy of his life. In short, the business from the *Amphitruo* was ideal for farce, provided Shakespeare had let Henri Bergson's stereotypes present it. Given credible characters, however, and characters who enlist our moral sympathy, we get a hint of domestic tragedy—a wife estranged from her husband at the very moment she is beginning to believe she has avoided estrangement, and a husband driven into the house of a prostitute without really wanting to go there. We also get a hint of what the solution to Shakespeare's complicated intrigue will have to be.

Elizabethan audiences would almost certainly have rejected the bigamous solution of Plautus's *Amphitruo*. Even two mortal husbands would have been intolerably immoral, but a solution with one mortal husband and one divine would have been blasphemy under any but the most delicately controlled circumstances. Furthermore, once Shakespeare had presented the marriage between Antipholus of Ephesus and Adriana as worth saving, he had committed himself both to preserving that marriage and to getting a suitable mate for Antipholus of Syracuse; for clearly that still-eligible Antipholus, with his demonstrable power to attract Adriana, could not have been allowed to remain unattached. Such a disruptive force on the loose would have unbalanced the comedy and frustrated its restorative function. Besides, the ethos of comedy, as English audiences seemed to understand that ethos, still required that an ability to stimulate affection and a capacity to receive it be accounted for in the course of any play that was supposed to end happily. A decade or so later, audiences would be ready to allow a Mariana and a Helena to be married to less-than-desirable husbands, though even they would not quite be prepared to settle for the tears of a Beaumont and Fletcher's Arethusa. Thus if Shakespeare in 1592 or thereabouts had not already planned to add a Luciana to Plautus's scheme, he would have found it mandatory to do so at this point. From here on in his planning and plotting it was clear that *The Comedy of Errors* would have to have two matings in it, one new and one renewed. With the addition of the frame story it would have to receive yet a third mating, this one recovered from the dead.

The interesting thing about Luciana is that Shakespeare found and presented in her an image of the larger action of the play. Normally the young girl in a romantic comedy is what the French call an ingenue, a naive young woman whose principal function is to be sought after by men and whose role in the play is fulfilled when she has allowed herself to be found and seized by the right one. This is the role and fate of Anne Page in Shakespeare's *The Merry Wives of Windsor*, and it is almost the role of Bianca in *The Taming of the Shrew* and of Hero in *Much Ado about Nothing*. It is not the role of Miranda in *The Tempest*, however much Prospero and Ferdinand may want Miranda to play that role; and it is not the role of Luciana, who is knowledgeable beyond her experience and wiser than her appearance of naiveté would lead one to suppose. When we first encounter Luciana, it is two o'clock in the afternoon an she is trying to argue with her sister, Adriana, that a man has a right to be late for dinner if he chooses:

> Good sister, let us dine, and never fret;
> A man is master of his liberty:
> Time is their master, and when they see time,
> They'll go or come; if so, be patient, sister.
> [II.i.6-9]

She also has a philosophical basis for her opinion:

> There's nothing situate under heaven's eye
> But hath his bound in earth, in sea, in sky.
> The beasts, the fishes, and the winged fowls
> Are their males' subjects and at their controls:
> Man, more divine, the master of all these,
> Lord of the wide world and wild wat'ry seas,
> Indu'd with intellectual sense and souls,
> Of more pre-eminence than fish and fowls,
> Are masters to their females, and their lords:
> Then let your will attend on their accords.
>
> [II.i.16-25]

Adriana is understandably contemptuous of her sister's defense of wifely complaisance, which she terms servitude. She recognizes in Luciana's words the familiar clichés of a presumptive world order that places all women at a disadvantage, and she knows very well that the world as a whole will use the same clichés, to her own sorrow and eventually to Luciana's as well. She tells her sister bitterly:

> . . . thou, that has no unkind mate to grieve thee,
> With urging helpless patience would relieve me;
> But if thou live to see like right bereft,
> This fool-begg'd patience in thee will be left.
>
> [II.i.38-41]

Luciana, as we have seen, is not entirely blind to the nature of at least some men in the world that men dominate. When Antipholus of Syracuse woos her, she thinks he is her sister's husband and dutifully reports what she takes to be an infidelity. Still, she has wavered slightly—replying to Antipholus's "Give me thy hand" with a half-meant "I'll fetch my sister to get her good will" (III.ii.70). Nevertheless, as we have also seen, she defends Adriana in the end and denies the charge of jealousy that the Abbess would bring against her sister.

There is really no point in debating who is right and who is wrong in all this; for the play does not tell us, and we have no other arbiter. One suspects that formal comedy almost never does tell, though when it speaks publicly on such matters, it frequently does so with Luciana's sentiments. We in the audience know that Antipholus of Ephesus is at best a dutiful but scarcely attentive husband, that Adriana is a disappointed wife, jealous but no shrew, and that in the unexciting union of these two lies the image of many marriages that degenerate when left to their own devices. What Luciana has said about the principle of order may very well be true in some unfallen world (apparently many Elizabethans believed that it might be true in their fallen one); but given the specific data that Shakespeare's play sets before us, the principle of order offers very little hope of a satisfactory resolution to the problems that confront either of the two sisters.

Their real hope (and the day's events have done much to diminish even that) lies in the naive, unarticulated faith that buttresses both Luciana's recourse to cliché and Adriana's stubborn will to deny the evidence of her senses—their child-like trust in the essential goodness of at least some human beings and their feeling (it is now scarcely more than that) that somehow things must turn out favorably for those who behave themselves reasonably well and do not perversely run into danger. For the audience, that faith has already been challenged absolutely by the threat of death to innocent Egeon. For the other principals in the play, it has been challenged by the specter of permanent disaster that grows moment by moment as they stumble from one ludicrous error to another. A resolution for Egeon can only come through the intervention of some kind of *deus ex machina*. For the others, however, the coincidences that have undone them all may yet make things right, provided a single condition can be met. The resolution for any romantic comedy (and this is as much a romantic comedy as any Shakespeare ever wrote) requires that the eligible young woman in it be at least free to say, without reservation, the "yes" she has been longing to say to her young man. By this rule, therefore, Shakespeare's *Comedy of Errors* cannot end until Luciana can believe that most men usually mean well even when they fall short of doing well and that the Antipholus who professed his love to her is in fact free to do so, in her sight and in the sight of all the rest of the world. In short, she must be reassured that the world she has accepted naively in her ignorance is equally attractive and worthy of acceptance in the glaring light of truth.

Unfortunately, Luciana reverts to stereotype at the end and does not speak for herself. She does not, as Kate in *The Taming of the Shrew* is shortly to do, discourse sagely but ironically on the relationship between the sexes; nor is she yet able, like the Cleopatra of a much later and very different kind of play, to speak movingly and memorably of the vision that may be generated by erotic love. It is probably enough for the conclusion of this early comedy that she seem destined to win by being wedded to a young man whom she clearly wants to marry and that she seem unlikely to prove a shrew. Antipholus of Syracuse presumably gives her all the reassurance that she requires when he turns to her in the last scene and says, "What I told you then [in my brother's house] / I hope I shall have leisure to make good, / If this be not a dream I see and hear" / (V.i.375-77). Beyond this the play does not show us or invite us to speculate.

Admittedly, attention in the present chapter has been concentrated on certain elements in the play at the expense of others. There is perhaps enough of the "knockabout farce" in *The Comedy of Errors* to justify Professor Levin's calling it one, but it is a knockabout farce with a difference. To the principal characters in the play the issues involved are serious ones: love (both young love and love that is no longer young), fidelity, and personal honor. Because of forces neither they nor we ever fully understand, the values they most cherish have been thrust suddenly into jeopardy. We who read or stand apart in the audience can see that the dangers that threaten are hardly so serious as they seem to the two couples; yet we recognize that, left unchallenged, those same dangers can prove as life-threatening as the dangers besetting the relatively innocent old man of the piece, Egeon, whose only fault is that he loved his children and wanted to insure their safety. And nothing at all in the play prepares us for the resolution of difficulties in the appearance of the Abbess, a wife who returns Alcestis-like from the dead to provide an essential miracle; so that when all things do finally come together for good in those final moments, we are never quite able to put out of our heads the last line of Antipholus's concluding speech to Luciana: "If this be not a dream I see and hear." By this time we ourselves may have glimpsed that dimension of comedy which stretches miles beyond Plautus into a realm where the commonplace begins to take on an aspect of the mysterious and miracle seems to have become a possibility; but these are boundaries which only the greatest writers have penetrated successfully and which Shakespeare himself never seriously attempted until, approaching the end of his career, he wrote the last two acts of *The Winter's Tale.*

3

The Two Gentlemen of Verona

The Two Gentlemen of Verona may well represent another kind of first excursion into the field of comedy. *The Comedy of Errors* is, after all, something that Shakespeare might have produced largely out of his academic experience at the Stratford Grammar School, where Terence and possibly Plautus would have been staple fare, acted as well as read.[2] *The Two Gentlemen*, with its abundant echoes of the currently popular Lylyean mode and its affinities with the Italian *commedia dell'arte*, is the sort of play he could have written only after some contact with the manifestations of urban sophistication.[2] Nevertheless, *The Two Gentlemen of Verona* contains parallels with his imitation of Plautus that might be construed as attempts to repeat a pattern which had already proved workable: two young men in a brotherly relationship (especially noteworthy in view of the fact that Shakespeare's principal source, Gil Polo's *Diana Enamorada*, had called for only one), a young woman for each man, a pair of servants, and a fair number of errors (the missent letter, the miscarriage of the gift of a lapdog, and Proteus's "white" lie that prompts his father precipitously to send him off to Milan).[3]

The differences, of course, between *The Comedy of Errors* and *The Two Gentlemen of Verona* are far more numerous and important than the few resemblances. None of the errors in the latter play has serious consequences, and all of them taken together would hardly lead one to speculate about the intrusion of some *deus ex machina*. Nothing whatever in *The Two*

Gentlemen can be considered a matter of life and death, nothing presented there is of notably significant "philosophical" import, and nothing in its exploration of human love quite reaches for the depths of experience and wisdom exemplified in the brief appearance of Abbess Aemilia at the end of *The Comedy of Errors*. This is not to suggest that triviality characterizes the entire play. On the contrary, *The Two Gentlemen of Verona*, like *The Comedy of Errors* (presumably earlier) and *Love's Labor's Lost* (presumably later), constitutes a serious assault on the domain of comedy and concludes with triumphs that Shakespeare was to make use of thereafter; but more than either of the other two plays it makes its assault under the cover of popular stereotypes and thus tempts the inattentive spectator or reader to settle for less than it actually offers.

In an early version of one of her earliest poems, now somewhat staled by excessive quotation, Marianne Moore wrote that poets must be "literalists of the imagination" and present for inspection "imaginary gardens with real toads in them."[4] She might have made the same observation about writers of comedy like Shakespeare, whose gardens are invariably imaginary but contain a variety of real creatures. One of the most notable of these in *The Two Gentlemen of Verona* is the clown Launce, whose descriptions of his family, his newly found sweetheart, and his mongrel Crab are engaging precisely because they combine native intelligence with independence of spirit and bespeak a courage to deploy the force of those endowments in oblique assaults upon the pretentiousness of the society he has been destined from birth to serve.[5] A memorable example comes near the end of the play when Launce, having lost the "squirrel" lapdog he was instructed to deliver to Madam Silvia, has substituted Crab, only to find that Crab has no instinct for courtly manners. Launce soliloquizes thus about (and to) the animal:

I was sent to deliver him as a present to Mistress Silvia from my master; and I came no sooner into the dining-chamber but he steps me to her trencher and steals her capon's leg. O, 'tis a foul thing when a cur cannot keep himself in all companies! I would have (as one should say) one that takes upon him to be a dog indeed, to be, as it were, a dog at all things. If I had not had more wit than he, to take a fault upon me that he did, I think verily he had been hang'd for't; sure as I live he had suffer'd for't. . . . I have sat in the stocks for puddings he hath stol'n, otherwise he had been executed; I have stood in the pillory for geese he hath kill'd, otherwise he had suffer'd for't. Thou think'st not of this now. Nay, I remember the trick you serv'd me, when I took my leave of Madam Silvia. Did not I bid thee still mark me, and do as I do? When didst thou see me heave up my leg and make water against a gentlewoman's farthingale? Didst thou ever see me do such a trick?

[IV.iv.6-39]

Launce's companion in clownage, Speed, whom most critics of the play have treated unfairly, also has lively moments, though unfortunately too few of them. One of his better sallies comes early in Act II. He has been standing by, indulging in knowing asides, while his master Valentine engages in a hopeful exchange with Lady Silvia. Afterwards, he tries without much success to persuade the young man that Silvia does not require courting but is in fact making overtures of her own. Nevertheless, seeing that Valentine has too little self-confidence to be convinced of Silvia's forwardness, Speed pertly improvises four lines of more or less relevant doggerel and adds a moderately witty conclusion, "All this I speak in print, for in print I found it." Then abruptly changing to a more productive topic, he asks, "Why muse you, sir? 'tis dinner-time"; and when Valentine replies that he has already eaten, Speed answers with an observation which points to the solid earth of the play. "Ay, but hearken, sir," he says; "though the chameleon Love can feed on the air, I am one that am nourish'd by my victuals, and would fain have meat" (II.i.169-74). Speed, of course, is not to the manner born and can afford to indulge his ties to the soil; but the play in its unfolding makes clear that this is where most of the lords and ladies of Verona and Milan also stand, on plain earth—even the Lady Silvia, who has recognized at least for a brief moment that human love may sometimes require one to circumvent convention.

Valentine, who is one of the additions to the plot that Shakespeare took from Gil Polo, is the signal exception. From beginning to end he embodies and thus keeps steadily in our view the imaginary world of the Italianate romance. Soon after his arrival in Milan, we find his servant Speed gleefully recounting the standard symptoms of the courtly lover as he has observed them of late in his now deeply smitten master: the repeated flailing of arms, the massive sighing, the inexplicable weeping, and, of course, the total lack of interest in food. Valentine expresses mild surprise at being thus transparent, but he does not deny that he "stands affected" to the lady. Nevertheless, even after Silvia herself has succeeded in tempting him to play the lover, he continues to follow meticulously the prescriptions of courtesy books and romantic fiction. To Proteus, newly arrived, he boasts of his mistress's status: "If not divine, / yet let her be a principality, / Sovereign to all the creatures on the earth" (II.iv.151-53). He makes her the subject of extravagant comparisons:

> Why, man, she is mine own,
> And I as rich in having such a jewel
> As twenty seas, if all their sand were pearl,
> The water nectar, and the rocks pure gold.
> [II.iv.168-71]

He dutifully plans an unsuccessful elopement via rope ladder, stoically suffers banishment to the hostile forest, meets a band of robbers there, but so impresses them with his valor (actually he lies about the occasion for his banishment) that they make him their captain. At the beginning of the final scene he stands alone in the wilderness and proclaims a fashionable combination of primitivism and melancholy:

> How use doth breed a habit in a man!
> This shadowy desert, unfrequented woods,
> I better brook than flourishing peopled towns:
> Here can I sit alone, unseen of any,
> And to the nightingale's complaining notes
> Tune my distresses and record my woes.
> [V.iv.1-6]

Valentine has a few set pieces that are rhetorically interesting. For example, there is another soliloquy in Act III, scene i:

> And why not death, rather than living torment?
> To die is to be banish'd from myself,
> And Silvia is myself: banish'd from her
> Is self from self, a deadly banishment.

What light is light, if Silvia be not seen?
What joy is joy, if Silvia be not by?
Unless it be to think that she is by,
And feed upon the shadow of perfection.
Except I be by Silvia in the night,
There is no music in the nightingale;
Unless I look on Silvia in the day,
There is no day for me to look upon.
She is my essence, and I leave to be,
If I be not by her fair influence
Foster'd, illumin'd, cherish'd, kept alive.
I fly not death, to fly his deadly doom:
Tarry I here, I but attend on death,
But fly I hence, I fly away from life.

[III.i.170-87]

Nicely balanced as this speech is, it bears no relation to anything we may call the life of the play, and it is sincere only in
that it is conventionally so. The best that can be said of this sort
of thing, as of the half-hearted complaint that opens the concluding scene, is that it prepares us to accept in the final
moments Valentine's equally conventional "proof" of his continuing friendship for a penitent Proteus:

. . . once again I do receive thee honest.
Who by repentance is not satisfied
Is nor of heaven nor earth, for these are pleas'd;
By penitence th' Eternal's wrath's appeas'd:
And that my love may appear plain and free,
All that was mine in Silvia I give thee.

[V.iv.78-83]

In making this gesture, of course, Valentine completely overlooks any claim that Silvia herself might have to human identity. One can hardly help recalling here Sir Arthur Quiller-
Couch's tart observation that by this time there are no gentlemen at all in Shakespeare's play.[6]

Long before reaching this point, however, many critical
readers will have lost interest, deciding by default that *The Two
Gentlemen of Verona* is best dismissed as an early work, or at
least one that did not fully engage Shakespeare's attention.
Such flickers of interest as remain probably focus on the fact

that here Shakespeare turned for the first time to popular fiction, which was henceforth to serve as a source for some of his happiest creations. *The Two Gentlemen* shows that he was already familiar with the field; and although he obviously took the core of his plot from Gil Polo's *Diana*, he just as obviously used other sources as well, particularly for his theme of friendship. As has already been intimated, the addition of this theme might have come about naturally, as a consequence of his success in working with pairs of characters in his Roman play; but friendship, sometimes portrayed in opposition to erotic love, was a popular topic with numerous precedents in literature, and Shakespeare could have been doing nothing more than adding another successful cliché to a play that already had a fairly full complement of them. Some years ago Ralph M. Sargent made out a case for Shakespeare's using Sir Thomas Elyot's *Boke of the Governor* for the friendship motif.[7] Others have suggested that he went to one of John Lyly's two novels or to Sir Philip Sidney's *Arcadia*, or perhaps to George Peele's *Old Wives' Tale*, all of which present versions of the stereotypical conflict between friendship and erotic love. Shakespeare probably knew some or all of these, but he did not require any of them absolutely. We should keep in mind that the friendship he presented here is tenuous from the outset, that it never goes more than skin-deep on either side, and that Valentine's *beau geste* at the end is one with the magnanimous gesture of the lover Eumenides in Peele's play, who, upon being reminded that he had agreed to share everything with his sworn friend (who also happens to be a ghost), prepares to cut his beloved in half. Valentine in his brief speech makes a show of invoking spiritual considerations; but in Shakespeare's presentation (as clearly in Peele's) the whole business appears a bit silly, as perhaps he meant it to be. Shakespeare, to the extent that he is serious in the rest of *The Two Gentlemen of Verona*—and he is serious to a much greater extent than he has been given credit for being—is concerned with the reality of flesh and blood and the consequences of setting that reality in a context, thinly veiled, of contemporary society's artificial ideals, aspirations, and pretensions.

So far we have noticed two characters who contribute to the reality of flesh and blood in this play: Launce, who comes to life briefly, and his more mercurial counterpart Speed, who qualifies as flesh and blood mainly by declaring, "I am one that am nourish'd by my victuals." For the most part, however, these are conventional clowns who amuse by performing the business expected of them; but there are two other characters, and a possible third, who share the responsibility for breathing real life into material that already was rapidly becoming dated and for turning what might have been a routine Italianate comedy into one with some capability of surviving the taste of the time. Julia is one of these; Proteus, another. The third is Julia's maid Lucetta. All three come from the part of the play that Shakespeare borrowed from Gil Polo, where he found a counterpart for Silvia but none for Valentine—and hence no theme of friendship.

Lucetta is the least complicated of the three. In the garden scene with Julia (I.ii) she is the outspoken confidante to her mistress and the sounding board for her opinions. Here, knowing Julia's mind and recognizing Julia's embarrassment at having it known, she shrewdly nourishes the young woman's love for Proteus with teasing comments and thus is probably responsible for the warm letter from Julia that Proteus is reading in the following scene. Later, however, Lucetta advances sensible arguments against Julia's proposed journey to Milan in pursuit of her beloved—advising that a woman disguised as a man must wear an indelicate codpiece in order to be convincing, and warning that Proteus may not be altogether pleased to have a woman following after him. In both scenes (the only ones she has in the play) Lucetta appears as a woman worldly wise but compassionate, who knows men as men but distrusts them as gentlemen and expects that as gentlemen they will be no better than Proteus in fact proves to be before the play is over.

Julia, by contrast, is as naive as she is devoted. In the first of these two scenes she betrays the intensity of her affection by the embarrassment she displays on realizing that a letter from Proteus has reached her, quite by accident, through the hands of Lucetta, who is therefore in a position to suspect that something is afoot between them. In the second, having put aside all dissembling, she confronts her own feelings and accepts them; then, disregarding properties and the unsettling contingencies that Lucetta has suggested to her, she acts with dispatch. Her parting words to Lucetta in this scene bear credible witness to her determination and her sincerity:

> Now, as thou lov'st me, do him not that wrong,
> To bear a hard opinion of his truth:
> Only deserve my love by loving him,
> And presently go with me to my chamber,
> To take a note of what I stand in need of,
> To furnish me upon my longing journey.
> All that is mine I leave at thy dispose,
> My goods, my lands, my reputation;
> Only, in lieu thereof, dispatch me hence.
> Come; answer not; but to it presently,
> I am impatient of my tarriance.
>
> [II.vii.80-90]

In Julia's first scene with Proteus (II.ii), who is never at a loss for words to accommodate a situation, she convinces us of her seriousness by the ring she gives him (though he gives her nothing), the kiss that she asks for but appears not to get, and the subsequent flood of tears that wells up as she suddenly becomes silent and then flees from his presence. After these early scenes the play moves forward with mechanical efficiency until Julia, now disguised in men's clothing, reappears as a cautious tourist eavesdropping on the serenading of Lady Silvia in the Duke's garden. Here the play comes poignantly to life again as we hear Proteus declare to the protesting Silvia, "I grant, sweet love, that I did love a lady; / But she is dead" (IV.ii.104-5), and hear Julia's bitter aside, "I am sure she is not buried." Minutes later she tells her amiable companion, the Host of the Inn, that "it hath been the longest night / That e'er I watch'd, and the most heaviest" (IV.ii.139-40), and we are once more reminded that this play moves in a world where wounds can bleed and at least some people must be held accountable for their actions.

Proteus, Julia's male counterpart, never becomes her equal in credibility, yet he is far superior in both credibility and interest to Shakespeare's Valentine, who for all his prominence in the play does little more than serve as a foil to the two principals. Proteus's speeches at their best have an intensity and a firmness of wit that Valentine's utterances never approach. When he first declares his love for Julia, we believe him:

> Thou, Julia, thou hast metamorphis'd me,
> Made me neglect my studies, lose my time,
> War with good counsel, set the world at nought;
> Made wit with musing weak, heart sick with thought.
>
> [I.i.66-69]

We also believe him when he declares at greater length that he has fallen in love with Silvia:

> O sweet-suggesting Love, if thou hast sinn'd,
> Teach me, thy tempted subject, to excuse it!
> At first I did adore a twinkling star,
> But now I worship a celestial sun.
>
> [II.vi.7-10]

Then when he remarks, early in the play,

> O, how this spring of love resembleth
> The uncertain glory of an April day,
> Which now shows all the beauty of the sun.
> And by and by a cloud takes all away.
>
> [I.iii.84-87]

we recognize that we have been told something true about young love in the flesh—indeed about all flesh, which, like April, can be gloriously beautiful but can also change without warning; and because Proteus's way of saying so is in itself lovely and memorable, these lines of his linger in our minds as a subliminal guide to the meaning and action of the rest of the play.

Change, of course, is what Shakespeare concentrates on in *The Two Gentlemen of Verona*, but not merely the conventional familial and social change that is the staple of all romantic comedy. Here, to a much greater extent than in *The Comedy of Errors*, Shakespeare focuses on a more fundamental manifestation of change: metamorphosis (to use a variant of the term which occurs twice in this play), the phenomenon whereby creatures surrender one life as a means of advancing to another, turning their youth into maturity, spring into stable summer. It is understandable, therefore, that he not only gave his principal character the name of that ancient sea-god best known for his readiness to change shape, but also used in this single play two of his four references to the chameleon.[8] In another play, *3 Henry VI*, probably written at about the same time as this one, he brought both terms together in the conclusion to Richard of Gloucester's most memorable soliloquy: "I can add colors to the chameleon, / Change shape with Proteus for advantages, / And set the murtherous Machevil to school" (III.ii.191-93). The young Proteus of *The Two Gentlemen*, one should note, has the same kind of vitality as Richard Crookback—diminished in degree, to be sure, but similarly unpredictable, potentially destructive, and undeniably human. The difference is that Proteus's aberrant vitality, unlike Richard's, proves to be redeemable; but, if we take the play at face value, his transformation cannot come about until "gentle Julia" has accepted as her own mode of procedure the principle of change that her lover has perverted, and risked her integrity and self-respect to move him forward to a new level of living. In short, it is the business of redeeming the "metamorphosing" Proteus that principally concerns us in this play, not the matter of his friendship with a faceless Valentine or the conventional comic matrix in which both friendship and redemption are embedded; and once we have seen where the emphasis lies and where it does not, we begin to be less troubled by some of the details that have exercised academic critics over the years.

The artificiality of Valentine's soliloquies in and of itself should signal to us that the conventional comic plot of this play was not meant to be taken seriously. Of course, change of a mechanical kind does take place in the plot, and the accomplishment of that type of change is celebrated at the end with conventional pairings off and promises of marriage; but such finalities, institutionalized over the centuries in countless comic exercises, in tales told and printed, and in plays on the stage, had long since become sterile. Shakespeare inherited the procession to the altar as the normal denouement of a comic intrigue and dutifully exhibited something like it in almost all of his comedies, but he never depended on that device alone for the resolution of the significant action of a play, as, for example, his contemporary Thomas Dekker did in *The Shoemakers' Holiday*. Invariably, Shakespeare went after rare game, as is evident in *The Two Gentlemen* in the lovely lines, already quoted, about the uncertainty of human love; in Julia's moving speeches in Act IV, scene iv, about the sadness that unrequited love has caused her; and at the end, where all the shifts and uncertainties have been faced up to and re-demptive love has begun its work. There Julia initiates the following exchange with her irresponsible lover:

> O Proteus, let this habit make thee blush!
> Be thou asham'd that I have took upon me
> Such an immodest raiment—if shame live
> In a disguise of love!
> It is the lesser blot, modesty finds,
> Women to change their shapes than men their minds.
>   *Pro.* Than men their minds? 'tis true. O heaven, were man
> But constant, he were perfect; that one error
> Fills him with faults; makes him run through all th' sins:
> Inconstancy falls off ere it begins.
> What is in Silvia's face, but I may spy
> More fresh in Julia's with a constant eye?
>   *Val.* Come, come, a hand from either.
> Let me be blest to make this happy close;
> 'Twere pity two such friends should be long foes.
>   *Pro.* Bear witness, heaven, I have my wish for ever.
>   *Jul.* And I mine.
>
> [V.iv.104-20]

H.B. Charlton in commenting on this passage refers to "were man / But constant, he were perfect" as an example of Proteus's "fatuous self-conceit" and, like much else in the play, hardly worth taking seriously.[9] One can, and should, disagree. A wish to be constant is not fatuous simply because constancy is impossible, and Proteus's wish to be so is best seen as a first, faint indication that his maturity is at last beginning. No one else in the play has such an intimation of perfection, and most certainly not Valentine, who has already solved the conflict between love and friendship by switching rapidly and pointlessly from one to the other. The prescription for love found in courtly manuals has no rules for what will henceforth transpire between Julia and Proteus; a relationship involving friendship as well as love and demonstrating that the two, insofar as they are attainable by human beings, are the same. Julia, in short, has gone seeking the young man she loves and, like a true friend, has proved herself willing to lay down her life for him if need be. It is she, therefore, who is the exemplar of friendship and the only true "gentleman of Verona."

We assume that according to the expectations offered by romantic comedy Valentine and Silvia will live happily ever after. We may wish the pair well if we like, but convention guarantees them happiness in any case. As for Proteus and Julia, convention guarantees them nothing, despite their professed wishes for constancy; for these two are an early example of Shakespearean romantic comedy wrought with passion and brought down to earth, and convention does not apply. Julia must acknowledge without embarrassment the "immodest raiment" that human love has brought her to, and Proteus must be able to declare that all the icy perfection he once thought he adored in Silvia's face he now spies "more fresh in Julia's with a constant eye." What these two have discovered, and discovered movingly for the attentive spectator or reader, is the need to accept one another, irregularities and all; and this is the only development that truly concerns us or interests us.

In many other Shakespearean comedies acceptance between pairs transcends expectation and makes our rejoicing genuine; one thinks of Petruchio and Kate, Hippolyta and Theseus, Rosalind and Orlando, Beatrice and Benedick, Helena and Bertram, Mariana and Angelo, Hermione and Leontes. Here in *The Two Gentlemen of Verona* the relatively slight development of characters may prevent our seeing that Shakespeare has already begun to make a choice between developing romantic comedy as an end in itself and using the mode of that comedy as a device for exploring and testing the world we all know and participate in. It is good to rejoice that the world has once more allowed a pair of constant lovers to come together and renew a society which previously attempted to keep them apart. This kind of reassurance is the benefit we expect—even demand—of romantic comedy, and for most comedies this is benefit enough. It is even better, however, to rejoice that lovers who once naively thought themselves constant, as here, have confronted the realities of their circumstances and condition, discovered the inevitable imperfections in one another, and found in themselves the charity to forgive and accept. When a union like this can be presented convincingly, we are reassured indeed.

4

Love's Labor's Lost

Superficially *Love's Labor's Lost* provides less reassurance than either *The Comedy of Errors* or *The Two Gentlemen of Verona*. The play abounds in lovers, but none of them at the end has found a mate. No society in it finds renewal; and the death of the *senex*, or parent (here the King of France), offstage, removes from the proceedings the most determined and forthright advocate of mating that the plot has to offer. Thus, instead of providing a release, the removal by death of the Princess's father brings everything to an indefinite halt. "Our wooing doth not end like an old play," says Berowne; "Jack hath not Gill" (V.ii.874-75). And he will not be consoled. Moreover, the songs which were to have concluded the entertainment within the play, a dialogue between the owl and the cuckoo, winter and spring, conclude the play itself but in reverse order, with winter having the last word and Don Armado pronouncing, "The words of Mercury are harsh after the songs of Apollo" (V.ii.930-31). It is as if the candlelight in a performance of some fairy play, with fantastic settings and seemingly immortal characters, had suddenly gone out, leaving in its place only harsh daylight, a crude stage, and all the hard circumstances of the world of common affairs.

And this is, in fact, what has happened. The songs of Apollo here dealt with "love, first learned in a lady's eyes . . . the right Promethean fire" (IV.iii.324;348); and these have given way to animal lust in the springtime and survival in the winter, to meadow flowers, adventurous cuckoldry, and aired linen, to icicles, muddy roads, cold churches, and red noses. Suddenly the world of petty local officials, foresters, and country clowns, which previously in the play has intruded only to the point of being a subject for ridicule has now entered into full view and seems likely to stay there. Thus we see that common life prevails in spite of death and the despair that it has precipitated among the group of sophisticated and well-meaning but blind young men, who scarcely the day before presumed to seek a life of the mind to the exclusion of any other kind. The late George L. Kittredge gave the two-part song that embodies this vision of common life high praise, calling it one of the best in the world.[1] Most would agree. The words of Mercury may be harsh to Armado's way of thinking and perhaps to the temporarily dispirited young people in his company, but they remain the "joy forever" to others who may have also labored vainly to find erotic love but have matured sufficiently in that process to find charity instead, learning thereby to accept rather than condemn the world of people and things:

> When icicles hang by the wall,
>   And Dick the shepherd blows his nail,
> And Tom bears logs into the hall,
>   And milk comes frozen home in pail;
> When blood is nipp'd, and ways be [foul],
> Then nightly sings the staring owl,
>   "Tu-whit, to who!"—
> A merry note.
> While greasy Joan doth keel the pot.

For those who know such joys in real life, the words of Mercury mitigate the absoluteness of the death of the King of France and suggest that the denial it seems to entail is only temporary—a deferral, as the wiser young ladies have all suggested it may be. Thus in this play is the business of comedy served, which otherwise might have gone begging. Even at the risk of seeming intolerably moralistic, one might suggest that the effect here is something like that of the last stanza of A.H. Clough's poem, "Say Not the Struggle Nought Availeth":

> And not by eastern windows only,
>   When daylight comes, comes in the light,

In front, the sun climbs slow, how slowly,
But westward, look, the land is bright.

In brief, the songs at the end of *Love's Labor's Lost* remind us that we have been in the mansion of real comedy all along—damp, earthy, vital comedy—despite the best efforts of a team of gallants to make it into something new and pure and sterile.

This is a good place to note at least one aspect that unites the three early comedies of Shakespeare: in none of them does the romantic comic pattern stand forth clearly as the main business at hand. That is, the classic action whereby young lovers, with or without the help of accomplices, circumvent parental opposition and join hands and hearts seems almost peripheral to our concerns. In *The Comedy of Errors* we look primarily at the concatenation of errors that leads the characters to cry witchcraft, and that leads us at times to suspect they may be right. In *The Two Gentlemen of Verona* we concern ourselves with the apparent contest between love and friendship. Here in *Love's Labor's Lost* we focus our attention primarily on the pretentiousness of fashionable Neoplatonic love. Yet throughout all three the basic action of comedy is there: the same pulsebeat struggles to reassert itself and eventually succeeds in doing so—completely though perfunctorily in *The Comedy of Errors*, where we are invited to look no farther than the gossips' feast; less obviously in *The Two Gentlemen*, where the fact that young Proteus has wavered once leads us to suspect he may waver again; and least obviously of all in *Love's Labor's Lost*, where the lovers go their separate ways, unfeasted and unwed and all in one kind of mourning or another.

The basic action of comedy in *Love's Labor's Lost* is further obscured, as in *The Comedy of Errors*, by the fact that the *senex* has aggressively sought the "wedding" and virtually pushed his child toward it. To be precise, one should say that Egeon of *The Comedy of Errors* unwillingly "hazarded the loss" of his remaining son (I.i.124-31), but his motive is still the unconventional one for comedy of being willing that his child move forward and take his place in the world; moreover, the forces opposed to the fulfillment that he seeks for Antipholus turn out to be even more hostile to him than they are to the boy. In *Love's*

Labor's Lost something like the traditional situation of comedy is announced soon after the beginning of the play, but all the furniture for it remains offstage. Berowne, in arguing against the King of Navarre's proposal to impose a three-year vow of celibacy, reminds his colleagues:

> . . . well you know here comes in embassy
> The French king's daughter with yourself to speak—
> A maid of grace and complete majesty—
> About surrender up of Aquitaine
> To her decrepit, sick, and bedrid father;
> Therefore this article is made in vain.
>
> [I.i.134-39]

The situation that Navarre has created is an absurdity to begin with, but complicating it is France's presumption in asking him to surrender territory to someone describable as "decrepit, sick, and bedrid" and the ostensible folly of sending a daughter to make such a request. What the embassy really means we learn almost as soon as the Princess arrives at the King of Navarre's park with her "three attending Ladies and three Lords." There one of the lords, the somewhat elderly Boyet, says to her:

> Now, madam, summon up your dearest spirits;
> Consider who the King your father sends,
> To whom he sends, and what's his embassy:
> Yourself, held precious in the world's esteem,
> To parley with the sole inheritor
> Of all perfections that a man may owe,
> Matchless Navarre; the plea of no less weight
> Than Aquitaine, a dowry for a queen.
> Be now as prodigal of all dear grace
> As Nature was in making graces dear,
> When she did starve the general world beside
> And prodigally gave them all to you.
>
> [II.i.1-12]

That the King of France still has some force in international politics is evident from Navarre's admission that he must receive the embassy, male or female, "on mere necessity" (I.i.148). France, it would appear, is still France; and the attractiveness of the young girl is never in question. Nevertheless, we are expected to infer the root of the matter: a dying sovereign is making a final desperate effort to insure the future of a dowerless but beautiful daughter, and he is prepared to go to some lengths to save his own face as well.

What those lengths are becomes clear as soon as Act II gets under way. The King does meet the Princess "on mere necessity" and graciously agrees to let her camp in the park. As soon as their conversation drifts from courteous pleasantries to business, however, the difficulties of the official purpose of the embassy become painfully evident (II.i.128ff.). From the King of Navarre's point of view (which is probably defensible), his father has in the past spent some 200,000 crowns in support of France's wars, in token of which the King of France gave the elder King of Navarre a portion of Aquitaine as security. The present King of Navarre, the young king of the play, maintains that neither he nor his father has received further payment. The French king now declares, through his daughter's embassy, that he has already paid half the debt in cash, a sum of 100,000 crowns; nevertheless, he says, he will let the portion of Aquitaine go permanently, provided Navarre will pay an additional 100,000. Navarre is nonplussed by the arrogance of the suggestion. He already controls his part of Aquitaine and can continue to do so without paying anything at all. Even so, he agrees to "return" the 100,000 crowns to France or give up Aquitaine, provided France can prove that the 100,000 crowns were actually paid in the first place. The Princess says that the payment will be confirmed in documents that Boyet will provide the following day. The King promises to yield to "all liberal reason" and meanwhile allows the Princess and her entourage the liberty of the park, though to protect his vow of celibacy he declines to invite them to come inside the gates. Suffice it to say, we hear little more about debts and documents in this play—which is just as well, for audiences cannot be expected to apprehend the substance of such casuistry so briefly presented any more than they can be expected to comprehend the Archbishop of Canterbury's explanation of the "law Salique" in the second scene of *Henry V*. Moreover, these details are not relevant.

The real purpose of the embassy is to woo the King of Navarre, who is now doubly difficult to woo because of the vow he has taken; and the only reason for all the bother about Aquitaine is to provide the appearance of a dowry for the Princess, who is as poor as she is beautiful. The French strategy begins to succeed almost immediately, if one may judge by the flirtatious behavior of Dumaine, Longaville, and Berowne and by what Boyet tells us of the King. "Navarre is infected," he says; and when the Princess demands his reasons for thinking so, the canny old courtier details the symptoms of the young man's infatuation, ending with, "I'll give you Aquitaine and all that is his, / And you give him for my sake but one loving kiss" (II.i.248-49).

The inclination of the Princess herself in this regard comes out in the hunting scene in Act IV. We have already seen signs of erotic stirrings in Maria, Katherine, and Rosaline; but the Princess up to this point has been discreet, especially with Boyet, who is almost too knowledgeable about such things for her comfort. She lets her hair down, so to speak, in our hearing when she stands with the forester assigned to attend her and discusses the stand she is to take. Her first question sets the tone for the entire scene:

> *Prin.* Was that the king that spurr'd his horse so hard
> Against the steep-up rising of the hill?
> *For.* I know not, but I think it was not he.
> *Prin.* Whoe'er 'a was, 'a show'd a mounting mind.
> Well, lords, to-day we shall have our dispatch;
> [On] Saturday we will return to France.
> Then, forester, my friend, where is the bush
> That we must stand and play the murtherer in?
> *For.* Hereby, upon the edge of yonder coppice,
> A stand where you may make the fairest shoot.
> *Prin.* I thank my beauty, I am fair that shoot.
> And thereupon thou speak'st the fairest shoot.
> *For.* Pardon me, madam, for I meant not so.
> *Prin.* What, what? First praise me, and again say no?
> O short-liv'd pride! Not fair? alack for woe!
> [IV.i.1-15]

One does not have to be bawdily inclined to catch the shadow of a double entendre in "spurr'd his horse so hard / Against the steep-up rising of the hill" or to catch the confirmation of that shadow in "mounting mind." Presumably the forester catches some of both, for he quickly betrays his uneasiness when the Princess bawdily puns on "fairest shoot" and continues to protest his innocence even after she has tipped him with the mock admonition, "Fair payment for foul words is more than due." The Princess now turns the punning in another direction, which suggests that her intentions are serious also in ways that are not exclusively erotic:

> Glory grows guilty of detested crimes,
> When for fame's sake, for praise, an outward part,
> We bend to that the working of the heart;
> As I for praise alone now seek to spill
> The poor deer's blood, that my heart means no ill.
>
> [IV.i.31-35]

At this point the clown Costard enters with letters from Berowne to Rosaline and from Armado to Jaquenetta. The Princess means to intercept the letter to Rosaline, but Costard by mistake gives her Jaquenetta's, which deals extensively with King Cophetua's wooing of "the pernicious and indubitate beggar Zenelophon," a subject inadvertently quite appropriate to the hopes of a beggar Princess and, as it turns out, prophetic as well. The scene continues as Boyet, Maria, and Costard pick up the punning on *deer* and *shoot* and to the juggling add such terms as *horn, hit, prick, cleaving the pin,* and *clout.* It is no wonder that Maria is finally moved to say to Costard, "Come, come, you talk greasily, your lips grow foul," and again inadvertently appropriate that Costard should leave the scene rejoicing, "O' my troth, most sweet jests, most incony vulgar wit! / When it comes so smoothly off, so obscenely as it were, so fit" [IV.i.142-43).

The point to be noted is that the Princess and her attendant ladies have come to Navarre with men in their sights and sex on their minds. They are the true hunters in the King's park, and the deer they seek are real, warm, and breathing regardless of how one spells the word. It is no wonder that some have considered the main business of the play to be that of the love game; yet the women never lose sight of the comprehensive action of which the love game is merely a part. They play the game with determination and vigor, but they never forget that their objective is something richer and more meaningful than conventional marriage. Apparently, at the play's end they have won the game, but they decline the prize.

For most of the males in the play—that is, those who play—the game is an end in itself. One speaks of *the* game, but it is a game of several modes. The mode most congenial to both Costard and Boyet, males at opposite ends of the social and intellectual scales, is the erotic one, best articulated in Costard's maxim, "Such is the simplicity of man to hearken after the flesh" (I.i.217-18); and the method of both men is to hearken after the flesh that is nearest, which for Costard turns out to be the wench Jaquenetta, whom he seduces. For Boyet, who is restrained by age and responsibility, the nearest targets are the Princess's ladies-in-waiting, with whom he dallies and engages in bawdy talk; but his inclinations are the same. Don Armado, who also has similar inclinations, is restrained by his own fatuousness and by his pretensions to the high philosophical seriousness professed by Navarre and his fellows. Having caught Costard and Jaquenetta in the midst of compromising activity, he promptly turns Costard over to the constable for delivery to the King. Nevertheless, the same "devoted and heart-burning heat of duty," he tells the King in a letter, disposes him to keep Jaquenetta "as a vessel of thy law's fury, and . . . at the least of thy sweet notice, bring her to trial" (I.i.274-76). No one doubts the kind of trial he himself would subject the girl to, given half a chance. All three men exemplify Berowne's assertion that every man is vulnerable to passion and powerless to overcome it without outside help: "Every man with his affects is born, / Not by might mast'red, but by special grace" (I.i.151-52). The play, as we know, never puts this assertion to the test, there being no man in it who is really much inclined to master his affects or anything else that might require discipline and self-denial.

Nevertheless, the King and his fellows, with the exception of Berowne, pretend at the beginning to have mastered these same affects. "Brave conquerors," the King calls his friends, declaring that Navarre shall shortly be "the wonder of the world" and its court "a little academe, / Still and contemplative in living art" (I.i.12-14). Berowne's outspoken ridicule of such pretensions does little to change them, but the appearance of the ladies does a great deal; upon the arrival of these, all four men fall quickly in love, each fortunately with a different lady, and as quickly forswear themselves. The King, as is appropriate in formal comedy, fixes his gaze on the Princess; Berowne, Longaville, and Dumaine fix their attentions on Rosaline, Maria, and Katherine respectively. All write poetry or letters to their beloved, and all are subsequently exposed as "traitors" in the conventional exposure scene in Act IV. At this point Berowne, who has since the first act established himself as the intellectually resourceful one of the group, gaily replaces ascetic Platonism with Neoplatonism and suggests that the courtships now be pursued openly:

> . . . when Love speaks, the voice of all the gods
> Make heaven drowsy with the harmony.
> Never durst poet touch a pen to write
> Until his ink were temp'red with Love's sighs:
> O then his lines would ravish savage ears
> And plant in tyrants mild humility.
> From women's eyes this doctrine I derive:
> They sparkle still the right Promethean fire;
> They are the books, the arts, the academes,
> That show, contain, and nourish all the world,
> Else none at all in aught proves excellent.
> Then fools you were these women to forswear,
> Or keeping what is sworn, you will prove fools.
> [IV.iii.341-53]

The King's response re-establishes them all as conquerors: "Saint Cupid, then! and, soldiers to the field!"—to which Berowne adds, "Advance your standards, and upon them, lords." The men are now finally in open pursuit of women who have shown themselves eager to be pursued, and thus the action of the play begins at last to resemble that of comedy, at least superficially. One must insist upon "superficially," however, for Berowne's recourse to Neoplatonism is precisely the course of action celebrated in Lylyean comedy, courtly romances, and countless sonnets of the more spiritual kind, in which winning the mate has no visible connection with community or the larger rhythms of human life.

In fact, one can best characterize *Love's Labor's Lost* up to this point as Shakespeare's exploration, evaluation, and condemnation of courtly comedy. To call the play satire, as many have done, is not enough. Shakespeare has gone all the way to challenge the presupposition of a sophisticated society that could take seriously as a description of ideal human affection the passage from Cardinal Bembo's ecstatic prayer to Love as Lord in the fourth book of Castiglione's *Courtier*:

Accept our soules that bee offred unto thee for a sacrifice. Burne them in the lively flame that wasteth all grosse filthinesse, that after they be cleane sundred from the bodie they may bee coupled with an everlasting and most sweete bond to the heavenly beautie. And wee, severed from ourselves, may bee changed like right lovers into the beloved, and after we be drawn from the earth, admitted to the feast of the angels, where fed with immortall ambrosia and nectar, in the end we may dye a most happie and lively death, as in times past died the fathers of olde time, whose soules with most fervent zeale of beholding, thou didst hale from the bodie and coupledst them with God.[2]

This eloquent articulation of a tradition that properly bears Petrarch's name and dominates the fashionable poetry of Shakespeare's early years had already made its way into respectable drama well before Shakespeare came upon the scene, notably in the work of John Lyly. Indeed, the best example of it is probably Lyly's *Endymion* of 1585, with its representation of the young shepherd's spiritual adoration of Cynthia, the moon goddess, as an illustration of passion at its noblest. Shakespeare's answer to the sonneteers eventually saw print in 1609 as Sonnet 130, "My mistress' eyes are nothing like the sun." His answer to Lyly and by implication to all who wrote in the Neoplatonic tradition stands for our inspection in *Love's Labor's Lost*, where he gave the Neoplatonic Pegasus full rein and let it run headlong into the prickly thicket of the human condition.

To the extent that it is a satire directed against fashionable attitudes and the persons who held them, the play arrests attention by its exhibition of the ancient devices of analogy and parody that Shakespeare was to go on exploiting, usually for other purposes, throughout the rest of his career. A good example of this is the business with Don Armado, with his Costard-like attraction to Jaquenetta on the one hand and his pretension to inclusion in the King's academe on the other. Seeing the Spaniard in action, with his telltale addiction to euphuism, one quickly recognizes the unacknowledged absurdities of those other characters in the play whose fashions and behavior he imitates—just as, one may suppose, some people in Shakespeare's audiences saw in the absurdities of the King, Holofernes, Berowne, and the rest a reflection of the vagaries of such contemporary figures as John Florio, Gabriel Harvey, George Chapman, Sir Walter Raleigh, and Thomas Nashe.[3] By the end of the 1590s, however, the fashion of euphuism had run its course, and courtly comedy had lost, for the time being, its bid to provide fare for the popular stage. One reason for that failure was Shakespeare—not simply because he had ridiculed courtly comedy and its fantastic rhetoric but because in so doing he had identified and resisted the power that always stands behind such things regardless of the guise in which that power may appear, whether Platonism, Puritanism, or the sophisticated pedantry of academia. In short, Shakespeare had resisted the Elizabethan version of the broader Renaissance attempt to keep comedy from honoring its ancient commitment to rank earth and the perennial generation of human life.

Thus, in *The Two Gentlemen of Verona* the Platonic preference for friendship over erotic love, the "marriage of true minds," a preference which had dominated more than one work of literature before Shakespeare, came off as an absurdity when put to the test of Shakespeare's re-creation of story as dramatic poetry. The same thing had already happened in Peele's perceptive *Old Wives' Tale*. In any case, Shakespeare's central male figure in comedy was never the true Renaissance gentleman, platonic lover, and ideal friend, but simply a young adult of basically good intentions with a healthy disinclination to be constant in anything except the pursuit of the opposite sex. His comedies suggest that for him the "songs of Mercury" were preferable to those of Apollo, who, as part-time occupant of the shrine at Delphi, certainly smiled on Shakespeare occasionally, as he did on Chapman and Ben Jonson. One suspects, however, that Shakespeare was more inclined to taste of the Castalian spring when Dionysius was in residence.

At any rate, Shakespeare's sympathies (and ours) are never with the brave young men in *Love's Labor's Lost*, who do not waver (at least not until near the end) in their attempt to escape the onus of the temporal and rise to the status of angels. The King puts it in almost these terms when he expresses the hope that the fame they earn will "grace us in the disgrace of death," man's ultimate shame, and "make us heirs of all eternity" (I.i.3-7). Fame will serve them thus, he continues, if they can all successfully "war against [their] own affections / And the huge army of the world's desires" (I.i.9-10). Yet live in the world these young gentlemen must; and when the arbitrariness of that world refuses to let them maintain their Promethean flame angel-like in mind alone—as both Plato and Calvin undoubtedly would have preferred them to do—they attempt, like Petrarch before them, to find it in the "lamping eyes" of a beautiful woman.[4] Moreover, throughout their questing they display their aspirations to heavenly harmony and divine orderliness in patterned behavior and formal rhetoric.

No scene in the entire play is more orderly than the third scene of Act IV, in which the series of exposures and confessions reveals that all have been more or less disorderly in keeping their vows; and at the end of that scene, Berowne argues with specious logic and beautiful rhetoric that they have from the beginning been yearning towards a higher principle that can redeem even the "necessary" pursuit of sex from the unpleasant physicality to which the details of courtship sometimes reduce it. In short, what the King and courtiers of Navarre are participating in is not comedy but a courtly masquerade; and though such masquerades sometimes preface a marriage or even precipitate one, a marriage that comes of nothing more substantial is usually perfunctory at best.

The triviality of the young men's courtship is symbolically presented in the two episodes that take up much of Act V: the masquerade of the Muscovites and Holofernes's pageant of the Nine Worthies. The great irony of the first of these is that the gentlemen, for all their pretensions to wisdom and learning, cannot tell one lady from another; and the ladies appropriately mock them with tongues that Boyet aptly describes as "keen / As is the razor's edge invisible" (V.ii.256-57). The irony of the second is that while the originals of the worthies are all conquerors, just as the King and his men pretend to be, the representations of them are absurdities, just as the King and his men in fact are. This time, however, the mocked men are the principal mockers; and missing the point that the joke may be on them, they treat with ridicule and contempt the show Holofernes and the others have devised and executed in good faith. One by one they put the would-be performers down: Costard dressed up as Pompey the Great, Nathaniel the curate as Alexander, Holofernes as Judas Maccabaeus (they do bypass the boy Moth as Hercules), and Armado as Hector. Costard is too simple-minded to recognize that he has been put down; and honest Nathaniel, whom some critics have mistakenly described as a hedge-priest,[5] retires in confusion. Costard says of him, "You will be scrap'd out of the painted cloth for this"; but he goes on to excuse the embarrassed Nathaniel as "a foolish mild man, an honest man, look you, and soon dash'd. . . . a marvellous good neighbor, faith, and a very good bowler; but for Alisander . . . a little o'erparted" (V.ii.575-84). Holofernes is less complaisant. The ridicule of him touches first on the name *Judas* ("a kissing traitor"), then on his old man's face, and finally on "ass," the latter part of his assumed name. He responds finally with a line that lingers in the mind for the rest of the play: "This is not generous, not gentle, not humble" (V.ii.629).

The line merits a moment's reflection. What strikes one immediately, of course, is its aura of pathos: the humiliation of a pretentious, pompous, but harmless old schoolmaster with an absurdly inappropriate name (Americans must think at once of Ichabod Crane), who has never been expected by any-

one except himself to be wise in the ways of the world but who
has allowed himself to be beguiled into giving what the world
can only regard as folly. It was different with "great-limbed"
Costard, who like the mechanics in *A Midsummer Night's
Dream* presented his absurdity in innocent ignorance before
royalty ("I here am come by chance, / and lay my arms before
the legs of this sweet lass of France") and received the Princess's amused but sincere thanks (V.ii.554-57). Holofernes is
capable of being humiliated, and the young lords have under-
taken to humiliate him in the presence of his curate, his constable, and a witty young page, to say nothing of a gentleman
from Spain. He is quite right to term their taunts ungenerous,
though he himself probably did not fully deserve generosity;
and he is correct in calling them "not gentle," for gentility in
this scene is displayed only by the well-mannered Princess.
The young gentlemen, so-called, for all their pretensions to
high-mindedness, stand with Boyet in their boorish behavior
toward inferiors. They lack the humility to perceive their own
folly, shortly to be revealed to all the world; and with the
possible exception of the King they do not see that the baiting
of Holofernes has caused a cloud briefly to touch their summer
sun. The King's remarks hereafter are restrained, though one
recalls that he opposed having the pageant in the first place
(V.ii.511-14); and the Princess's are as generous as anyone
could wish—sympathetic even with Holofernes ("poor Maccabaeus") and kindly to Armado as Hector. The rest plunge
unfeelingly ahead, piling mock on mock, until Costard accuses
Armado of seducing Jaquenetta. Armado takes offense ("Dost
thou infamonize me among potentates?"), and the two prepare
for a fight that is prevented by the messenger Marcade's intrusion with news that the King of France has died.

Here finally we see, or should see, where Shakespeare has
brought us and where he has not. Clearly we appear now to be
at what might be called the turning point of a comedy, where
the old one dies, steps aside, or otherwise relaxes his threats
and where the young become free to marry and to inherit and
renew the decaying society. In this case, however, the "old
man" has not been an impediment to the union of the young

but rather the principal advocate of it; and even if his plan had succeeded in bringing about a union between his daughter and the King of Navarre, there would have been no justification in calling the action a comedy. What Shakespeare has done in *Love's Labor's Lost* is to give an almost archetypal action for courtly comedy (that is, the quest for "true" love, ideal love, or the marriage of minds, conceived of presumably as part of a larger quest for the source of our being) but set within the earthy conditions and commitments proper to the action of genuine comedy. The young men in the play see themselves as participating in the first kind of action; the Princess and her ladies-in-waiting attempt to participate in the second kind, and do so with complete but disguised seriousness. The result is that the courtly comedy part of the play, unprotected from the outside world by any kind of quarantine, falls victim to the ills of the flesh. The Princess, knowing full well what those ills are, hears of the death of her father and prepares to leave immediately for France. Death is one of the contingencies of her life, and she understands how to behave in the presence of it. The King and Berowne, by contrast, who still live and move in a world where death is the ultimate disgrace, can only seek to dissuade her.

The King argues as follows:

> . . . since love's argument was first on foot,
> Let not the cloud of sorrow justle it
> From what it purpos'd; since to wail friends lost
> Is not by much so wholesome-profitable
> As to rejoice at friends but newly found.
> [V.ii.747-51]

Berowne's argument is jesuitical and much lengthier, despite the fact that he has promised to use "honest plain words." The ladies have produced a radical change of purpose in their young men, he says, and therefore they are responsible for what the young men have become:

> Our love being yours, the error that love makes
> Is likewise yours. We to ourselves prove false,
> By being once false forever to be true
> To those that make us both—fair ladies, you;

And even that falsehood, in itself a sin,
Thus purifies itself and turns to grace.
[V.ii.771-76]

Either of these arguments would do for a sophisticated sonnet,
but both sound a bit strange being addressed to one on her way
home to a funeral, and neither is accompanied by any expression of sympathy or word of comfort. The men are still incapable of proffering anything more than the theoretical kind of
love they have been articulating for their own amusement, and
the Princess knows it. Her eloquence puts theirs to shame:

We have receiv'd your letters full of love;
Your favors, embassadors of love;
And in our maiden council rated them
At courtship, pleasant jest, and courtesy,
As bombast and as lining to the time;
But more devout than this [in] our respects
Have we not been, and therefore met your loves
In their own fashion, like a merriment.
[V.ii.777-84]

When they protest again, she responds sagely to the King,
"Your Grace is perjur'd much, / Full of dear guiltiness"
(V.ii.790-91); then she challenges him to spend a year in "some
forlorn and naked hermitage" fasting and meditating before he
repeats his declarations.

There is evidence that at least the King hears what she is
saying, but no evidence at all that the other three do. Berowne,
whose Rosaline adds visiting and comforting the sick to her
prescription of penance, cries out: "To move wild laughter in
the throat of death? / It cannot be, it is impossible: / Mirth
cannot move a soul in agony" (V.ii.855-57). His final exchange
with the King shows that even at the end he remains un-
enlightened:

Ber. Our wooing doth not end like an old play:
Jack hath not Gill. These ladies' courtesy
Might well have made our sport a comedy.
King. Come, sir, it wants a twelvemonth an' a day.
And then 'twill end.
Ber. That's too long for a play.
[V.ii.874-78]

The concluding songs, with which this examination of *Love's Labor's Lost* began, are used as a device to suggest the ultimate reconciliation of the King and the Princess.[6] Armado, who despite his braggadocio is actually one of the simple children of the earth, comes forward to offer the last part of their show, and the royal pair receive him graciously and hear his "dialogue" between Winter and Summer. Thus even though the Folio version of the play specifies that the characters leave the scene in different directions ("You that way: we this way"), it ends on a note of acceptance and in a hope of harmony for at least two of the participants; and the down-to-earth quality of the two marvelous songs (Mercury after Apollo indeed!) further suggests that real comedy may be possible after the prescribed twelvemonth and a day.

Love's Labor's Lost has sometimes been called an experiment or brilliant apprentice work; it is both of these in the sense that it puts an action customarily called comedy to the test of external reality—the measure that Shakespeare always used, from his first play to his last, in comedy as well as in history and tragedy. Shakespeare did not, and perhaps could not, produce "pure art" or explore art as a thing in itself; he may have recognized art or "creativity" as humankind's noblest gift, as Sir Philip Sidney did, but he saw it always as a means to knowing a creation not made by hands or human ingenuity. We can never be sure to what extent he looked out of the world he had made from time to time to test and measure the details of that external creation; even in *Love's Labor's Lost*, where it is clear he did just that, we can never be quite sure of what he saw. In any case, we can be sure that he repeatedly deployed the light of his art to see and know better the infinite ramifications of that heart of reality, the great action of human life to which in this study the term *comic* is limited.

5

A Midsummer Night's Dream

A Midsummer Night's Dream, Shakespeare's fourth comedy, marks the end of his early period of experimentation. Most scholars agree that the play came into being as a private entertainment devised for the wedding of some aristocratic couple.[1] Moreover, the marks of its occasional nature are such as to invite comparison with the court masque, though the masque in 1595 was still relatively amorphous.[2] Nevertheless, marks of the public playhouse also appear on all extant versions of the play—the first quarto of 1600, the Roberts quarto of 1619, and the Folio text—and some have speculated that the fifth act as we have it contains at least two and possibly three alternative endings, further proof of adaptation for the stage.[3] At any rate, stage comedy it is; and Frank Kermode has declared his willingness to maintain that *A Midsummer Night's Dream* is Shakespeare's best comedy.[4] One could certainly argue that it is the best introduction to Shakespearean comedy. Everything needful for the comedy of his day is there, and more besides: rustic clowns to grace three of the first four acts and dominate the last one, the lyric voices of children reminiscent of John Lyly's sophisticated productions, as well as Lyly's diminutive fairies, and the mysterious wood of George Peele's best comedy with lovers that Peele and perhaps even Robert Greene might have admired. More important, there is an action which expands the conflict of Roman comedy to include oppositions of generations, sexes, and social strata, to say nothing of the orders of creation, and contributes significantly to the continuing Renaissance inquiry into the nature of love. In addition, the play reflects a greater cosmic action which not only includes the scope of Roman comedy and its derivatives but also reaches out to embrace any human activity that has to do with transition and renewal. One may wonder how a piece of such variety and complexity could have provided entertainment for a wedding without distracting attention from the festivities it was supposed to enhance. Yet one may more profitably consider how Shakespeare, on being confronted with a special assignment, suddenly, perhaps for the first time, saw the whole brilliant design in the carpet of comedy ready to come together in his mind and, without giving further thought to the proprieties of the occasion, began to look for a combination of compatible devices to hold it all in focus.

That it all did achieve focus is implicit in Hippolyta's assertion near the beginning of the fifth act, where she responds to her new husband's brilliant but easy generalizations about fantasy and fiction. Hippolyta knows of the relationship between herself and Theseus, now mysteriously changed from hostility to something like affection; she knows the story of the young lovers and their night in the forest; and she dimly suspects forces are at work that she cannot begin to account for:

> . . . all the story of the night told over,
> And all their minds transfigur'd so together,
> More witnesseth than fancy's images,
> And grows to something of great constancy;
> But howsoever, strange and admirable.
>
> [V.i.23-27]

We, of course, know more than Hippolyta does, and what we know is the texture of the play that has now taken shape, all but completely, as a coherent action before our eyes. The objective of this chapter is to unravel enough of that texture to see at least the magic in it if not the larger mystery behind.

Any analysis of the design of *A Midsummer Night's Dream* should distinguish four motifs, all of which are present to some degree throughout most of the play. The initial motif, or subject, constitutes the periphery of the comprehensive action (we begin and end with it), and it is the part of the play most serviceable as a complement to a wedding. This is the business of Theseus and Hippolyta, a slender thing, encountered briefly but memorably in the printed text and by no means inconsequential; without this motif the play as we know it would disappear. It surrounds and protects the next motif, that of the four young lovers, which is much more extensive; and it has a real, though tenuous, link with the third motif, that of Oberon and Titania, which provides the center for the play and its cosmic reference. The fourth motif, provided by the mechanics of Athens, grounds the whole in real earth, recognizable as English earth, and in the play of Pyramus and Thisby presents an unforgettable if parodic reminder of the precariousness of love between the sexes. It also momentarily bridges, in the unlikely person of Bottom the weaver, the seemingly impossible gulf between humanity on earth and the prototypes of humanity in the suprahuman world of the fairies. In fact, one commentator finds the play centered in Bottom, the transformer and the transformed, who consorts with the Queen of the Fairies, and who carries all the other creatures of earth with him into the glittering spaces of the Duke's palace.[5] Bottom is easily the most arresting character in the play, of course; more than any other he holds the disparate parts together, and he can be made to stand at the center of it all. But he does not belong there.

The characters at the center of the action are indeed Oberon and Titania,[6] and their problem is the failure of love, which in one way or another is the problem that preoccupies the other groups also. Whether this failure in the case of the fairy monarchs represents simply a deficiency, something that has always been lacking in their relationship, or a falling away, the play does not make clear. They are at odds when we first see them, and the immediate occasion for their disaffection is Titania's reluctance to give Oberon an orphan boy that he is particularly fond of:

> A lovely boy stolen from an Indian king;
> She never had so sweet a changeling.

> And jealous Oberon would have the child
> Knight of his train, to trace the forests wild.
>
> [II.i.22-25]

Clearly the trouble is deeper than this. Titania notes that Oberon has come to Athens solely because of a nostalgic fondness for Hippolyta, who was once his mistress, and a wish to bless the bed that Hippolyta will share henceforth with Theseus; she notes also that Oberon has had other favorites (II.i.64-73). Oberon retaliates by charging Titania with an illicit love for Theseus that presumably has made her interrupt the Greek hero's philandering on at least four occasions. This charge she denies ("These are the forgeries of jealousy"), but she continues in a soliloquy of almost forty lines to acknowledge the estrangement from her lord and to find in that estrangement the cause of current abnormalities on earth—fogs, floods, and pestilence:

> The seasons alter: hoary-headed frosts
> Fall in the fresh lap of the crimson rose,
> And on old Hiems' [thin] and icy crown
> An odorous chaplet of sweet summer buds
> Is, as in mockery, set; the spring, the summer.
> The childing autumn, angry winter, change
> Their wonted liveries, and the mazed world,
> By their increase, now knows not which is which.
> And this same progeny of evils comes
> From our debate, from our dissension;
> We are their parents and original.
>
> [II.i.107-17]

Regardless of what relationship may have been between Titania and Oberon in the beginning, the bickering that characterizes their relationship here makes one think of the Greek Zeus and Hera rather than of traditional English fairies and calls to mind Zeus's philandering, Hera's justifiable anger, and the reflections of their subsequent quarreling on human counterparts down below. In the manner of Zeus, what Oberon wants from Titania is wifely complaisance rather than love or affection in any of its commonly recognized manifestations. By her own admission she has recently forsworn his bed and company; but this, as we know, is not really the issue. Oberon has usually been able to find agreeable bedmates. He wants the boy, partly because it is in the nature of fairies to want such changelings, but mainly, we believe, because he needs a show of obedience from his wife. Failing to achieve that, he needs to inflict some appropriate punishment for her obstinacy. Thus when Titania offers to let him rejoin her company of fairies and be a spectator at their moonlight revels, he once more demands the boy. "Not for thy fair kingdom," she replies, whereupon he promptly dispatches his self-appointed jester, Robin Goodfellow, to bring him the flower love-in-idleness, with its mysterious color and power derived from one of Cupid's spent shafts. Both the agent and the flower he fetches require comment at this point.

Robin Goodfellow, according to the unnamed fairy who makes an entrance with him at the beginning of Act II, is of a different "shape and making" from the other supernatural characters in the play. K.M. Briggs, one of the more recent commentators on the representation of fairies by Shakespeare and other writers, supports this observation, noting that Robin Goodfellow's race is quite distinct from that of the trooping fairies, to which Oberon, Titania, and company belong.[7] He is a puck, to use the name we usually give him—a hobgoblin, or, as people in Shakespeare's time sometimes called such creatures, a "bug" or "bogey." We ourselves may best think of a puck as a domestic spirit, one who, as the unnamed fairy says (II.i.34-42), delights in doing small chores about a friendly patron's house or in playing practical jokes. This is why Shakespeare's contemporaries regarded pucks with much friendly feeling, even though, as Briggs notes, the Church had for centuries held them to be devils and sometimes lumped them along with fairies under one condemnation with "ghosts," who wander about in the night, "damned spirits all, / That in crossways and floods have burial" (III.ii.382-83).[8] Oberon enlightens Robin on this point: "We are spirits of another sort," he says; and as far as the limits of the play go, that settles the matter. Clearly Oberon himself is kindly disposed towards well-behaved human beings and uses Puck to minister to them, much as Prospero uses Ariel to minister to other human beings in *The Tempest*. Nevertheless, we should note and keep in mind that Puck does not possess efficiency commensurate with his loyalty to his master. He can bumble on occasion and does so conspicuously when he mistakenly applies the powerful juice of love-in-idleness to the eyes of Lysander, thus momentarily destroying the young man's love for Hermia. Robin's penchant for error gives us a puck who is vulnerable to a fate he does not fully understand and apparently does not particularly care to. For him such a limitation is no great problem, but for Oberon it is cause for a certain amount of vexation. Being king to a race of trooping fairies loses much of its savor if he cannot be king in his own household. There, as in the Athenian wood generally, he cannot be fully master without resorting to the special power of a tiny flower.

Love-in-idleness is, in fact, the one infallible agent in this play about creatures natural and supernatural; and Shakespeare has Oberon give Puck a pretty explanation of how the plant came to have its peculiar character and potency:

> . . . I saw (but thou couldst not),
> Flying between the cold moon and the earth,
> Cupid all arm'd. A certain aim he took
> At a fair vestal throned by [the] west,
> And loos'd his love-shaft smartly from his bow.
> As it should pierce a hundred thousand hearts;
> But I might see young Cupid's fiery shaft
> Quench'd in the chaste beams of the wat'ry moon.
> And the imperial vot'ress passed on,
> In maiden meditation, fancy-free.
> Yet mark'd I where the bolt of Cupid fell.
> It fell upon a little western flower,
> Before milk-white, now purple with love's wound,
> And maidens call it love-in-idleness.
>
> [II.i.155-68]

Modern scholars have noted the compliment to the Virgin Queen here and surmised that the Queen herself, if she heard it, took note and was amused. Actually, as glosses and the *Oxford English Dictionary* tell us, the flower is the common pansy, or *Viola tricolor*, which goes by the name "heartsease" as well as

by Shakespeare's term, "love-in-idleness." Paul Olson's suggestion that the last of these names involves the notion of lust,
commonly and anciently associated with idleness, probably
puts us off the track.[9] The love that Oberon's flower produces
differs only in intensity from any of the kinds it may displace;
and this is as it should be, for there is no suggestion anywhere
in the play that love can be differentiated into kinds.

The love we see in *A Midsummer Night's Dream*, regardless of
how it is manifested, is always the impulse that looks forward
to the attachment of one being to another—or, consummated,
it is the tie that binds. The best statement of it comes in
Helena's description of the friendship that she and Hermia
enjoyed before other manifestations of love began to make
contradictory claims:

> We, Hermia, like two artificial gods,
> Have with our needles created both one flower,
> Both on one sampler, sitting on one cushion,
> Both warbling of one song, both in one key,
> As if our hands, our sides, voices, and minds
> Had been incorporate. So we grew together,
> Like to a double cherry, seeming parted,
> But yet an union in partition,
> Two lovely berries moulded on one stem;
> So with two seeming bodies, but one heart,
> Two of the first, [like] coats in heraldry,
> Due but to one, and crowned with one crest.
> And will you rent our ancient love asunder,
> To join with men in scorning your poor friend?
> [III.ii.203-16]

This is love as postulated roughly midway through *A Midsummer Night's Dream*, and the rest of the play goes on to show how
a measure of harmony is eventually re-established between
these two and also between their distractable and distracted
lovers. Shakespeare does not presume here or elsewhere to
penetrate the mystery of love's source or the nature of its
awesome power. He is content to symbolize both in the fiction
of the flower that he assigns to Oberon, and there he leaves
them. Nevertheless, his fiction does tell us that the power of
love is loose in the world; and it is this power that Oberon in his

frustration, with Puck's help, proceeds to deploy against his recalcitrant spouse. "Fetch me that flower," Oberon says to his willing servant, and from this desperate and dangerous command all the events of the midsummer night and those of the last act follow.

Nothing, of course, quite follows as the fairy King intends it should. Even before Puck can return with the flower, Oberon has espied Helena's futile pursuit of Demetrius and vowed to turn the young man's churlishness into affection; then, ignorant of the second pair of lovers in the forest, he gives the order to Puck that results in the estrangement of Hermia and Lysander. When Oberon tries to correct that mistake, this time applying the juice himself, he succeeds only in estranging both pairs of lovers and turning two erstwhile friends, Hermia and Helena, into brawling enemies. That he does somewhat better in his attempt to triumph over Titania is due in part to Puck's inspired improvisation whereby Titania, prompted by the juice of love-in-idleness in her eyes, falls in love with a metamorphosed Bottom. Oberon admits as much. "This falls out better than I could devise," he exclaims delightedly (III.ii.35); yet on seeing her innocently sleeping in the weaver's arms he is unexpectedly moved to pity. Titania, moreover, having found love in her induced affection for Bottom, transfers it readily to her legitimate husband and so makes it possible for them both to bless the nuptials in Act V, "hand in hand, with fairy grace" (V.i.399). This is a far better blessing for all concerned than the one Oberon had originally planned to give singly to Theseus and Hippolyta, and he assumes charge of the reconstituted operation with as much confidence as if he had planned it all in advance: "Every fairy take his gait, / And each several chamber bless" (V.i.416-17). "Honest" Puck in his bid for applause, immediately following, is more candid and refers to the "unearned luck" (V.i.432) which may enable them all to escape the London audience's hiss of disapproval.[10] Even the young lovers, characters not traditionally given to modesty, assume no credit for the resolution of their differences and the achievement of their suits, but take Duke Theseus's word for it that they have somehow "fortunately met" and willingly follow him to the temple to plight their troths in the publicly approved fashion.

Thus chance, or some undefined and perhaps undefinable power, ultimately governs things in *A Midsummer Night's Dream*. This is nothing new, of course; Shakespearean comedy generally runs on some kind of "unearned luck," and characters who suddenly recognize that they are not in control of events are prone to cry witchcraft or fairy. One recalls how Dromio and Antipholus of Syracuse came early to the conclusion that Ephesus was some kind of enchanted city and likewise recalls that faery or its equivalent was invoked by Shakespeare's characters in a number of other plays, from *The Merry Wives of Windsor* to *The Tempest*. To be sure, affirmations of faery, in all but one or two instances, cannot be taken to mean the actual presence of supernatural beings; but they all point to the fact that in Shakespearean comedy, human ability to account for even purely human events inevitably fades in a mist of uncertainties if pressed far enough. As Demetrius waking puts it, "These things seem small and undistinguishable, / Like far-off mountains turned into clouds" (IV.i.187-88). It remains a mystery that Egeon should find his Aemilia after thirty-three years of thinking her dead. It is a mystery worthy to be set down "with gold on lasting pillars" that things work out as they do on Prospero's isle (V.i.208); and it is no less a mystery that such disparate couples as Theseus and Hippolyta, the two immature couples in the wood, and the anciently incompatible Oberon and Titania should all end in charity with one another. The last is, in fact, even more of a mystery than the others, for in *A Midsummer Night's Dream* Shakespeare has peeled back the layers of appearance to show us what is presumably a symbol for the primal reality at the source, and what we see there is only a mystery within a mystery, more unearned luck, as firmly established at the center as it is at the surface.

This is why one should exercise a degree of caution in applying Northrop Frye's brilliant generalizations about the role of the "green world" in Shakespearean comedy. The presence of such a world, Frye has suggested, "charges [Shakespeare's] comedies with a symbolism in which the comic resolution contains a suggestion of the old ritual pattern of the victory of summer over winter."[11] So it does. Nevertheless, in *The Two Gentlemen of Verona*, one of Frye's examples, the presentation of that world is at best perfunctory and of itself effects very little. Moreover, in *Love's Labor's Lost*, where the entire action takes place in the King of Navarre's park, immersion in what might be called a green world shows the action to be something different from the contest between summer and winter, or youth and age, that in fidelity to the expected pattern of comedy it might well have been. Admittedly a green world figures more prominently in *A Midsummer Night's Dream*, in which the fairy manipulators have their habitat in the Athenian wood and all the other characters happen to go there to experience their actions of metamorphosis. The irony in *A Midsummer Night's Dream*, however, is that the green world of the Athenian wood is itself in serious trouble; and Oberon and Titania, who are responsible for the trouble, are king and queen of that world. Furthermore, the young lovers who lose and find themselves again within it, do so not because of the wood but because of their "unearned luck" in encountering there the juice of love-in-idleness, which brings a full measure of mature love into their relationship for the first time—even for the first time into the relationship beween Lysander and Hermia—and confirms in their lives the mature presence of that rhythm, the early stirring of which sent them scurrying out of Athens in the first place.

Indeed, Puck's phrase "unearned luck" seems to provide a better key to the meaning of the action of *A Midsummer Night's Dream* than does the combination of setting, human characters, and supernatural agents that gives the play its distinctive character. By its very nature that phrase precludes explanatory commentary, but it suggests both the mysteriousness of the mainspring that runs our lives and the inexplicable benefits we sometimes receive; and it symbolizes the optimism that to some degree marks all of Shakespeare's comedies, with the possible exception of the anomalous *Troilus and Cressida*. Here it is the pansy-like flower in the wood rather than the wood itself which is Shakespeare's symbol for the mystery at the heart of things; and that symbol, moreover, does not focus our attention on any of the struggles that theoretically precede a comic resolution—not the immemorial struggle between winter and summer, though that is perhaps alluded to in the play, nor the struggle between high estate and low, nor even that between old and young. Some such opposition is presented, at least briefly, in most of the comedies that Shakespeare wrote, and the third of those mentioned—the struggle between old and young—appears conspicuously in *A Midsummer Night's Dream* in the opening confrontation between Egeus and his daughter Hermia; but neither here nor elsewhere does such an opposition appear to generate the action that follows. The dynamo that generates and drives a Shakespearean action of renewal, with or without actual death preceding, remains a mystery. Moreover, Shakespeare's agent of transformation is more often than not some unlikely person—an eccentric male suitor or an aggressive female in disguise—or even, as here, a seemingly innocuous flower that acts with all the power of a cosmic ray and appears unexpectedly on the scene to effect or hasten beneficent metamorphoses in men, women, or other sluggish creatures. We never penetrate to the full meaning even of the visible agent in this play, or for that matter in any of Shakespeare's other plays; but we see the effect of the agent on all who are amenable to change—here, by direct action on the four young lovers, and by indirect action on Theseus and his captive bride, on Oberon, who thinks he is making use of the flower rather than being used by it, and on Titania, of course, who is Oberon's principal concern.

We also see its effect on Bottom, who, even as a monster, becomes the Adonis to Titania's Venus and then survives to report the fact of his "translation" in a rare but apparently quite unconscious parody of 1 Corinthians 2.9 (IV.i.204-19). The important thing to note about Bottom, however, is that he remains essentially unchanged. His name would have led the Elizabethan audience to expect nothing of him, "bottom" being the common term for a weaver's irreducible bobbin, spool, or clew to hold a skein. Peter Quince, on seeing the ass's head on his friend's body, may cry out in amazement, "Bless thee, Bottom! bless thee! thou art translated" (III.i.118-19); but Bottom, for all that, is still Bottom the irreducible in a world that is to be accepted rather than transcended. His dream is "a most rare vision," also irreducible and without bottom; and the man who sees such a vision presumably becomes wiser as a consequence. Bottom, however, does nothing different from what he would have done in any case, and even to the astonished Peter Quince he remains the same man. This point is important because it reminds us that, despite our talk about transformation, the other characters in the action of this play are not *essentially* different after their midsummer night's dream. They have simply developed, much as one imagines that nature intended them to develop. In short, they have become themselves, recognizable human beings rather than puppets to custom or convention. This is not quite Ovid's type of metamorphosis, but it is metamorphosis of a more credible kind—still mysterious, not entirely inconsonant with Ovid, and distinctively Shakespearean.

Regardless of its origin, however, the transforming love that appears in this play—love in idleness, which is to say, love dangerously on the loose—is presented as a normal part, perhaps even as the *sine qua non*, of growing up.[12] Granted that Theseus equates it with madness (V.i.4) and that Oberon refers to it as "dotage" (IV.i.47), we are not to assume that either diagnosis is adequate or accurate. Throughout Shakespeare's work, the erotic urge, what Victorians sometimes called "the mad abandon of love," is treated as something quite appropriate to youth, and indeed appropriate to the first stages of love at any age. For example, Armado's erotic love for Jaquenetta in *Love's Labor's Lost* would be dotage by Oberon's definition; but the foolishness that is compounded with Armado's love is derived from Armado's total being, not merely from his being in love, and would have been conspicuous in his character in any case. In fact, his being in love is treated with respect in the play. He knows the girl is lowborn but loves her in spite of that, wins her away from Costard (obviously her peer), gets her with child in defiance of the edict, and accepts the moratorium at the end with better grace than almost any other male in the play. "I am a votary," he says; "I have vow'd to Jaquenetta to hold the plough for her sweet love three year" (V.ii.883-84). Likewise, by Oberon's definition the love of Romeo for Juliet, which Shakespeare was probably putting into dramatic form at about the same time as he was writing *A Midsummer Night's Dream*, would be dotage.[13] Friar Lawrence would certainly have called it that had he not had an ulterior motive in letting it be the prelude to a marriage. Yet Romeo's love, like Juliet's, is an affection of high seriousness and intensity, and readers almost without exception have accorded it the respect that the play with its compelling poetry invites us to grant. By contrast, Malvolio's love in *Twelfth Night*, which Olivia calls "midsummer madness" (III.iv.56), is tainted with the folly of its sole progenitor, whose principal motives are self-love and avarice and, in any case, not some essence derived ultimately from Cupid's shaft.

In the first scene of *A Midsummer Night's Dream* the loves of Lysander and Demetrius for Hermia, though different in degree and respectability, fall somewhere between Romeo's initial infatuation and Malvolio's transparent masquerade, and the resulting contention between the two, though excellent material for New Comedy of the classical kind, carries with it the romantic expectation that one or both of them will indeed find the love they have presumed to declare. Lysander has courted in the approved fashion and has persuaded Hermia to transfer her loyalty from father to suitor. Demetrius, who has previously sued in similar fashion for the hand of Helena (I.i.106-14), has now turned his attentions to Hermia, who appears to be a more profitable venture, and has succeeded in convincing Egeus, her father, that he is the preferable choice for his daughter. Lysander puts forth his claim, mixing protestations of love with quantitative arguments presumably designed to sway a pragmatic old man. To Theseus serving as arbiter he declares:

> I am, my lord, as well deriv'd as he,
> As well possess'd; my love is more than his;
> My fortunes every way as fairly rank'd,

> (If not with vantage) as Demetrius';
> And (which is more than all these boasts can be)
> I am belov'd of beauteous Hermia.
> Why should not I then prosecute my right?
>
> [I.i.99-105]

Except for the fact that "preferr'd" might serve better here than "belov'd," all this is true enough, though "right" strikes a discordant note. We shall presently look at the evidence that Hermia's love is also something less than complete. Nevertheless, at this point, she and Lysander stand on the threshold of love and, drawing on their reading knowledge of the matter, comment more sagely than they realize on the difficulties of young love and above all on its brevity and uncertainty, calling it

>   . . . momentany as a sound,
> Swift as a shadow, short as any dream,
> Brief as the lightning in the collied night,
> That, in a spleen, unfolds both heaven and earth;
> And ere a man hath power to say "Behold!"
> The jaws of darkness do devour it up:
> So quick bright things come to confusion.
>
> [I.i.143-49]

These magnificent words are Lysander's.[14] One may wonder whether the callous youth is aware just how many bright things in this world come to confusion; but everything he says at this point is borne out fully in the events of the night that is almost upon them: the young lovers separate, Oberon makes his move, confusions abound, and before dawn comes, all concerned fall into despair and thence exhausted into sleep. Although true love is within their grasp and has been so almost from the beginning, they do not quite know it; and they achieve a happy outcome of their difficulties only as a result of the intervention of Theseus, who ends the impasse in their lives by forgiving youth's defection and requiring age to accede to the inevitable. One can hardly avoid casting a mental glance here at Prince Escalus in *Romeo and Juliet*, who intervened with his authority too late to remove the obstacles in the path of his young lovers and thus perforce found them dead. Without Theseus these lovers in *A Midsummer Night's Dream* might well have encountered the defeat that befell their counterparts in Verona or the ill-fated Pyramus and Thisby, whom the mechanics portray in Act V. Indeed, but for Theseus the lovers in the wood might well have come short of New Comedy altogether and made a double tragedy.

Two details in the play suggest as much. One suspects that Shakespeare hit upon the first of these as he went about the routine business of constructing his plot. To make use of the flower and account for Puck's mistake in infecting Lysander rather than Demetrius, he had somehow to separate an ardent and aggressive suitor from a companion grown strangely cautious in the depths of the forest. To do this he might have invoked a bear, or robbers, or even a rainstorm. Instead he had the two young people lose their path, grow momentarily weary, and settle themselves for a brief respite. The exchange at this point runs as follows:

> *Her.*   Find you out a bed;
> For I upon this bank will rest my head.
>   *Lys.* One turf shall serve as pillow for us both.
> One heart, one bed, two bosoms, and one troth.
>   *Her.* Nay, [good] Lysander; for my sake, my dear,
> Lie further off yet; do not lie so near.
>   *Lys.* O, take the sense, sweet, of my innocence!
> Love takes the meaning in love's conference:
> I mean, that my heart unto yours [is] knit,
> So that but one heart we can make of it;
> Two bosoms interchained with an oath,
> So then two bosoms and a single troth.
> Then by your side no bed-room me deny;
> For lying so, Hermia, I do not lie.
>   *Her.* Lysander riddles very prettily.
> Now much beshrew my manners and my pride,
> If Hermia meant to say Lysander lied.
> But, gentle friend, for love and courtesy,
> Lie further off, in humane modesty;
> Such separation as may well be said
> Becomes a virtuous bachelor and a maid,
> So far be distant; and good night, sweet friend.
> Thy love ne'er alter till thy sweet life end!
>   [II.ii.39-61]

Whatever his intentions may be, Lysander's sentiments here anticipate but fall considerably short of Helena's "Two lovely berries moulded on one stem . . . two seeming bodies, but one heart" (III.ii.211-12). Even so, Hermia declines to put her sweet friendship for the young man to a test by consenting to the arrangement that both he and prudence urge upon her. Her response, referring to "courtesy," "humane modesty," and virtue, is the response of an Athenian maid who thinks she is still in Athens and who has forgotten that in repudiating the social context for such phrases she has forfeited her right to insist upon them. In any case, the two lie apart as always and fall asleep so; and when Hermia awakes to find Lysander gone indeed, she recalls in horror the dream she has just had of a serpent at her breast. Self-love, perhaps? A casual observer might say that Lysander begins to wander dangerously at this point only because of Puck's intervention; but such an observer, if he or she missed seeing Puck's hand in the matter, might just as easily conclude that Lysander, cooled by Hermia's continuing prissiness in the face of raw life, has simply wandered afield and cast his unappreciated ardor on the first pretty girl in view; and the observer would, of course, be at least partly right. For all the events of this night, from the confusion of the lovers to the "translation" of Bottom, however much they may have been prompted by puckish intervention, derive their significance from causes far more deeply embedded in the observable grain of things than a prankster's activity.

The second discordant note in this portion of the play is that both Puck and Oberon intervene in their New Comedy plot at the wrong place for a true comic intervention and do so for the wrong reasons. The roles these two assume, uninvited, are those of the wily servant and the good friend respectively—Brainworm and Wellbred, to use the names that Ben Jonson gives them in his own version of conventional New Comedy, *Every Man in His Humor*—and the function of puck and fairy king in these borrowed roles is to frustrate Egeus and his favorite, Demetrius, so that Hermia and Lysander may get to the aunt's and a proper wedding with as little fuss as possible.

In Jonson's play we see much of Brainworm and Wellbred and their distracting activity but nothing of young Nowell and Bridget after they have eloped until they return at the end to receive congratulations and join in the feasting. So it is, in fact, with Shakespeare's next pair of eloping lovers, Anne Page and Fenton, in *The Merry Wives of Windsor*; but in his *Midsummer Night's Dream* Shakespeare pulls back the curtain to show what goes on between lovers on the way to the altar, to demonstrate that the course of true love indeed "never did run smooth," and to reveal that sometimes agents we had assumed to be on the lovers' side are as likely to hinder as to help.

In short, what makes a comic action go on to its expected end remains as mysterious as love itself, which, despite what this play shows us, we never fully understand.[15] Whether it be a psychological response or a divine impulse, a force amenable to reason and will or one totally capricious, such knowledge is beyond us. We can be certain only that when treated carelessly and directed incautiously, the awesome power of love can cause great damage, bring its victims to madness, or do even worse. We do not know much more about those supernatural beings who are said sometimes to be the lovers of mortals— whether they are the movers of the universe, as Titania suggests (II.i.117), or evil spirits, such as Puck originally was in English folklore and such as Oberon intimates he and his own kind have been accused of being (III.ii.378-88). All we know for certain is that when love is uncontrolled, the fat is in the fire. Then old worlds may burn, and things may change; and people are lucky indeed if the new world that emerges is one in which their lives may find renewal, thereby enabling them to escape once more the annihilation that lurks always at humanity's elbow, whether one remains in a well-lighted Athens or wanders into the potentially sinister wood that lies a league beyond.

The role of Theseus, to carry the comparison with Jonson's *Every Man in His Humor* one step farther, is analogous to that of Justice Clement; that is, he arbitrates, cuts the stubborn knot, calms fears, makes peace all round, and thus makes it possible for the audience to go home reassured. Yet there is one key difference: Theseus participates extensively in the action of the play. Whereas Jonson's Clement does not. Before the beginning of *A Midsummer Night's Dream*, Theseus, to credit Oberon's report about him (and Plutarch's), was an abuser of females and at one time (this on Oberon's report alone) paramour of Titania herself. As the play opens, he has just captured another queen, Hippolyta of the Amazons, and is proceeding with plans to wed her four days hence. Hippolyta is understandably a bit reluctant to see the days go by; but her only choice is to submit, and after four and a half lines at the beginning of the scene, she keeps her reluctance to herself. At this point old Egeus arrives to complain that his daughter, Hermia, is insisting on marrying Lysander, a young man of her own choice rather than his; and Theseus, confronted by this threat of youthful rebellion, takes a stand on principle, sides manfully with the father, and orders the girl either to obey or to take the consequences. The law, one should note, would have allowed Egeus to take the girl's life if she proved obstinate. Theseus qualifies that regulation, allowing Hermia to choose a cloister if she cannot follow the wishes of her parent: "For aye to be in shady cloister mew'd, / To live a barren sister all your life, / Chaunting faint hymns to the cold fruitless moon" (I.i.71-73). Nevertheless, he is much kinder to Demetrius, who stands justly charged with having won and then abandoned the unfortuante Helena. Theseus is fully aware of the young man's fickleness:

> I must confess that I have heard so much,
> And with Demetrius thought to have spoke thereof;
> But, being over-full of self-affairs,
> My mind did lose it. But, Demetrius, come,
> And come, Egeus, you shall go with me;
> I have some private schooling for you both.
>
> [I.i.11-16]

The best one can say of this performance is that it shows one philanderer dealing with another.

From this point on we see no more of Theseus until the end of Act IV, when we meet him with Hippolyta and company on their way to a hunt at the edge of the Athenian forest. It is of considerable importance to keep time and dates in mind here. Apparently only something under forty-eight hours has elapsed since the beginning of the play, when Theseus and Hippolyta noted they were four days short of the new moon, the time at which Hermia had been instructed to return her decision about marrying Demetrius. Lysander and Hermia agreed to elope "tomorrow night" (I.i.164), and they have since spent only a single night in the forest. Theseus and Hippolyta thus come upon the four weary young people sleeping on the ground only two days after Egeus stormed into Theseus's chamber with his demand for just application of the law. We are still two days short of the appointed wedding day for the royal pair; and the date, whatever else it may be, is not May Day, as Theseus shortly suggests (IV.i.132-33). Most editors, noting the title of the play, say that it suggests something written for a performance at Midsummer's Eve—that is, for the festivities of the night before June 24, which is also the eve of the feast of St. John the Baptist. Pagan or Christian, that date had long been an occasion for games, bonfires, and merrymaking; and in some areas, notably in Scandinavia, where spring comes later than in most places, it had also served as a time for choosing mates.

Some editors go on to say, however, that in spite of its title, *A Midsummer Night's Dream* is a May-Day play. Glosses indicate that their error derives from a misunderstanding of the remarks made by Theseus when he discovers the couples: "No doubt they rose up early to observe / The rite of May; and hearing our intent, / Came here in grace of our solemnity." (IV.i.132-34). Theseus's mention here of "rite of May" apparently causes some to take his "now our observation is perform'd" a few lines earlier (IV.i.104) as a reference to his own observance of the rite of May with Hippolyta, an observance which in view of their previous betrothal would have been rather pointless even were it May and not June.[16] A far more reasonable supposition is that the royal pair have got up to attend early mass, or whatever observance is appropriate to their "temple" in this Shakespearean Athens, and that Theseus, having come upon young people in a compromising situation, gallantly tries to put the best possible appearance on his discovery. It is not May Day, and it is not St. Valentine's either, though he playfully chides them with a reference to that day also: "Good morrow, friends. Saint Valentine is past; / Begin these wood-birds but to couple now?" (IV.i.139-40). The immediate occasion for both references is undoubtedly the angry countenance of old Egeus, who even in these circumstances is prepared to repeat his demand that Hermia either accept his choice of a mate for her or else remain single for the rest of her life. Theseus, having found love himself, sees the discovery of love reflected in the sleeping faces of the young people before him and, perhaps prompted by the image of peace they present, magnanimously reverses himself on the spot. The time for choosing mates and making preliminary arrangements is past. The young people have chosen and, for all he knows, have already acted upon their choice. It is midsummer, a time in England for celebrating weddings rather than for making preliminary sallies; the bridegroom is at hand. Thus Theseus cancels the morning's hunting and the rest of the waiting period before his "sealing day" and bids the couples return immediately with him to the temple for instant weddings—then back to Athens, where "three and three" they will hold "a feast in great solemnity" (IV.i.184-85).

Theseus's sudden action, betokening humility and charity, betokens also a larger change of heart, for his newly displayed virtues continue in Act V. One notes his forbearance with Hippolyta when she contradicts him on the subject of poetry, his charitable treatment of the simple mechanics and their absurd play, and his gentle concern for the young people he has just taken under his care. Theseus the conqueror and philanderer has grown in stature in the course of the play, it would seem; though whether he has indeed been moved by the power of love-in-idleness reflected in the younger lovers' eyes, the play does not allow us to say for certain. In any case, the miraculous transformations of Puck's doing are nothing to compare with what has taken place in the heart of this mature ruler, where love is no longer idle but active and growing in wisdom and stature as well as in beauty.

We can also see in Theseus's role a reflection of the theme of appearance and reality that pervades *A Midsummer Night's Dream* and frequently moves critics and scholars to comment. In fact, the play opens with Theseus's declaration, already noted, that the four days remaining before the wedding will move much too slowly, followed by Hippolyta's rejoinder that, on the contrary, they are likely to be as swift as anyone could ask—an exchange that is perhaps to be taken simply as an opposition of the two points of view to be expected in a prospective groom and bride; yet both of them contemplate the reality that Lysander is shortly to declare

> Brief as the lightning in the collied night,
> That, in a spleen, unfolds both heaven and earth;
> And ere a man hath power to say "Behold!"
> The jaws of darkness do devour it up.
>
> [I.i.145-48]

In other words, all three here look upon love as an objective, something to be reached for or perhaps avoided. Helena, by contrast, in a speech delivered some hundred lines later, near the end of the scene, sees love as an agent or force: "Things base and vile, holding no quantity, / Love can transpose to form and dignity" / (I.i.232-33). Happily, her view of the reality of love is vindicated in the several actions of the flower and in the transformation referred to by Hippolyta, who in Act IV can speak of the cacophony of the hounds in Crete as "all one mutual cry. . . . So musical a discord, such sweet thunder" (IV.i. 117-18), and by Theseus, who can good-humoredly postulate a seemly reality beneath the undeniable appearance of two pairs of young lovers sleeping together on the turf. The lovers themselves, as we have seen, awake, hear the Duke's revised judgment, and linger to wonder about the reality of all they have seen and experienced during the past few hours:

> *Her.* Methinks I see things with parted eye,
> When every thing seems double.
>   *Hel.*   So methinks;
> And I have found Demetrius like a jewel,
> Mine own, and not mine own.
>   *Dem.*   Are you sure

That we are awake? It seems to me
That yet we sleep, we dream.

[IV.i.189-94]

Finally, as soon as all the others have left the stage, a restored Bottom appears on the scene to declare his vision: "The eye of man hath not heard, the ear of man hath not seen, man's hand is not able to taste, his tongue to conceive, nor his heart to report, what my dream was" (IV.i.211-14). This scene in Act IV, in short, brings the mortals together, removes the supernatural machinery from control, and leaves them all variously, but happily, confronting the contradictory world of appearances (which is the only reality most people ever know), but still wondering timidly about the meaning of those intimations of an ultimate mystery that have come to them.[17]

Act V continues with an exchange between the two mature lovers, who at the end of Act IV had not yet articulated their wonder openly. Poetry, Theseus is saying grandly (in a frequently quoted passage), is only an unreliable imagination's creation of the appearance of reality:

I never may believe
These antic fables, nor these fairy toys.
Lovers and madmen have such seething brains,
Such shaping fantasies, that apprehend
More than cool reason ever comprehends.

[V.i.2-6]

As we have already noted, Hippolyta persists in seeing the situation differently and speculates that the poetic process may be a means of discovering the presence of a reality behind the appearances of reality, however incredible those appearances may be. The exchange between Theseus and Hippolyta reveals (as one suspects that Shakespeare thought it should) what the play as a whole does: that is, it speaks of a concatenation of disparate actions—an enforced marriage, a marital quarrel, a tragedy, a romantic adventure of lovers in a wood, all explicitly presented as forms of comedy that one might expect to encounter on the stage or in print—and invites us to see behind the whole patchy fabric, lurking in the shadow, something inordinately substantial, "something of great constancy; / But howsoever, strange and admirable" (V.i.26-27). That constancy, regardless of how it is described or defined in abstract terms, speaks of an indestructible reality immanent in every comic action—a reality that Shakespeare's concatenations of the tangible, more frequently than those of any other writer in history, touched and made known. *A Midsummer Night's Dream,* being fantasy for the most part, presents concrete symbols of that reality which stand out all the more sharply for having been embedded in something evanescent, like cherries in ice. There is no mistaking them, and yet all such symbols are at best faint clues to what lies behind both the symbols and the evanescent dream. We cannot ignore either of these or make the mistake of taking them lightly.

Indeed, they are probably the best reason for calling *A Midsummer Night's Dream* our best introduction to the study of Shakespeare. Of all his early works this onetime much neglected play speaks most explicitly and eloquently of Shakespeare's greatness, of the mode of his mature perceptions, and of the sympathy that that mode engenders. The play works best for us if we bring a minimum of special knowledge to it. Knowing that it may have been used in celebration of somebody's wedding contributes little to our understanding or appreciation; knowing that it anticipates the Jacobean masque contributes even less. Its relation to specific classical myths is only name-deep in most places; and its relation to Elizabethan fairy lore, important as that is, is practically explained in the text itself. In fact, one book-length study of such matters compels us to the conclusion that Shakespeare here created considerably more folklore than he perpetuated.[18] To get into the play, one has only to read it a couple of times with that whole heart and free mind with which Mark Van Doren once asked us to read all of Shakespeare.[19] After that, if unearned luck be our lot as well as that of the principal characters, the action may take control and carry us backwards—or down or upwards, who knows?—to Roman or Greek comedy, to rite, to a primitive yearning for a life beyond life or, equally likely, to the savage child's impulse to reach for more than a child's grasp can accommodate. Before *A Midsummer Night's Dream*, says Leo Salingar, Shakespeare's interest was to develop an intricate plot.[20] Granted, but after that play he was bold to write comedies with plots that are open-ended, comic plays to be performed on a simple stage, the backdrop of which in the course of things turns out to be neither a curtain nor a theater wall but the smoky depths of the universe itself.

6

The Merchant of Venice

No one who has ever read Plato's *Symposium* is likely to forget that haunting picture near the end, of Socrates still drinking and still clear-headed, talking on past cock-crow of such things as the relation between tragedy and comedy, and insisting to his befuddled listeners that the writer of tragedy ought to be a writer of comedy also. In a sense we are all still very much Socrates' befuddled listeners, but we can at least recognize that no piece of work in any literature more brilliantly exemplifies the consequences of a playwright's following that suggestion of his than Shakespeare's does. Unfortunately, no body of work also demonstrates more effectively the special problems an author temperamentally inclined to work in both comedy and tragedy can create for his academic interpreters. This chapter will address some of these special problems as they arise in *The Merchant of Venice*, which, as we have seen, was certainly not the first of Shakespeare's comedies to exhibit such difficulties. Nor was it to be the last. The comedies that Shakespeare wrote near the middle of his career—*All's Well That Ends Well, Measure for Measure*, and the anomalous *Troilus and Cressida*—show a particularly disturbing kind of confusion, for in these the traditional somber tones of tragedy everywhere mingle indiscriminately with the gaiety, such as it is. Indeed, some details in these plays are so "uncomic" by most standards that modern critics have made a point of calling them "dark comedies" or "problem comedies" or, most recently, simply "problem plays." As for Shakespeare's late comedies, encumbered as they are with odd things like monsters, brothels, beheaded villains, and dead children, one can understand why critics from Ben Jonson to modern academic scholars have been tempted to leave them out of the comic category altogether, dubbing them "romances" or even "tragicomedies."

The Merchant of Venice is different from all these in that its special mixture of the tragic and the comic has seemed to invite drastic reduction by critics and producers; and, in fact, for two centuries this play, which now sometimes is treated as little more than a gorgeous fairy tale, had to make its way in public theaters as a near-tragedy. One might say that *The Merchant of Venice*—like *A Midsummer Night's Dream,* which has been wrenched from its comic category only in recent years—throughout has a tendency to make the attentive reader divide "one thing entire to many objects, / Like perspectives," a quality which Bushy in *Richard II* attributes to tears (II.ii.17-18). Perspectives, or optical toys, can be fun, of course; but serious audiences and readers, at least in our own time, seem to be suspicious of unresolved doubleness in a literary work and seek to be reassured that somewhere beneath all the appearance is an unambiguous core of solid meaning. As mentioned earlier, such a core in *A Midsummer Night's Dream,* if one exists, will probably continue to resist explication indefinitely; but the disturbing thing about *The Merchant of Venice* is that doubleness in it extends to the ethical dimension of the play, so that one's wonder at the mystery behind it all begins to give way to an uneasy suspicion that the stark truth behind the surface of this comedy might just be uncomfortable and perhaps even intolerable.

This is why most inquiries into the meaning of the play begin with Shylock. He is not the whole play by any means; but he is the most memorable figure in it, and he provides the most memorable illustration of the problem that concerns us. People were beginning to sense Shylock's special kind of doubleness early in the eighteenth century, when Nicholas Rowe suggested (1709) that Shakespeare had probably designed his play as a piece about a savage Jew. The nineteenth century, more humanitarian than the eighteenth, elected to treat it as a play about a savage Jew deeply wronged. The twentieth was dissuaded from both emphases, in large part by E.E. Stoll's famous essay of 1911, which set forth a well-substantiated case for the historical propriety of seeing Shylock as a comic villain, "a sordid miser with a hooked nose";[1] but Stoll's view has not prevailed absolutely, and nowadays the consensus, if one may risk calling it that, is that Shakespeare's Shylock is a character of contradictions compounded, both unjustly sinned against and variously and sometimes mysteriously sinning, and that he belongs in the play principally because of his part in a plot that has mainly to do with friends and lovers.[2]

Acceptance of this view, unfortunately, has frequently been accompanied by a tendency to treat the play pretty much as the fairy tale that Harley Granville-Barker thought it to be.[3] In the midst of all the pageantry, singing, dancing, and lovemaking stands Shylock as the incredible intruder, oftentimes vicious, usually devious, sometimes almost admirable, and occasionally pitiable. He is like the wicked witch of "Snow White," who must be discredited and destroyed so that the good people can live happily ever after. In some interpretations, however, Shylock is made to resemble those victims of racial persecution that have tormented the consciences of men and women of good will in our own times; and whenever this is the emphasis, his downfall, richly deserved as it may be, makes us all feel uneasy, as if we ourselves were somehow to blame for the humiliation that comes to him. In short, we are either asked to treat Shylock as a scarecrow villain or invited to respond to him with feelings that preclude our attempts to understand him; in both cases our comprehension of the play as a whole suffers. We need very much to see in the text and on the stage that hateful-sympathetic Shylock of the better modern studies and productions; but, more important, we need to see whether such a richly endowed character, not reduced but presented in all his complexity, can be legitimately unified with the action of a play with which in one way or another he has for so long been merely associated.

One noteworthy attribute of Shylock's that can bring his

character together for us, regardless of how we happen to interpret it, is his capacity for rage. In this at least the Jewish usurer of Giovanni Fiorentino's *Il Pecorone*, which provided the story of the bond and much of the rest of the plot except for the caskets, is at one with the miserly parent—perhaps taken from the fourteenth tale of Masuccio's *Novellino*—who became hysterical when his daughter stole all his ducats and jewels and eloped with her lover.[4] Rage, however, is always a symptom rather than a thing in itself, and the response of readers and spectators to a presentation of rage must depend upon the circumstances they can mentally bring forward to account for it. Thus the raging usurer of *The Merchant of Venice* can easily seem pathological or inhumanly monstrous to those who, because of prejudice or because of details stressed in the performance before their eyes, are made to think primarily of Shylock's undying antipathy to a generous Antonio; yet the same usurer may seem pathetic to those who elect or who are led to see primarily a lonely Jew who against his better judgment tries to come to terms with snobbish Christians and finds himself mocked and robbed of his wealth and his only daughter. Clearly, however, the play as written suggests both possibilities to us throughout; and as for the rage itself, the play also equivocates on that, letting us first see a hilariously distraught Jew through the eyes of that heartless pair Salerio and Solanio, and then bringing us into his presence to hear directly his eloquent claim to human consideration and his lament over the loss of a turquoise that his dead wife Leah had given him before she became his bride. If we read or see all this without the impediment of intellectually imposed restraints, we can and should experience a series of widely differing reactions during the course of the play; but if Shakespeare has done his work properly, the end should find them all focused in a single impression. Otherwise we have a choice of Shylocks and a choice of plays, and any *Merchant of Venice* that satisfies us must be a reduction.

Focusing here is not impossible, however; for all aspects of Shylock's rages, the hateful as well as the pathetic, can be seen to derive from a single attitude: his preoccupation with self.

Never in the play do we catch more than the most dubious glimmer of altruism in Shylock. He would love to catch Antonio on the hip, he says, and "feed fat" the ancient grudge he bears him (I.iii.41-52); and thus when he breaks custom, offering to lend Antonio money gratis and proposing only a "merry bond" in lieu of interest, he does so with the ancient grudge in mind—that, and perhaps the expectation of a renewal of Bassanio's perfunctory invitation to a Christian's dinner. At home he starves his household and views the departure of the ebullient Launcelot with a reflection that his going will be an economy. Presumably Shylock does feel something like love for Jessica, his only child; yet he sequesters her as if she were no different from ducats and jewels, and when she escapes he laments the loss of all three in a single outcry. Even his much praised declaration to Salerio and Solanio—"Hath not a Jew eyes? Hath not a Jew hands?"—turns at the end into a threat of revenge. It does not really extenuate his fault to say that persecution and oppression have made him the way he is. Many Christians—Gratiano, for example—are bullies and apt for revenge; and Christians like these have tormented Jews for centuries. But the Duke of Venice seems not to be so minded, and Antonio clearly is not; nor is revenge characteristic of their Christian faith (as Shylock intimates that it is), for Christianity like Judaism teaches forgiveness. Sanctioned or not, however, revenge is everywhere in the Western world and usually serves as a device for reducing justice to a matter of personal satisfaction, something that Shylock can understand. In any case, preoccupation with self is the ground upon which the two "Shylocks" of Shakespeare's sources come together. In this the Jew of *Il Pecorone* coalesces with the miser of Masuccio's brief tale, and the result is a character that is by turns frightening, pitiable, and laughable but consistently self-centered from first to last.

Self-centeredness also constitutes the ground upon which the play as a whole most conspicuously displays its unity, and it is that quality which relates Shylock to all the other well-developed characters in the play. Readers fearful of losing the romance and what they consider to be the true comedy of *The*

Merchant of Venice might urge that this point be treated lightly; but erring in overemphasis, even if that were a danger, would probably be preferable to pressing too little or not at all. What Shakespeare did in this unorthodox specimen of comedy was to take the action seriously—endow it with veritable substance—at precisely that point where some of us prefer to take it for granted. In romantic comedy we tend to want villains that are villains and lovers that are innocent. Most especially we resist the implications that those on whom the continuation of the community will depend are no more selfless than those who would hoard and sterilize its sustenance and its life. Admittedly, in their degree of affliction with self-interest the characters who dominate the scenes at Belmont come considerably short of Shylock in being villainous or selfish. Their preoccupation with self is of the degree that characterizes most fallible, redeemable human beings; thus, the members of the Belmont group are contrasted with the Jew even in their cardinal point of resemblance. Moreover, being capable of reform, they move in the action as human beings move and not as stereotypes: that is, they move towards enlightenment and renewal and not merely in the direction of a denouement.

The play hardly shows us anything like that, of course, in such undeveloped characters as the Duke of Venice, or Launcelot Gobbo, whose lively performance consists almost entirely of stage conventions, or even Gratiano, whose childishly savage baiting of the defeated Shylock in Act IV might have been cited earlier in this chapter to illustrate the young man's aptitude for revenge. Among the principals, however, there is none who consistently avoids the preoccupation with self and also none who does not in some way resist, escape, or try to hide it. It shows up in Lorenzo and Jessica, despite their occasional protestations to the contrary. One suspects that Lorenzo might have been less inclined to run away with Jessica had she not been able to bring along financing for the expedition; and Jessica, who despises Shylock's blood in her and regards his house as a very hell, cannot be said to have run away solely for love. Bassanio's self-centeredness is even more explicitly presented. He begins as the selfish young wastrel (Shylock calls him a prodigal) who, having been tempted by wealth and a vision of feminine beauty, does not hesitate to impose disastrously on the generosity of a friend. Thereafter a succession of traumatic experiences—the choosing of the casket, the trial, and the surrender of the ring—brings him out of his childish preoccupation; and in the end a very different Bassanio wins not only wife and wealth but also his wife's love and deep respect. What is more important, he achieves his own integrity. This progressive transformation of Bassanio serves as the main vehicle for the action of the play.

Many undoubtedly would argue that Antonio does not belong in such selfish company. The prevailing view seems to be that he is a good and generous man, troubled through no fault of his own by unaccountable premonitions. Mark Van Doren, for example, calls him "one of Shakespeare's gentlemen" and absolves him completely of anything like a taint of self-love.[5] Not long ago, however, Professor Thomas H. Fujimura in a full study of the problems of *The Merchant of Venice* gave us an Antonio who is afflicted by hubris in the opening scenes of the play ("the product of his spiritual condition, of his lack of charity and his ignorance of self") but who comes through suffering to recognize his weakness (in the trial scene) and thus participates fully in the comic resolution in Act V.[6] One may question Professor Fujimura's description of growth in Antonio, but self is certainly at the root of the troubles Antonio encounters, in the beginning and throughout the rest of the play. It is a topic he enjoys dwelling upon in conversation, and to keep it available he must imagine some malaise that he alone suffers from, preferably one with fuzzy edges that can escape diagnosis indefinitely. In the first scene of the play Salerio and Solanio give him occasion to refute two explanations for his current melancholy; then Lorenzo enters with Gratiano, who also joins the conversation, only to receive the following response: "I hold the world but as the world, Gratiano, / A stage, where every man must play a part, / And mine a sad one." (I.i.77-79). To this piece of unsubstantiated melancholia Gratiano replies tactlessly but acutely:

> I tell thee what, Antonio—
> I love thee, and 'tis my love that speaks—
> There are a sort of men whose visages
> Do cream and mantle like a standing pond,
> And do a willful stillness entertain,
> With purpose to be dress'd in an opinion
> Of wisdom, gravity, profound conceit,
> As who would say, "I am Sir Oracle,
> And when I ope my lips let no dog bark!"
> O my Antonio, I do know of these
> That therefore only are reputed wise
> For saying nothing; when I am very sure
> If they should speak, would almost damn those ears
> Which hearing them would call their brothers fools.
> I'll tell thee more of this another time;
> But fish not with this melancholy bait
> For this fool gudgeon, this opinion.
>
> [I.i.86-102]

Finally, only Bassanio and Antonio remain on stage, and Bassanio for the moment is too preoccupied with his own interests to provide much occasion for the examination of Antonio's. Still, Bassanio, ever in need of funds, has been the most consistently attentive of Antonio's companions; and Antonio—in friendship certainly but partly also, one may believe, out of a need of friends—listens to one more request and decides to do whatever he must in order to meet it.

What Antonio does is to go to Shylock, for his supply of ready cash has at last come to an end; and granted that friendship has provided him with a need he cannot ignore, Antonio clearly needs Shylock more than Shylock needs him. Thus his resentful and arrogant behavior to the Jew, contrasted as it is with Bassanio's restraint, should give us cause for concern about Antonio's ethical stature. It is possible to say that Shylock here in his opening scene is simply the stereotype of a usurer and that Antonio's insulting of him is only conventional business, but the play as a whole provides too many ways of looking at Shylock for that explanation to be convincing. It is also possible to say that Shakespeare himself is being anti-Semitic here, but the whole text of the play renders that possibility most unlikely. Moreover, it is not merely this one instance of bad manners that makes us uneasy about Antonio, but the sum of all his dealings with Shylock. We note that he treats the Jew with consummate arrogance when he has no cause to fear him (I.iii) and with more caution when the Jew has the upper hand (III.iv). After the trial is over, he does move to see that Shylock is able to survive and perhaps amend his life; but that public display of generosity has been prompted by a request from the triumphant Portia disguised as a young lawyer, and mercy has just recently been the topic of conversation. There are reasons, in short, and some would say compelling reasons, for seeing Antonio as successively arrogant, servile, and charitable only for purposes of self-interest.

First, there is the letter to Bassanio, which arrives at Belmont just after the betrothal of Bassanio and Portia has been compared: "Sweet Bassanio, my ships have all miscarried, my creditors grow cruel, my estate is very low, my bond to the Jew is forfeit; and since in paying it, it is impossible I should live, all debts are clear'd between you and I, if I might but see you at my death. Notwithstanding, use your pleasure; if your love do not persuade you to come, let not my letter" (III.ii.315-22). The sober tone of the letter is perhaps understandable, but it is worth noting that nothing in it bespeaks a continuing concern for Bassanio's welfare. Conceivably Antonio, thinking that he knew his man, surmised at the outset that nothing much was likely to come of the expedition to Belmont; but as we are beginning to see at this point in the play, he underestimated his young friend, who has now already succeeded beyond any realistic expectations. Nevertheless, Antonio for the personal satisfaction of having Bassanio attend his execution has unhesitatingly put in jeopardy his friend's chance for a lifetime of wealth and happiness; and before the play is over, he will do so again.

More to the point is Antonio's attitude just before and at the beginning of the trial. He does not really give the Duke a chance to say whether or not he has a plan to save a fellow Venetian's life but instead launches into some laudatory comments about his own fortitude in the face of oppression:

> . . . since he stands obdurate,
> And that no lawful means can carry me
> Out of his envy's reach, I do oppose
> My patience to his fury, and am arm'd
> To suffer, with a quietness of spirit,
> The very tyranny and rage of his.
>
> [IV.i.8-13]

But, as we eventually learn, the Duke does have a plan. First, he calls Shylock into the courtroom and urges him to be merciful. Then when Shylock, after much wrangling, refuses as expected, the Duke makes clear something that we as observers of these proceedings should have suspected all along. "Upon my power I may dismiss this court," he says; then he adds, "Unless Bellario, a learned doctor, / Whom I have sent for to determine this, / Come here to-day" (IV.i.104-7). Dr. Bellario is one of the mysteries in this play. He is Portia's cousin, or so she says (III.iv.50); but whether she has been doing some spying or whether she merely knows that Bellario is in the habit of helping the Duke with embarrassing cases we never learn. It does not greatly matter. We do learn that the Duke has decided not to let the affair go all the way to the taking of flesh, and that is the only point that really concerns us. Antonio's life, in short, is never really in jeopardy in the play. Almost at once Bellario's young friend is announced, and the trial goes forward with what appears to be a lawyer from Rome in charge. Our suspense is dependent now not upon what the Duke may do but upon whether the young lawyer (whom we recognize as Portia in disguise) will prove equal to the occasion.

One does not imagine that Antonio perceives any of this. He is too completely absorbed in self-pity, opposing patience to fury, urging the Duke to give up urging the Jew to relent, and declaring to Bassanio (who vainly urges him to be of good cheer and have courage) the following:

> I am a tainted wether of the flock,
> Meetest for death; the weakest kind of fruit

> Drops earliest to the ground, and so let me.
> You cannot better be employ'd, Bassanio,
> Than to live still and write mine epitaph.
> [IV.i.114-18]

After this Antonio continues in his role of self-appointed scape-goat until Portia triumphs, and then he demonstrates to her, the Duke, and all assembled his comprehension of mercy:

> So please my lord the Duke and all the court
> To quit the fine for one half of his goods,
> I am content; so he will let me have
> The other half in use, to render it
> Upon his death unto the gentleman
> That lately stole his daughter.
> Two things provided more, that for this favor
> He presently become a Christian;
> The other, that he do record a gift,
> Here in the court, of all he dies possess'd
> Unto his son Lorenzo and his daughter.
> [IV.i.380-90]

We are probably right to take all this for evidence of Antonio's intent to be merciful, but nagging difficulties remain. Scholars still disagree about the exact meaning of the first six lines of the speech, and moralists bridle outright at the eighth line. Moreover, the last three give approval to an abduction which can be approved only if Shylock is totally villainous or if he is simply a stereotype of the despicable miser of New Comedy.

In any case, Antonio serenely resumes his sober course, apparently unaware that his motives may be questionable. When Bassanio objects to giving the young lawyer Portia's ring, protesting first that it is a "trifle" and then admitting the significance of it, Antonio chides him for misplacing his values: "My Lord Bassanio, let him have the ring. / Let his deservings and my love withal / Be valued 'gainst your wive's commandement" (IV.i.449-51). Later, when Portia seems to be challenging Bassanio's faithfulness, Antonio will remind her that having once lent his body to save his friend, he is now prepared, like a benevolent Faustus, to lend his soul "upon the forfeit, that your lord / Will never more break faith advisedly"

(V.i.252-53). This is a noble and dramatic gesture, allowing for the fact that souls are normally not ours to pledge; but Portia ignores Antonio's inadvertent presumption and the self-esteem that has generated it, accepts a statement of good intentions at face value, and joyfully returns the ring that she certainly never meant to keep. Antonio is, of course, no soul-pledging Faustus here, nor even a Malvolio sick of self-love. He has not presumed to seek a lady who does not want him, and he has condemned no revelers. He is, like most of us, merely human, stronger than Bassanio and perhaps even spiritually larger. Unlike the more deeply tainted Shylock, he has prospects of getting better; but Antonio has only just arrived at his point of change, and he still has a good distance to go.

After Antonio only Portia remains to be accounted for in this play about selfish people. Like her husband, Portia manages to grow out of self-love in the course of the action, but the beautiful thing about her transformation is that she manages it almost entirely on her own. In the beginning, one notes, Portia is humanly restive under the restraint imposed by her father's will: "O me, the word choose! I may neither choose who I would, nor refuse who I dislike; so is the will of a living daughter curb'd by the will of a dead father" (I.ii.22-25). It is the simple waiting-woman Nerissa who sets her on a healthier course at this point with the admonition: "Your father was ever virtuous, and holy men at their death have good inspirations; therefore the lott'ry that he hath devis'd in these three chests of gold, silver, and lead, whereof who chooses his meaning chooses you, will no doubt never be chosen by any rightly but one who you shall rightly love" (I.ii.27-33). Later, when Bassanio comes to his crucial moment of choosing, impatience recurs and almost gets the better of her; but this time she herself puts selfish concern aside and finds her own interests more than amply rewarded thereby with the husband she wants.

The greatest test for Portia comes moments after her betrothal, when Salerio brings Antonio's letter. At first she is equal to the challenge, putting friendship before love and telling her husband, "You shall hence upon your wedding-day"

(III.ii.311). Afterwards she is less certain, and though she conceals her uneasiness (Lorenzo speaks of her "godlike amity, which appears most strongly / In bearing thus the absence of your lord"), she betrays her concern in a number of ways. To Lorenzo she rationalizes about her situation with a skill that would do credit to a sophist, but she almost trips on her own cleverness:

> I never did repent for doing good,
> Nor shall not now: for in companions
> That do converse and waste the time together,
> Whose souls do bear an egall yoke of love,
> There must be needs a like proportion
> Of lineaments, of manners, and of spirit;
> Which makes me think that this Antonio,
> Being the bosom lover of my lord,
> Must needs be like my lord. If it be so,
> How little is the cost I have bestowed
> In purchasing the semblance of my soul,
> From out the state of hellish cruelty.
>
> [III.iv.10-21]

Then, catching herself at the brink of a relapse, she breaks off with, "This comes too near the praising of myself, / Therefore no more of it." Nevertheless, we shortly learn that she has embarked on a course of action with a determination and energy that earlier in her career might have been used to propel her into collision with Antonio. Indeed, a Portia still immature and still selfish would have had no quarrel with the Jew, who might even have served her cause by removing from the scene a serious rival for the affection of her husband. Shakespeare's Portia, however, transcends her own interest and by working to preserve the friendship of two men effects the transformation of her childlike husband, makes possible the transformation of the melancholy Antonio, and in her demonstration of mercy provides the murderous Jew with the only shock that has even the remotest chance of penetrating his solipsistic prison.

Act V has often been credited with providing the cap of meaning to this comedy, and rightly so. This is the expected function of the fifth act in almost any conventional comedy, where lovers and their supporters have at last arrived at the point of celebrating with banqueting and other festivities a triumph over the tyranny of their elders. The Belmont of Act V, however, glittering in its candlelight, is not to be taken as a symbol of that earthly paradise towards which all good lovers in comedies hope to move; rather, it serves as a reminder that the imperfections of Venice continue even here and must continue beyond the limits of the play. This is the point of that incredibly beautiful opening passage in which Jessica and Lorenzo exchange allusions to lovers famous in literature—Troilus, Thisby, Dido, and Medea. One notes that, for all our beautiful memories of their stories, not one of these was happy in his or her love; and the two young lovers at Belmont know that. This is why, against the background of music that must surely be more suggestive of satisfaction than satisfying in itself, Lorenzo speaks of perfection elsewhere:

> Look how the floor of heaven
> Is thick inlaid with patens of bright gold.
> There's not the smallest orb which thou behold'st
> But in his motion like an angel sings,
> Still quiring to the young-ey'd cherubins;
> Such harmony is in immortal souls,
> But whilst this muddy vesture of decay
> Doth grossly close it in, we cannot hear it.
>
> [V.i.58-65]

And this is why a few minutes later, as Portia is arriving from her secret expedition to Venice, we get her pleasant and meaningful exchange with Nerissa on the subject of universal imperfection:

> *Por.* That light we see is burning in my hall.
> How far that little candle throws his beams!
> So shines a good deed in a naughty world.
>   *Ner.* When the moon shone, we did not see the candle.
>   *Por.* So doth the greater glory dim the less:
> A substitute shines brightly as a king
> Until a king be by, and then his state
> Empties itself, as doth an inland brook

Into the main of waters. Music, hark!
    Ner. It is your music, madam, of the house.
    Por. Nothing is good, I see, without respect;
Methinks it sounds much sweeter than by day.
    Ner. Silence bestows that virtue on it, madam.
    Por. The crow doth sing as sweetly as the lark
When neither is attended; and I think
The nightingale, if she should sing by day
When every goose is cackling, would be thought
No better a musician than the wren.
How many things by season season'd are
To their right praise and true perfection!
                      [V.i.89-108]

Part of what Portia is saying here is that most of the things we call perfect are only relatively so; and surely we are to understand that her observations apply also to gentlemen and their ladies, lovers, Venetian merchants, and servants. At any rate, it is with Portia's words still fresh in mind that we move to the expanded scene, the last of the play, where stand all the other characters (Shylock excepted) with their flaws very much about them—Lorenzo the abductor; Jessica the thief; Launcelot the seducer, heartless prodigal, and serving-man; Bassanio the husband, faithless in spite of himself; garrulous Gratiano; and Angelo with his sadness intact. Portia still has her imperfections, too; she has much confessing to do and, with regard to Dr. Bellario, some explaining. Yet unlike most of the others and very much unlike Antonio, Portia is aware of her imperfections; and it is she who has just articulated that principle which unites Shakespeare's comedies with his tragedies: the principle whereby we are urged to accept substitutes until a true king be by, to take things as they come to us, at face value whenever that is possible but always as a gift deserving of our respect and our effort at understanding.

There is nothing mindless or servile about this kind of acceptance. The world that Shakespeare sees has plenty of evil in it and plenty of people with courage to take arms against their sea of troubles, but it is also a world informed by a will that was good in its original intention and continues to be so in the main. Accepting Shakespeare's world means correcting whatever is obviously in need of correction and continuing to hope that the rest will in good time either correct itself or prove the critics wrong. It may well be that Hamlet's initial fault lay in imagining that the ghost's command to do one specific thing was a command to set the whole age right. Portia has too much humility and too much good sense to undertake any such giant task, but her powerful presence in the workings of *The Merchant of Venice* keeps the denouement from being merely an escape from Shylock. Without her there could have been no transformations, no love, no laughter except a few sighs of relief raised to hilarity, and no acceptance at the end.

Such acceptance Shakespearean comedy regularly requires of us in lieu of the poetic justice and other kinds of distortion that we are sometimes tempted to impose upon it. This is the bittersweet truth that we all too often fail to perceive because our vision of imagined harmony blinds us; but the bittersweet is there, and only an acceptance of both parts of that compound can make the plays truly satisfying, as they stand, without reduction. More important, perception of the quality of Shakespeare's comic achievement can help us to bring the force of his plays from scene to audience as a power in people's lives rather than as diversion or soporific. If we are fortunate, or unfortunate, enough to escape confrontation with the challenges of normal daily existence, we may continue to stand in self-absorption with Antonio in a world where absolute perfection remains a hypothetical possibility. If like most people we must expect daily disappointments, mediocre wine, and rain in the afternoon, then the implicit admonition in this play may be of some relevance to us. It is fitting that the play should end with an indirect presentation of this admonition by way of a piece of action that is virtually required by the movement of the scene. It comes when Gratiano looks at his untried bride of several days and says:

> The first inter'gatory
> That my Nerissa shall be sworn on is,
> Whether till the next night she had rather stay,
> Or go to bed now, being two hours to day.
> [V.i.300-303]

Nerissa does not answer at this point in the play, for Gratiano has Shakespeare's last word; but most producers know what to have her do. She looks at her husband, frowns playfully at him, kisses him full on the lips, and then, clasping his hand as tightly as she can, races for the nearest bedchamber.

7

The Taming of the Shrew

For many students the really interesting questions about *The Taming of the Shrew* have to do with the circumstances of its composition. No one knows for certain when Shakespeare wrote the play or, indeed, whether he wrote it once or twice. Since Francis Meres makes no mention of it in the *Palladis Tamia* of 1598, scholars in the past have sometimes given it a date as late as 1602; but in recent years most have tended to follow E.K. Chambers in assigning the play to 1594, thus grouping it with the earliest comedies, *A Comedy of Errors, The Two Gentlemen of Verona*, and *Love's Labor's Lost*. One good reason for settling on 1594 is the entry for May 2 of that year on the Stationers' Register of a similar but anonymous play called *The Taming of a Shrew*, which was either the play Shakespeare revised or an early version that Shakespeare himself wrote and came back to at a later time.[1] In any case, the appearance of a second version of the popular *Shrew* play on the stage in 1594, the one we now unhesitatingly assign to Shakespeare, may very well have prompted Shakespeare's company to enter the superseded version for publication.

Yet some aspects of *The Taming of the Shrew* give it a sophistication that makes one uneasy with the early date. Thematically it resembles the somewhat later *A Midsummer Night's Dream* and *The Merchant of Venice*; and thus in the absence of firm evidence one way or another, one is tempted to assign a tentative date of 1596, suggesting thereby its advance over the earliest comedies and its affinities with the two comedies of

1595-96. *The Taming of the Shrew* also has obvious affinities with *Much Ado about Nothing*, which seems not to have been performed until the winter of 1598-99, and that relationship has sometimes tended to overshadow its connection with the earlier "middle" comedies. To be sure, both *The Taming of the Shrew* and *Much Ado* develop from a situation involving a complaisant marriageable female and a shrewish unmarriageable one, and both provide instances of Shakespeare's early fondness for disguises and mistakings. The earliest comedies also have disguises or mistaken identities of one kind or another, but for the most part these are mistakes of the surface: twins who happen to look alike, women who put on men's clothing, dancers masked, and nighttime wanderers transformed by magic. *The Merchant of Venice*, for example, although like *Much Ado* it turns upon a superficial but carefully engineered error in identity, derives its distinctive character from mistakes of a more serious kind—miscalculations about the relationship between parent and child, between spouses, and between friends; so that a fully satisfying resolution of the whole intrigue (and most today feel that it is *not* fully satisfying and was perhaps not meant to be) would have required most of the principals to make substantial concessions and end wiser, and soberer, than they began. For *The Taming of the Shrew* Shakespeare seems to have gone out of his way to enliven his basic text with mistakes of the more superficial variety, even to the extent of heavily mining George Gascoigne's *Supposes* in the process; and this suggests either a continuation of the strategy that had worked brilliantly for him in *The Comedy of Errors* or at least a temporary return to it. Nevertheless, in reworking the text of an older play—if that is in fact what he did—he produced a comedy that exhibits considerably more of the serious kind of mistaking than it has sometimes been given credit for.

A probable reason for the long-standing neglect of the subtleties of *The Taming of the Shrew* is that its frame plot, with its crude but funny practical joke on the drunken Christopher Sly, almost automatically signals audiences to prepare for a farce.[2] Scholars regularly observe that the earlier version of the story,

The Taming of a Shrew, completes the frame plot, allowing Sly to wake after the last act and go home vowing to tame his own shrewish wife; and some have regretted that Shakespeare in the revised version permits Sly to disappear from view after the first scene of the first act. Alexander Pope assumed that the corresponding ending in Shakespeare's version had somehow got lost in transmission and without noticeable misgivings concluded his edition of *The Taming of the Shrew* with the last scene of the anonymous play. Pope's judgment was not entirely faulty here. *The Taming of a Shrew* remains good theater to this day, and we have every reason to suppose that it was fairly successful in its own time: an amusing, uncomplicated farce with clean lines, written in full awareness of the popularity of the London theater's brightest young playwright, Christopher Marlowe, echoes of whose lines appear here and there throughout. Thus if *A Shrew* came first, as most now seem to agree that it did, Shakespeare in a second version of the play was giving his audiences a story they already knew and could enjoy seeing presented again. They had come prepared first to enjoy the joke played on old Sly and then to settle down with him to an evening of fun at the expense of a headstrong female who should be brought to heel properly by a madcap wooer. The audience knew that even without an ending Sly had to wake up; and given their memory of the relatively simplistic version of the story in the older play, in which Sly's conclusion was predictable, they were probably prepared to hear him say again:

> . . . I know now how to tame a shrew,
> I dreamt upon it all this night till now,
> And thou hast wakt me out of the best dreame
> That ever I had in my life, but Ile to my
> Wife presently and tame her too
> And if she anger me.
>
> [xix.15-20]

For us today, however, who have at most a scholar's memory of the simpler taming in *A Shrew*, the old conclusion of the Sly frame plot jars with the Kate-Petruchio action that Shakespeare has provided for his revised play, and his new Sly, though re-created in believable flesh and blood, is constitutionally incapable of reaching across the threshold of the farce that surrounds him to touch even briefly a real world beyond. The less believable Sly of the older play does see an exemplum, for him a lesson in practical morality; and although he can conceive of applying it only in a peasant's world where there is no shading and no ambiguity, he has found at least some meaning in what he sees. Shakespeare's Sly apparently finds no meaning at all in the play that is presented for his pleasure. We see that much clearly at the end of the first scene, where Shakespeare before consigning him permanently to Limbo gives him one final speech: " 'Tis a very excellent piece of work, madam lady; would 'twere done!" This Sly is totally unable to comprehend the notion that he may be (indeed, *must* be in any fulfillment of his humanity) figuratively both tinker and lord, slave and master, mean and glorious, all at once—cousin to the notion that taps insistently at our awareness as we watch the Induction and remains at the edge of our consciousness until an awakened Katherina ushers it in fully developed at the end of the play. The young lord in the anonymous play had observed of his victim, "Fie, how the slavish villaine stinkes of drinke"; but for that peasant Sly, as the sequel showed, there was still some faint hope of rehabilitation. The young lord in Shakespeare's version declares, "O monstrous beast, how like a swine he lies! / Grim death, how foul and loathsome is thine image!" (Induction, i.34-35). This Sly, for all his liveliness, is beyond enlightenment, redemption, or even a temporary reprieve. His early dismissal serves to warn us, at least in retrospect, that in watching this play about conventional and unconventional wooing and marriage, we do well to avoid being blinded by conventional judgments, however hallowed by custom those judgments may be, and to take a fresh look at a familiar tale.

In any case, *The Taming of the Shrew* has continued to require a fresh look, even from audiences and readers predisposed to find a norm of sorts in the Roman-comedy plot that gives the play its backbone; for what we have there is not the usual Roman-comedy plot. In focus throughout most of the play is what one might call the "backside" of Roman comedy: the attempt of a good-natured parent, who is nothing like the traditional *senex*, to achieve a satisfactory marriage for a favorite daughter. He encourages eligible men to court her and gives every indication of approving marriage with the person who legitimately wins her hand. A more typical Roman comedy would have focused on Lucentio, the young man, who has left Pisa with his father's permission and come to Padua to study the arts but who instead falls in love and enlists the aid of a wily servant to help him circumvent his father's intentions and win the young woman he fancies. The presumptive obstacle to the fulfillment of the young man's wishes and his nature would be, as it is in many such comedies, the opposition of his parent; and the denouement for him would come, as it normally does, when the parent finally concedes defeat and accepts the situation as a *fait accompli*.

Yet in neither version of this play is Lucentio at the center of the plot. Bianca is; and the primary obstacle to Bianca's marriage is not a parent's opposition but the presence of Katherina, an unmarried and presumably unmarriageable elder sister. Our attention throughout most of the play is thus diverted to the need to get Kate married so that Bianca may proceed with the business of choosing a suitable husband and completing the comic action.

Most scholars now agree, however, that the important difference between the two versions of the play is Shakespeare's development of the character of Kate, which distorts the image of the Roman-comedy model even further.[3] *The Taming of a Shrew* gives us a conventional stereotype who decides to marry the madcap tamer for the expected reasons: "But yet I will consent and marrie him, / For I methinkes have livde too long a maid, / And match him too, or else his manhoods good" (v.40-42). By contrast, Shakespeare's Kate is a girl desperate for love. She would be happy to love her father Baptista, but she sees that he dotes upon the relatively colorless Bianca—hence her detestation of the girl. When Baptista rebukes her for giving vent to her resentment, her frustration and anger spill over:

What, will you not suffer me? Nay, now I see
She is your treasure, she must have a husband;
I must dance barefoot on her wedding-day,
And for your love to her lead apes in hell.
Talk not to me, I will go sit and weep,
Till I can find occasion of revenge.

[II.i.31-36]

Thus, whereas in *The Taming of a Shrew* we see the story of a young woman who learns to her chagrin that she cannot tame a man who has made up his mind to dominate, in *The Taming of the Shrew* we see the story of a young woman who penetrates the façade of custom and social institutions to find in her iconoclasm an intimation of the true nature of love. In other words, Shakespeare's rehabilitated play, whether or not he wrote the earlier version of it, transcends the format of Roman comedy and becomes the story of Katherina, who, confronting life in the suburbs of comedy, reaches a degree of self-knowledge that lifts her in stature far above both her sister and her lover and places her along with Julia and Portia, also rebels to custom, among Shakespeare's most intriguing portraits of women.

A word should be added about Petruchio at this point. Ostensibly he is simply the generic tamer who disciplines with a heavy hand and brings the obstinate female into submission, much as one would tame a falcon, a savage dog, or a high-spirited horse.[4] Seen in the light of the Roman-comedy pattern, however, he can be regarded as a version of the traditional interloper, who for once has been given something constructive to do. Note that Petruchio arrives in Padua with a dual aim: "Happily to wive and thrive as best I may" (I.ii.56). By almost anyone's standards, however, he is not a suitable husband except for some woman whom others would like to get rid of, and his principal objective, openly acknowledged, is to acquire money. As Grumio puts it: "Nay, look you, sir, he tells you flatly what his mind is. Why, give him gold enough, and marry him to a puppet or an aglet-baby, or an old trot with ne'er a tooth in her head, though she have as many diseases as two and fifty horses. Why, nothing comes amiss, so money comes withal" (I.ii.77-82). But for the accident of Kate's presence, Petruchio on entering the scene would almost certainly have taken his place as one of the prime suitors for the hand of Bianca; and in view of his aggressiveness, one might suppose he would have had by far the best chance of winning her. As it is, Petruchio, more responsive to challenge than to easy opportunity, steps into the wings and picks up his own diamond in the rough, leaving the other young men to play out the conventional comedy and marry with, presumably, some hope of living happily ever after.

The irony that the final scene of this part of the play in both versions underscores, however, is that nothing of the sort appears likely to happen for the two who take the conventional path to achieve their happiness. We know, as all the principal participants come to know, that Lucentio's Bianca and Hortensio's widow are both shrews, no worse than most but no better, and that life for the two grooms is likely to get more troublesome before it begins to improve. Furthermore, lest we be inclined to call Petruchio clever, we should keep in mind that he gets from his marriage only what he asks of it, most of which he sums up in his description of Bianca to the bemused Vincentio on the Padua road:

> . . . be not grieved; she is of good esteem,
> Her dowry wealthy, and of worthy birth;
> Beside, so qualified as may beseem
> The spouse of any noble gentleman.
>
> [IV.v.64-67]

In addition, Petruchio receives the gift of obedience from his wife so that she will agree with him on any issue, however absurd, kiss him on any public street, fetch and deliver with the alacrity of a tamed falcon, and go to bed on command. This should make him a winner extraordinary, a candidate for happiness, and the principal object of our attention. Winner he is, and a candidate for happiness he may be, though we have no guarantee of that; but for all his violent activity and loud manners, he is not the object of our attention. Kate is that object, and Shakespeare clearly meant her to be; and whatever happiness she achieves in the "after" following this play, she will achieve on terms that are irrelevant to the action of comedy. To repeat, Kate is both at the center of the play and peripheral to the conventional comedy in it; and since that comedy is typical of New Comedy as a whole, she provides an intellectual critique of all such plays and enables us to see what the comic action in them is and what that action is not.

As has already been suggested earlier in this study, the happiness that concludes a comedy is not always what it seems to be. The illusion of happiness is probably real enough, but that illusion derives in part from the sense of relief that participants and spectators alike feel at seeing absolute death averted one more time; and the revelry that naturally follows that sense of relief is joyous in proportion as resisting parents can be made to relent, interlopers be pacified, and unsuccessful or stupid suitors be made to see and confess their folly—that is, in proportion as the illusion can be made to approach completeness. To shatter the illusion, one has only to do what Edgar Allan Poe did in "The Masque of the Red Death": allow death (or its surrogate) to sneak in and join the unsuspecting revelers. The shapers of Greek myth did that when they represented the uninvited Eris, Goddess of Discord, as coming with her golden apple to the wedding feast of Peleus and Thetis. Shakespeare did the same thing explicitly in *Love's Labor's Lost* with the intrusion of Marcade in Act V, and only slightly less so in *The Merchant of Venice*, where the thought of Shylock is only one of several things that becloud the moonlight of Belmont.

A hint of chill is present also in this play of a shrew, regardless of which version we happen to be looking at. In *The Taming a Shrew* there are two younger daughters, Emilia and Philena, both of whom are presented as being constitutionally arrogant and quite unloving. For example, when Polidor, who corresponds to Shakespeare's Lucentio, delivers himself of an extravagant courting speech to Emilia (Bianca) and concludes, "O faire *Emilia* I pine for thee, / And either must enjoy thy love, or die," she replies impertinently, "Fie man, I know you will not die for love" (vi.63-65). The young lovers, Aurelus and Polidor, continue with their verbal extravagances, but throughout they think of women as creatures to be tamed and at one point even speak of going to Ferando's (that is, Petruchio's) "taming schoole" (x.25-34). Their final scene is much the same as the one that Shakespeare developed for *The Taming of the Shrew*: there is a wager, the ladies are summoned, and Emilia and Philena refuse to follow their husbands' bidding, whereas Kate not only obeys but forces obedience on the other two, lectures them for their defection, and lays her hand beneath her husband's foot. The point of this relatively simple earlier play, therefore, is that women need to be tamed if the action of comedy is ever to be more than momentarily joyous or even tolerable. One suitor has done the necessary preliminary taming before marriage; the others have not; and thereby hangs the ending of the tale, which apparently justifies Sly's conclusion: "Ile to my / Wife presently and tame her too / And if she anger me" (xix.18-20). In short, control or domination of woman is presented as the only source of satisfaction in *The Taming of a Shrew*, both for Sly and for his audience. The world will go on, of course, but it has been established clearly as a man's world. The play is also a man's play. For all the Marlovian rhetoric that the suitors use in their courting speeches, the female characters, tamed and untamed, have been reduced at the end to ciphers.

Shakespeare's revision, though it incorporates new details from Gascoigne's *Supposes*, presents a similar pattern of activity. The young man still goes off to improve his mind or otherwise better himself. He still, quite contrary to his father's plans for him, falls head over heels in love with a pretty face, successfully woos the wearer of that face and marries her, and in the end achieves a reconciliation with his father. Shakespeare has reduced Kate's two sisters to the single Bianca; hence the young man's friend becomes his rival and, on losing the contest, has to content himself with a wealthy young widow. Nevertheless, as before, both find that their brides are unreconstructed shrews and thus come to recognize that happiness at a wedding feast does not necessarily mean happiness ever after. Still, the context in which the pattern manifests itself is quite different from that of *The Taming of a Shrew* in at least two ways.

First, throughout the play Shakespeare has emphasized that chill which comedy is supposed to counteract if not remove. We have already noted that at the outset he draws our attention to the image of "grim death" in the visage of the drunken Sly, who vanishes at the end of the first scene of the first act, never—for whatever reason—to reappear. Shakespeare also complicates the Petruchio character, making him not only a fortune hunter (which he undeniably is) but a young man dislocated by the death of his father:

> Antonio, my father, is deceas'd,
> And I have thrust myself into this maze,
> Happily to wive and thrive as best I may.
> Crowns in my purse I have, and goods at home,
> And so am come abroad to see the world.
>
> [I.ii.54-58]

Bianca becomes more callous and unloving than her predecessor ever was. "Believe me, sister," she tells Kate, "of all the men alive / I never yet beheld that special face / Which I could fancy more than any other" (II.i.10-12); and to her would-be lover Hortensio, disguised as a lute player, she declares, "I am no breeching scholar in the schools, / I'll not be tied to hours nor 'pointed times, / But learn my lessons as I please myself" (III.i.18-20). To please herself is the constant aim of her life, and she has not changed at the end of the play. Hortensio's widow is no more gracious. Only minutes before her own exposure as a shrew she taunts Petruchio with "He that is giddy thinks the world turns round" and then unkindly explains to Kate, "Your husband, being troubled with a shrew, / Measures my husband's sorrow by his woe" (V.ii.20;28-29). Tranio's tormenting of the innocent pedant from Mantua is even more vicious. His counterpart in Gascoigne's *Supposes* simply tells the unfortunate traveler that the local duke will exact his substance as tribute and send him home in doublet and hose.[5] Tranio puts his victim in fear of his life, calling to mind the similar fate that actually befalls old Egeon in *The Comedy of Errors*: "'Tis death for any one in Mantua / To come to Padua. . . . To save your life in this extremity / This favour will I do you" (IV.ii.81-82;103-4).

Finally, the image of death arises also in the course of Shakespeare's transformation of the episode in which the madcap husband taunts ancient Vincentio, to him a total stranger, in the roadside scene. In *The Taming of a Shrew* Ferando begins with "Faire lovely maide yoonge and affable," which his Kate betters by piling on extravagances: "Faire lovely lady, bright and Christalline," etc. (xv.26;34-35). But Shakespeare's Kate transcends extravagance with her memorable lines:

> Young budding virgin, fair, and fresh, and sweet,
> Whither away, or [where] is thy abode?
> Happy the parents of so fair a child!
> Happier the man whom favorable stars
> Allots thee for his lovely bedfellow!
>
> [IV.v.37-41]

This is disturbing, addressed as it is to a man whom life has left virgin in no sense of that word and who will certainly never be in bud again. Ferando in the older play, seeing that his wife is willing to reverse herself, simply lets the matter drop and says no more; but Petruchio in *The Taming of the Shrew* is trapped into responding with what his eyes do in fact see. "This is a man," he shouts indignantly, "old, wrinkled, faded, withered, / And not a maiden, as thou say'st he is" (IV.v.43-44). It is difficult to say whose performance is the more appalling here, Kate's or Petruchio's, but between them they leave the old man in a state of confusion until Kate saves the situation with her gentle apology:

> Pardon, old father, my mistaking eyes,
> That have been so bedazzled with the sun,
> That every thing I look on seemeth green;
> Now I perceive thou art a reverent father.
>
> [IV.v.45-48]

Even so, one recalls here the chill that settles more or less permanently on *The Merchant of Venice* with the gulling of Shylock, whose vicious pursuit of revenge has too often blinded readers to the heartless abuse that prompted him to it. Vincentio, however, we should note, has offended or threatened no one, and certainly not the two young people who capriciously use him as a foil for their battle of wits; and he remains a neighbor to death despite their well-meaning apologies.

Nevertheless, most critics have ignored Vincentio here and focused attention on Katherina, who, on the surface at least, has capitulated to Petruchio's bullying and surrendered her identity. In both plays she soon reappears at Padua as a happily submissive wife, ready and willing to lecture Bianca and Hortensio's new wife on their duty to their husbands. Moreover, in both plays she cites a cosmic context to justify her womanly subservience. In the earlier one she lectures her hearers on biblical precedent: Adam's priority in creation, God's production of Eve out of Adam's rib, and Eve's subsequent introduction of evil into a sinless world. In the later play she omits the scriptural references but presents the burden of those references as a principle of universal order:

> Thy husband is thy lord, thy life, thy keeper,
> Thy head, thy sovereign; one that cares for thee,
>
> . . . .
>
> And craves no other tribute at thy hands
> But love, fair looks, and true obedience—
> Too little payment for so great a debt.
> Such duty as the subject owes the prince,
> Even such a woman oweth to her husband.
>   [V.ii.146-47;152-56]

Regardless of form, both arguments are calculated to bring approval from advocates of male supremacy, including Petruchio, his fellows on the stage, and the men in the Elizabethan audience round about; and they seem to signal a masculine victory on the main front of the war between the sexes. At least, they were interpreted in this fashion by most readers and viewers well into the present century; but the majority is not necessarily right, and it may in this case have been preserving the peasant blindness of a Christopher Sly.

Katherina's preamble to her argument, used only in *The Taming of the Shrew*, involves a subtle turn that is easily overlooked. Recognizing that beauty is the lure that presumably gains most women their husbands, she admonishes the two married women before her as follows:

> . . . unknit that threat'ning unkind brow,
> And dart not scornful glances from those eyes,

To wound thy lord, thy king, thy governor.
It blots thy beauty, as frosts do bite the meads,
Confounds thy fame, as whirlwinds shake fair buds,
And in no sense is meet or amiable.
A woman mov'd is like a fountain troubled,
Muddy, ill-seeming, thick, bereft of beauty,
And while it is so, none so dry or thirsty
Will deign to sip or touch one drop of it.

[V.ii.136-45]

Katherina, now fully rehabilitated in station and appearance, stands before us in this last scene as the most beautiful woman in view. In any production of the play hers is the starring role, and she is inescapably the focus of our attention. We should keep in mind, however, that physical beauty was no bargaining point in Petruchio's courtship of her: she was tamed, not wooed. Hence her reminder is aimed primarily at the other two women, Bianca and Hortensio's widow, both of whom are showing an unfortunate inclination to press the advantage of their evanescent natural endowments. We remember, as Katherina obviously does, the counters routinely used by wooing males in sophisticated circles, such extravagances, usually of literary origin, as slip easily from the lips of impassioned Renaissance gentlemen. Lucentio has provided some excellent examples early in the play.

> . . . I saw sweet beauty in her face,
> Such as the daughter of Agenor had,
> That made great Jove to humble him to her hand,
>
> . . . .
>
> . . . I saw her coral lips to move,
> And with her breath she did perfume the air.
> Sacred and sweet was all I saw in her.
>
> [I.i.167-69;174-76]

No one in the play has ever denied Kate's physical beauty, but her manner has always discouraged extravagant compliments, and Petruchio, declaring openly that his objective was money, has offered her none:

> . . . you are call'd plain Kate,
> And bonny Kate, and sometimes Kate the curst,

> But Kate, the prettiest Kate in Christendom,
> Kate of Kate-Hall, my super-dainty Kate,
> For dainties are all Kates, and therefore, Kate,
> Take this of me, Kate of my consolation—
> Hearing thy mildness prais'd in every town,
> Thy virtues spoke of, and thy beauty sounded,
> Yet not so deeply as to thee belongs,
> Myself am mov'd to woo thee for my wife.
>
> [II.i.185-94]

There is sincere praise in this speech, but it is unfashionable praise and tinged with sarcasm; and it is typical of the whole extraordinary set of maneuvers that brings Kate to the same altar as her sister and to a legitimate husband, though admittedly one who acts as if he were doing her a favor by marrying her.

A number of modern critics and directors have seen "contextual irony" in Kate's apparent acceptance of this unusual state of affairs and doubted the sincerity of her submission. One of these, Coppelia Kahn, goes on to interpret Kate's giving in as part of the perennial exchange between male and female, a revelation of "the dependency that underlies mastery, the strength behind submission."[6] Undoubtedly the play admits of such an interpretation, but what stands out above all else in this last scene of the play—and gives especial point to Lucentio's concluding line, " 'Tis wonder, by your leave, she will be tam'd so"—is Katherina's serenity, a quality not heretofore seen in *The Taming of the Shrew* and, indeed, a quality one does not normally expect to find in comic characters, male or female. The ancients usually treated serenity as an aspect of preeminence, which they seldom ascribed to anyone except a masculine god. Yet serenity is the aspect that Kate presents to the assembly of lords and ladies at Padua (who perhaps do not recognize it) and to us. She has achieved it by emerging a whole person from a comic action—or, one might say, an inverted comic action—that has threatened to deny her existence; and by so doing she has provided the second, and far greater, difference that lifts *The Taming of the Shrew* well above its anonymous predecessor and gives it a unique quality and meaning.

The comic action, as Shakespeare inherited it from the Western dramatic tradition, has never been the benign thing it sometimes appears to be. As we have seen repeatedly, it celebrates the continuation of life, which is a bloody affair at best, fraught with waste and the threat of death. Of the two dramatic actions transmitted to us from antiquity, that of tragedy is in many ways the kinder, ending as it often does in something approaching "calm of mind, all passion spent." Only in Dante's version of comedy is the harsh purgatorial action completed by anything like peace and permanent beauty, and there only because the action has been lifted from time into eternity. Shakespeare's temporal world does not admit of such a solution to the problem. Not even Navarre or Belmont, as we have seen, is immune to the threat of that mutability which is the subject and substance of comedy; and in Shakespearean comedy, as in all other forms of secular comedy in the West, the joy and laughter that we assume to be essential to any product of the comic spirit must be bought at the cost of pain and sometimes even bloodshed. This seems to be an aspect of human life itself, and, however much it may be suppressed, it is inescapably an aspect of any comedy that seriously presumes to reflect human life. Yet the hope of comedy is always that somehow the pain may be avoided, or if not avoided at least assuaged. This is why the most satisfying comedies usually manage to dry our tears at the end and lead us to think that possibly the next action will succeed in sparing us the need of such comforting. Thus the hope of a benign metamorphosis of comedy persists in all our Western theaters, including Shakespeare's; and the path in that direction taken by Shakespeare when he set out to transform the story of the intractable shrew is the path that he was to take again and again, producing along the route his most appealing heroines.

Interestingly, three centuries later George Meredith was to declare that same path as the *sine qua non* for the preservation of the comic spirit:

There will never be civilization where Comedy is not possible; and that comes of some degree of social equality of the sexes. . . . Where [women] have no social freedom, Comedy is absent; where they are household drudges, the form of Comedy is primitive; where they are tolerably independent, but uncultivated, exciting melodrama takes its place, and a sentimental version of them. . . . But where women are on the road to an equal footing with men, in attainments and in liberty—in what they have won for themselves, and what has been granted them by a fair civilization—there, and only waiting to be transplanted from life to the stage, or the novel or the poem, pure Comedy flourishes, and is, as it would help them to be, the sweetest of diversions, the wisest of delightful companions.[7]

Pure comedy does not yet flourish in Padua, but Kate's glory is that she has caught a glimpse of what pure comedy might be. Her serenity derives from an acceptance in charity (some would call it forgiveness)[8] of a world that is in many ways still primitive and, if unrestrained, would still deny her the social freedom that she has had the imagination to dream of. For some modern readers there can be nothing admirable in a response like this. Kate's perception and understanding, if genuine, demand an appropriate militancy; but she had already pursued that route and found it interminable. The turning point for her came on the road back from Petruchio's country house when in sheer weariness she conceded to her husband that the sun might be the moon: "Be it moon, or sun, or what you please; / And if you please to call it a rush-candle, / Henceforth I vow it shall be so for me" (Iv.v.13-15). Her transformation was complete when she stared at the visage of death and, to please Petruchio's obstinate perversity, declared it to be the face of life. In that brief denial of her senses she mocked not so much herself, or ancient Vincentio, as her capricious husband; and by her sudden compliance she forced him to the capitulation he never intended to make. From that moment on, Katherina—Kate—was a true winner in the perennial battle. She had begun the liberation of Petruchio from the prison of masculine vanity; but for herself she had found and declared for all to hear the hope of continuing vitality in the face of death itself, and the echo of that courageous voice was never again to be entirely absent from Shakespearean comedy.

8

The Merry Wives of Windsor

It is regrettable that *The Merry Wives of Windsor* has for many years remained an anomaly in the Shakespeare canon; yet several characteristics almost automatically set it apart from the other comedies. For one thing, more than any other the play declares openly by plot-line and device its derivation from both Italianate comedy and the classical tradition behind that, notably Plautus's *Miles Gloriosus*.[1] For another, it is the only comedy with an announced English setting, the consequence perhaps of the requirement, royally imposed, that Shakespeare write it about the Falstaff character from the Henry IV plays.[2] That link with Shakespeare's second history cycle is in itself a mark of the uniqueness of this comedy, and it is also one of the sources of the widespread dissatisfaction with the play that one encounters among English and American audiences and readers.

Dissatisfaction might never have developed had criticism of Falstaff kept to the hard line set down by Dr. Johnson; but Maurice Morgann's essay of 1777 opened up new possibilities, and by William Hazlitt's time English readers and viewers were prepared to assume indefinitely that Shakespeare had created two Falstaffs, one the fat knight of *1* and *2 Henry IV* and the other a pallid reflection of that same knight in *The Merry Wives of Windsor*.[3] What the romantics saw in the latter was little more than a discredited and banished rogue (though nothing in the text of *The Merry Wives* absolutely requires Falstaff to be at that final stage in his career) sadly reduced from the irrepressible figure most of them had taken to their hearts. Of his old group of followers, a few remain in *The Merry Wives*—Bardolph, ancient Pistol, Nym (who actually appears only here and in *Henry V*), and the young page; but poaching and filching have brought in far too little to support even that small group in meat and sack, and it disintegrates before their eyes as the comedy proceeds. Bardolph becomes a tapster; Pistol and Nym defect and betray their former leader and friend. Justice Shallow and Mistress Quickly appear, but to readers mindful of the two parts of *Henry IV* these two must have seemed to move like memories in a nightmare. Moreover, by the time the play comes to an end, Falstaff, though he is invited by the Pages to share in laughter around their country fire, seems to have no real friends left. He is already quite alone and almost ready for the death that Mistress Quickly describes in the second act of *Henry V*.

Given the popularity of this romantic view of Falstaff, it is not surprising that *The Merry Wives of Windsor* suffered a protracted eclipse. The reported death of Falstaff in *Henry V* was a pathetic fact, as was his rejection at the end of *2 Henry IV;* but sentimentality could, and did, link the two events with an assumption that callous opportunism had broken an honest old man's heart. Shakespeare's masterfully complex scene in the Boar's Head (II.iv) should have been enough to qualify that notion and prepare the way for his portrayal of decay in *The Merry Wives*, which, among other things, stands as proof that both Falstaff and the world he inhabits—the world of a classical hero, two kings, and a princess—are equally pathetic and tragic and real. The point of concern to us here, however, is that Shakespeare's instrument of proof was the action of formal comedy, which, for whatever reason, he thrust into the midst of his long historical sequence, giving it thereby a central position in his growing awareness of the uses of comedy and the dimensions of the comic form.

The outline of conventional comedy in *The Merry Wives* serves mainly to let us know that we are focusing attention on that sphere in which corporate human life perpetuates itself. This focus is provided by the Fenton-Anne plot, in which young love triumphs in good New Comedy fashion over a series of obstacles imposed by the girl's ambitious parents. Master Page, her father, supports the suit of young Abraham Slender, village ninny, who has additional advocates in his cousin, Justice Shallow, and the Welsh parson Sir Hugh Evans. Mistress Page supports the suit of a French physician, Dr. Caius; and Caius has at least nominal support from Mistress Quickly, who serves him as housekeeper and serves the rest of Windsor as general go-between. Fenton, the young country gentleman of sound mind and limb who eventually wins out, has really no support at all until halfway through the play, he begins to move the affections of the girl herself. By the end of Act IV he has also persuaded the Host of the Garter Inn to join him, and this advantage tips the three-sided contest in his favor. Laughter in this part of the play is provided by the plot itself as its details begin to mesh and satisfy our expectation, and by the series of farcelike episodes and embellishments: the fractured English of Parson Hugh and Dr. Caius, the absurd duel between these two that never comes off, the horse-stealing business, and the Latin lesson.

One should note that in the relatively simple mechanics of the Fenton-Anne plot there is no specific need either for the Fords or for Falstaff. With these characters out of the way Shakespeare might very well have resolved his plot with something like a parentally manipulated May Day followed by an inevitable backfire—at any rate, with something less improbable than the elaborately contrived nighttime episode in Windsor Park. Yet if the tradition is true, Shakespeare began with a need to satisfy his Queen's wish to see Falstaff in love, and the conventional comic pattern that he chose as matrix for the required Falstaff action served mainly to put his audience into a sphere where the activity of love—erotic love, that is—would be naturally intense and meaningful. The ending that he contrived, therefore, had to be appropriate for both actions and, in fact, to make them one.

The first problem, however, was to find a credible love action for a man who was both old and unattractively fat. The action Shakespeare hit upon has numerous affinities with

New Comedy themes and characters, but it is closer in point of evolutionary development to Old or Aristophanic Comedy and the antecedents of that comedy. Such a relation was noted briefly in 1948 by Northrop Frye, who wrote in an English Institute essay for that year that *The Merry Wives* contains "an elaborate ritual of the defeat of winter, known to folklorists as 'carrying out Death,' of which Falstaff is the victim."[4] To a generation brought up on the work of Sir James G. Frazer and the Cambridge anthropologists, the pertinence of such a re-mark—referring, one imagines, to Falstaff's series of humilia-tions—may have seemed self-evident; and perhaps it seemed so to Frye, who passed quickly on without bothering to probe further the implications of what he had said. Yet the suggestion remains to tantalize knowledgeable readers. The resem-blances between the first two humiliations of Falstaff and the European forms of "carrying out Death" are, of course, obvious to anyone who reads about the latter in Frazer's *The Golden Bough* or in the studies of such investigators as F.M. Cornford and Jane Harrison.[5] Falstaff undergoes his first humiliation, we recall, when he escapes from Ford's house in a buck-basket full of dirty linen. He describes the indignity as follows:

I suffer'd the pangs of three several deaths: first, an intolerable fright, to be detected with a jealous rotten bell-wether; next, to be com-pass'd like a good bilbo in the circumference of a peck, hilt to point, heel to head; and then to be stopp'd in like a strong distillation with stinking clothes that fretted in their own grease. Think of that—a man of my kidney. Think of that—that am as subject to heat as butter; a man of continual dissolution and thaw. It was a miracle to scape suffocation. And in the height of this bath (when I was more than half stew'd in grease, like a Dutch dish) to be thrown into the Thames, and cool'd, glowing-hot, in that surge, like a horse-shoe; think of that— hissing-hot—think of that Master [Brook].

[III.v.107-22]

Frazer records no observance in which laundry, as such, is used as part of a ceremony; but he gives several illustrations in which old and dirty clothing, symbolizing the ills of the com-munity, is begged from house to house and thereafter draped upon a crude effigy of some kind, usually made of straw or birch twigs, to be carried through the town and eventually tossed into the river. This is what happens at Debschwitz in Thuringia, where the young people afterward return to the village, break the news to the people, "and receive eggs and other victuals as a reward."[6]

Falstaff's second humiliation even more closely resembles ritualistic practice, especially that of "carrying out Death" in other parts of central Europe; for this time he is dressed in the clothes of an old woman, reviled, beaten out of the house, and chased through the streets. This is suggestive of mid-Lent observances in parts of Silesia:

In many places the grown girls with the help of the young men dress up a straw figure with women's clothes and carry it out of the village towards the setting sun. At the boundary they strip it of its clothes, tear it in pieces, and scatter the fragments about the fields. This is called "Burying Death." As they carry the image out, they sing that they are about to bury Death under an oak, that he may depart from the people. . . . In some Polish parts of Upper Silesia the effigy, representing an old woman, goes by the name of Marzana, the goddess of death. It is made in the house where the last death occurred, and is carried on a pole to the boundary of the village, where it is thrown into a pond or burnt.[7]

Neither of the pseudo-rituals in Shakespeare, however, proceeds to a proper conclusion. One of them ends simply as dirty linen in the river, and the other evaporates as soon as Falstaff has a chance to slip out of his disguise. In neither is Death carried out; and neither precipitates any kind of renewal, as practically all the genuine rituals of "carrying out Death" are expected to do.

Falstaff's third trial does have the efficacy of ritual, and that trial is suggestive of something far more ancient and more serious than the widespread forms of folk game that "carrying out Death" assumes in central and western Europe. In fact, Shakespeare, knowingly or unknowingly, seems to have arranged Falstaff's three humiliations in order of increasing seriousness so that the whole series has the painful effect of stripping away one by one the layers of civility that normally shield the primitive nerve in our psyche and make the darker part of our humanity bearable. Thus, while we laugh at the spectacle of Falstaff in the forest, we may also shudder at the same time; for this last humiliation, involving as it does the victim disguised as an animal and the people's participation in the punishment of that victim, suggests unmistakably the ancient castigation of the scapegoat, whereby an animal, or a man, or a man dressed as an animal was made to take upon himself—and suffer for—the sins of a whole community.

The word *scapegoat* indicates the form of this ritual that is familiar to most of us: that is, the one using an actual goat and practiced by the ancient Jews on their Day of Atonement (Leviticus xvi.8-22). Related modern survivals include the Yoruba (West African) custom of disguising with ashes and chalk paint a victim selected for sacrifice and parading him through the streets to allow people to lay hands on him and thus cast off their various guilts, sins, and symptoms of death.[8] In Siam the victim was a woman, but her function was the same: "It used to be the custom on one day of the year to single out a woman broken down by debauchery, and carry her on a litter through all the streets to the music of drums and hautboys. The mob insulted her and pelted her with dirt; and after having carried her through the whole city, they threw her on a dunghill or a hedge of thorns outside the ramparts, forbidding her ever to enter the walls again."[9] Elsewhere in the world the victim might be a cow, a bull, or a buffalo. All these practices constitute survival rituals, or ancient forms of what we call "carrying out Death"; and Frazer suggests that practices like them lie behind Europeans' seasonal dousing of puppets and playful chasing of victims in effigy.[10] In any case, Shakespeare's last humiliation of Falstaff reached beyond any existing practice in Windsor, Warwickshire, or the rest of Europe to provide for the old fat man a punishment that was, at least in part, directed at the expulsion of evil which was not entirely of his own generating.

Falstaff's principal fault at the time of the play, aside from some petty poaching and keeping of disreputable company, is that age has caught up with him. "It is as much as I can do to keep the terms of my honor precise," he tells the recalcitrant

Pistol. "I myself sometimes, leaving the fear of [God] on the left hand, and hiding mine honor in my necessity, am fain to shuffle, to hedge, and to lurch" (II.ii.22-25). His instincts are now for survival only, and the objective of his assault on the wives of Windsor is not the satisfaction of lust but the satisfaction of the belly. To everyone but Falstaff and Master Ford the whole business is a clear piece of senile folly, and even Falstaff himself is uneasy until Mistress Quickly relieves his anxiety with her false tales of the complaisance of the two women. Thus reassured, however, he is ripe to receive the fulsome flattery that Ford, disguised as Brook, heaps upon him: "You are a gentleman of excellent breeding, admirable discourse, of great admittance, authentic in your place and person, generally allow'd for your many war-like, court-like, and learned preparations" (II.ii.224-29). Finally, when Ford lays before him the temptation of tangible coin, Falstaff is completely undone and ready to believe almost anything. Even at this point, however, he sees himself only as a man of parts and undiminished vigor, not as a small-town lecher, the role in which Ford's jealousy flatteringly casts him. "Master [Brook]," he declares grandly (and gratefully for the last compliment), "thou shalt know I will predominate over the peasant, and thou shalt lie with his wife" (II.ii.281-83).

For Ford, by contrast, everything is colored by the almost insane sexual jealousy through which he views his world. Folly of this kind is conventionally presented as laughable in comedy, and it is so presented here; but here, as in the contemporary *Every Man in His Humor*, jealousy is given a dimension that renders it credible as well as funny. Mistress Ford warns us that her husband's problem is a recurring one even before he appears on the scene. "O that my husband saw this letter!" she says in her first reference to him; "it would give eternal food to his jealousy" (II.i.100-101). Ford's behavior shortly thereafter in his encounter with the informer Pistol and later in his interview with Falstaff leaves no doubt about the matter: Ford's mind leaps at the intimation of sex, and he is always prepared to suspect that his wife is indulging in it illicitly. Moreover, his malady is infectious or else it is endemic in

Windsor; for both wives seem to be especially chagrined at receiving an attempt on their virtue that cannot possibly come to anything except embarrassment; and even Page, for all his counsels of moderation, declares in the end for appointing "a meeting with this old fat fellow, / Where we may take him, and disgrace him for it" (IV.iv.14-15). Evans is speaking the truth when he observes, "You say he has been thrown in the rivers, and has been grievously peaten as an old oman. . . . methinks his flesh is punish'd, he shall have no desires" (IV.iv.20-24). Nevertheless, they proceed with their plan, burning and pinching Falstaff for the lust he never enjoyed, reviling him for being too old to make other men cuckolds (V.v.146-54), and finally even dunning him for the twenty pounds that he has received from the jealous Ford disguised as Brook.

The irony of all this is that only the victimizers here are physically vigorous enough to be even partly guilty of the charges they are making; their victim is too old for the performance of sex and almost, but not quite, too old to be stirred by the recollection of it. Furthermore, he is far too clumsy to serve as a pander even for middle-aged lovers like the Fords. Falstaff's fundamental awareness of his inadequacies is painfully suggested in the feeble wit of the extravagant mock prayer that he makes in the park just before his tormentors arrive:

The Windsor bell hath strook twelve; the minute draws on. Now the hot-bloodied gods assist me! Remember, Jove, thou wast a bull for thy Europa, love set on thy horns. O powerful love, that in some respects makes a beast a man; in some other, a man a beast. You were also, Jupiter, a swan for the love of Leda. O omnipotent love, how near the god drew to the complexion of a goose! A fault done first in the form of a beast (O Jove, a beastly fault!) and then another fault in the semblance of a fowl—think on't, Jove, a foul fault! When gods have hot backs, what shall poor men do? For me, I am here a Windsor stag, and the fattest, I think, i' th' forest. Send me a cool rut-time, Jove, or who can blame me to piss my tallow?

[V.v.1-15]

Harsh enlightenment follows shortly after this, and Falstaff's overt confession comes only one hundred or so lines later: "I do begin to perceive that I am made an ass" (V.v.119). To this, Ford, with the figure of a discredited scapegoat standing before him, replies aptly, "Ay, and an ox too; both the proofs are extant."

One can say a number of things about Shakespeare's treatment of the scapegoat theme here. It is, of course, broadly funny in the childish, rough-and-tumble way that good folk art often is, and for this reason alone it enhances the value of the play. Moreover, once we recognize clearly the presence of the scapegoat theme in *The Merry Wives of Windsor*, we may discover suddenly that we have also sharpened our perception of less well-defined treatments of the same theme in other plays of Shakespeare—notably those in *The Merchant of Venice*, in *Twelfth Night*, and, as pointed out by C.L. Barber, in *1 Henry IV*.[11] Most important, however, recognizing the scapegoat theme in *The Merry Wives* means finding a new dimension to the play, one of major significance without which the play would remain merely the more or less effective farce that most critics have found it to be. In this regard, two additional sets of observations should be made. First, the Fenton-Anne plot, the New Comedy element of the piece, is stiffly regular by comparison with the Falstaff plot and chiefly funny in its farcing or episodic detail; furthermore, it generates no proper resolution of its own. Second, the Falstaff plot, set in motion early in Act I and developed independently throughout most of the play, converges with the Fenton-Anne plot at precisely that point at which the scapegoat theme emerges explicitly; thus, it is the Falstaff plot that provides the solution by which the oppressiveness of Windsor's old order can be relaxed and Windsor's winter made to give way to the interests of spring. The two plots complement each other, and fitted together in this ingenious fashion they create both an entertaining play and one that makes visible within its scope something of the whole evolution of comedy.

The plot of the young lovers, to be sure, has a movement in the direction of renewal; but that movement is one that promises only an escape for the young lovers—an elopement rather than the general and potentially joyous acceptance of an alteration in the balance of constituent elements in the community. Susanne Langer has characterized the feeling given by mature comedy as a renewed awareness of the impetus and flow, the continuing rhythm, of human life; and she identifies the antagonist of comedy as the "World," meaning by that one of those artificial and temporary structures perpetually being established by the very same rhythm that promotes life's continuity.[12] One function of the Fenton-Anne plot is to present concretely that rigidly established structure, which collapses only with the sacrifice of Falstaff.

As *The Merry Wives* begins, economic considerations in Windsor have temporarily replaced genetic ones. Pretty Anne Page is of marriageable age. She is virginal but conspicuously fertile, and the senior members of the community are mightily concerned to see that she is disposed of to their advantage. Justice Shallow, noting that she is heiress to seven hundred pounds in her own right in addition to whatever she may expect from her father, is seeking to pair her off with his simpleton of a nephew, Abraham Slender, whom he controls. Parson Hugh and the girl's father both support him in this, again for economic reasons. No one of the older generation, with the possible exception of the Host of the Garter Inn, seems to remember the primary purpose of such pairings or to be aware that matches for money are often of the kind that bring a community to extinction. Even Fenton admits that money has until recently been his own motive in seeking Anne's hand:

> . . . I will confess thy father's wealth
> Was the first motive that I woo'd thee, Anne;
> Yet wooing thee, I found thee of more value
> Than stamps in gold, or sums in sealed bags;
> And 'tis the very riches of thyself
> That now I aim at.
>
> [III.iv.13-18]

In short, Windsor has for some time been shivering with the counsels and whispers of winter, old age, and death; and these must be "carried out" if Windsor is to survive for another cycle of life and living.

So it is that the business of Herne the Hunter, ostensibly devised as the climax of a series of humiliations for a Falstaff who has been doing his feeble best to peddle love for money, becomes the perfect scapegoat for the redemption of a community committed to the same sin. Fortuitously, it also provides an appropriate screen behind which Anne's unwanted suitors can be matched with boys in female dress and Fenton and Anne triumphantly become husband and wife; but actually it does much more than that. Through the sacrifice of Falstaff, the community's morbid preoccupation with monetary concerns is symbolically challenged if not altogether defeated (Ford still wants his twenty pounds back), the triumph of biology is assured for at least one more generation, and good will for the moment prevails. The elders are not fully enlightened by their adventures and misadventures. Ford falls back on cliché: "In love, the heavens themselves do guide the state; / Money buys lands, and wives are sold by fate" (V.v.232-33). Falstaff, as unaware as the rest of the service he has rendered, is simply glad to have fared no worse: "I am glad, though you have ta'en a special stand to strike at me, that your arrow hath glanc'd" (V.v.234-35). Still, the round of confessions and acceptances (including acceptance for Sir John) suggests that the spiritual ills of Windsor were perhaps never so grave as some of the early symptoms indicated. Forgiveness is not only possible here but in the air. This much, and it is a great deal, *The Merry Wives of Windsor* has in common with the other proper comedies of Shakespeare. Like them, it makes us once more sense the mysterious terms by which frail humanity continues to survive, and it encourages us to accept those terms—even though we do not fully understand them—and to concede that the game shall go on.

9

Much Ado about Nothing

It is customary to say that *Much Ado about Nothing* marks Shakespeare's advent into mature comedy, or joyous comedy, as some call it. But Shakespeare's recipe for his new play was approximately the same as the one he had used for *The Taming of the Shrew*, which, as noted earlier in this study, may well be a play that he had reworked from an older one, *The Taming of a Shrew*; and this, too, he may have had a hand in writing. Whether *Much Ado about Nothing* can properly be called joyous is a question best deferred until later in the chapter. For the moment it is enough to note that *The Taming of the Shrew* contains at least three elements which Shakespeare used in framing its successor. These are, first, that familiar variation of the marriage pattern in which a father seeks successfully to dispose of a marriageable daughter; second, the ancient battle of the sexes which surfaces repeatedly throughout Western literature, reminding us that although both sexes are essential to society's most important institution, they are not always consulted or considered equally in the perennial reconstitutions of that institution; and, third, the examination of the plight of the unsponsored or otherwise unmarriageable person, the ugly duckling, male or female, in a society that normally makes marriage a requirement for full membership. In *The Taming of the Shrew* Shakespeare mixed these elements well, framed them in the Sly plot, which gave one notably ugly duckling a brief illusion of being something else, and turned the whole into an exploration of the realities of woman's situation in a world dominated by men and masculine values.

The elements in *Much Ado about Nothing* are the same; but the proportions are different, and the effect is different. For one thing, the Roman or New Comedy plot—that is, the marketing of the marriageable daughter—is actually, not just nominally, the ground of the action. Regardless of what producers and critics may have done with it down through the centuries, *Much Ado* properly belongs to Claudio, Hero, Don Pedro, Leonato, and company rather than to Beatrice and Benedick.[1] The custom, fairly common in productions of *The Taming of the Shrew*, of telescoping the Roman-comedy plot into a series of "throwaway" scenes[2] is indefensible where *Much Ado* is concerned. Claudio must seek, plight troth with, repudiate, and finally marry Hero, or there is no play at all; Kate and Petruchio have no corresponding absolute need of Bianca and Lucentio. Moreover, the main plot of *Much Ado* is reinforced internally by characters who serve an important function similar to that of the Sly frame plot: they provide an earthy, commonsense scrutiny of what the principals are up to, though in *Much Ado* they provide that at points where the principals are most vulnerable. The most notable of these are Dogberry and company, purely Shakespeare's invention as far as scholars have been able to tell, who live in a relatively innocent or at least childlike world that surrounds the sophisticated court. Like most rustics and serving-men, they treat the inhabitants of their court with a respect that amounts to reverence (witness Dogberry's conviction that truth and salvation somehow lie in the art of writing), and they strive with good will to protect their betters from the tiresome distractions that characterize the daily concourse of common life. It has been said that these simple souls still inhabit an Eden, and in a sense they do; for they never fully comprehend the potential for evil in those sophisticates whom they admire and would protect. In the same sense, two other characters in the play—Friar Francis, who hesitates to believe in Hero's defection, and Antonio her uncle, who stoutly denounces those who accuse her of it—are not far removed from Eden; for they, too, contemplate the world as innocents, at least until Hero's misfortune shocks them into a recognition that the courtly system has been subverted and the comic movement that supports that system, frustrated absolutely.[3]

Beatrice sympathizes with this group and might be tied more closely to it were she more than tangentially related to the New Comedy part of the action. Unfortunately, as an orphan she belongs to the limbo of those whose status, or lack of it, precludes full identification with the society in which they happen to live. Don John the bastard and his friends Borachio and Conrade belong to this category also, as does Margaret; and all these, though free to love and be loved, must expect to embrace love purely for love's sake, not as the final step in their social maturation. Strictly speaking, this is presumably what lovers with established status also do, but such loves tend to follow accepted formulas and seek a combination of goals, none of which necessarily has much to do with love as a motion in its own right. The orphan Beatrice probably could never attract a man like Claudio because she has nothing to give such a man except love and devotion; thus it is to Benedick's credit (at least in our eyes) that as a young lord of Padua, presumably eligible to seek more profitable pasture elsewhere, he has fixed his attention upon Beatrice even before the play begins.

The first scene of Act I tells us a great deal about that. A messenger, come from the wars in advance of the returning army, is making a report to Leonato, Governor of Messina, when Beatrice, the Governor's niece, interrupts to engage the man in lengthy banter about young Benedick's role in the fighting. Her beginning is an impertinent "I pray you, is Signior Mountanto return'd from the wars or no?" (I.i.30-31), and she continues until Leonato finally interposes with an apology: "You must not, sir, mistake my niece. There is a kind of merry war betwixt Signior Benedick and her. They never meet but there's a skirmish of wit between them" (I.i.61-64). Benedick, however, on arriving shortly thereafter with Don Pedro, Claudio, and others, soon finds something temporarily more interesting than a "merry war" going on in the present assemblage of gentlemen and ladies. Leonato's daughter Hero is also standing silently by; and Benedick, as soon as he can draw Claudio inside, chides him for what is clearly his Florentine

friend's infatuation for the lady. Benedick's response to
Claudio's "she is the sweetest lady that ever I look'd on," however, reveals more than he meant to reveal: "I can see yet
without spectacles and I see no such matter. There's her cousin,
and she were not possess'd with a fury, exceeds her as much in
beauty as the first of May doth the last of December"
(I.i.189-92). Clearly the young people genuinely attracted to
one another here are Beatrice and Benedick; and the attraction
between these two, long noted (by Leonato's testimony) but
heretofore denied the encouragement of society (and perhaps
inhibited by fear of repulse on both sides), needs precisely the
sort of priming that Don Pedro, with the help of Claudio and
Hero, will shortly undertake to provide. One might wish that
the motives of the three courtly conspirators were as noble as
the image of love the literary conventions undoubtedly have
set before them, but this would probably be asking too much.
Hero, understandably, thinks principally of helping her cousin, whom she genuinely likes, to settle into a socially respectable marriage with a respectable husband; and Don Pedro
thinks only of the skill he will display in making an improbable
match, declaring that by so doing he will steal the title of love-
god from Cupid himself. Claudio, preoccupied with his own
conquest, simply follows along. In the end, by standards that
generations of viewers have been willing to apply, their efforts
are successful, and the marriage of Beatrice and Benedick is
assured. As far as we know, the matchmakers never comprehend the significance of their action. Nevertheless, this match,
which they have initiated more in sport than in earnest, is the
only relationship in the play, early or late, that gives any
promise of permanently transcending the artificiality of Messina's courtly society, in which sophisticated people live and
love and sometimes die by a code that has long since ceased to
define any of the realities of human life.

This is not to deny that *Much Ado*'s war between the sexes
has its moments of hilarity. Audiences never cease to applaud
the lively sparring between the lovers, and Benedick's futile
efforts to play the courtly wooer are probably as amusing
today as they ever were—marching off forthwith to get the

lady's picture (II.iii.263-64), shaving off his beard, washing his face, and putting on perfume (III.ii.40-62). He is charming as well as amusing in Act V, when, doggedly trying to emulate the sophistication of Claudio and Don Pedro, he is at last driven to ask Margaret for help with his poetry: "Marry, I cannot show it in rhyme; I have tried. I can find out no rhyme to 'lady' but 'baby,' an innocent rhyme; for 'scorn,' 'horn,' a hard rhyme; for 'school,' 'fool,' a babbling rhyme: very ominous endings. No, I was not born under a rhyming planet, nor I cannot woo in festival terms" (V.ii.36-41). Beatrice has a better grasp of the situation and tends to dispense with the formalities which preoccupy Benedick as soon as he has committed himself to courtship.

At the abortive Monday wedding, when Hero appears to have been totally destroyed by Claudio's rejection of her, she quickly maneuvers Benedick into making straightforward declarations:

Bene. I will swear by [my sword] that you love me, and I will make him eat it that says I love not you.
Beat. Will you not eat your word?
Bene. With no sauce that can be devis'd to it. I protest I love thee.
. . . .
Beat. I love you with so much of my heart that none is left to protest.
Bene. Come, bid me do anything for thee.

[IV.i.276-80;286-89]

At this point the unwary Benedick is trapped, for Beatrice, now mindful only of the Florentine gentleman's renunciation of her cousin Hero, promptly counters with a response calculated to put an abrupt end to all their courtly games. "Kill Claudio," she says.

With this peremptory demand Beatrice all but makes explicit the primitive and quite unconventional meaning that love has for her, and by it she also challenges Benedick to prove equal to her commitment. Benedick's evasion of the challenge marks the turning point of the action: the moment when he chooses the codified courtly love of Messina instead of the spiritual liberation that for an instant seemed to be within his grasp. At first he pretends not to take her seriously; then, reluctantly and much against his better judgment, he makes a half-hearted attempt at compliance. Apparently he whispers his first challenge so that none but Claudio shall hear it; moments later he repeats it aloud but so obliquely that both Claudio and Don Pedro put his behavior down to love-madness: "What a pretty thing man is when he goes in his doublet and hose and leaves off his wit!" (V.i.199-200). Only one scene later, he has resumed his pursuit of the skills of courtly wooing, asking Margaret, as we have just noted, for help in the composition of poetry; and at the end of the play he is once more hard at the business of "merry war," which he halts temporarily by silencing Beatrice with a kiss in order to join the "boys" in pleasantries about double-dealing and cuckoldry.

Beatrice is thus as much outside the sytem at the conclusion of *Much Ado about Nothing* as she was at the beginning of it. She has achieved her right to marriage (publicly acknowledged with Benedick's kiss) in a world that, after a momentary faltering, has regained its stifling equilibrium. For the time being, at least, Messina's female fury is silent, though one wonders whether she will continue to speak only when spoken to. Critics who see the play as a superficial comedy and who share Leonato's view of the "merry war" may be inclined to say that she will not remain silent and that the verbal sparring will shortly continue as an aspect of a unique pairing in Messina, a pleasant and quite tolerable anomaly in an otherwise normal courtly society. If this view be the one that Shakespeare's play invites, then the play itself is probably superficial, little more than a hyperbolic presentation of the froth and furor that traditionally attend approaches to the altar, the "much ado about nothing" that ends when the vows are said and the men and women go back to their customary roles—war or tea parties, politics or childbearing. One notes that Hero throughout says almost nothing except when the men are absent and that her mother, Innogen, says nothing at all—a circumstance so inexplicable in modern eyes that many editors suppress the fact of that lady's two appearances in the stage directions.[4] By the condition of these two we see the portrait of the Beatrice that is to be, and perhaps Beatrice sees it too.

Of all the characters in the play, however, it is Don John who most clearly perceives what being excluded from things means. One has only to mark his unpleasantly saturnine disposition or his dubious ethics to recognize that he is afflicted, as he says, with a "mortifying mischief" (I.iii.12), the overwhelming accident of his bastardy, which is enough in the world into which he is born to negate an otherwise favorable pedigree, an acceptable physiognomy, and an undeniable masculinity. Don John wants nothing more than to be what a disinterested Nature has decreed him to be: to "be sad when I have cause, and smile at no man's jests; eat when I have stomach, and wait for no man's leisure; sleep when I am drowsy, and tend on no man's business; laugh when I am merry, and claw no man in his humor" (I.iii.13-18). But, Conrade advises him, "you must not make the full show of this till you may do it without controlment"; for the surly Don is on probation, having lately "stood out" against his brother, Don Pedro, and only recently having received forgiveness. He has seen, moreover, as would have happened in any case, his brother give full fraternal attention to young Claudio, eligible by accident of legitimate birth to enjoy all the privileges denied himself, including that of marriage to a "very forward March-chick" like Hero. Don John's declaration of independence, as memorable as it has been subject to misunderstanding over the years, thus provides the context for his subsequent "crime," which is an attempt to get revenge on a society that cannot or will not recognize his full humanity:

I had rather be a canker in a hedge than a rose in his grace, and it better fits my blood to be disdain'd of all than to fashion a carriage to rob love from any. In this (though I cannot be said to be a flattering honest man) it must not be denied but I am a plain-dealing villain. I am trusted with a muzzle, and enfranchis'd with a cog, therefore I have decreed not to sing in my cage. If I had my mouth, I would bite; if I had my liberty, I would do my liking. In the mean time let me be that I am, and seek not to alter me.   [I.iii.27-37]

Don John, like his friends Conrade and Borachio, lives in a state of incorrigible alienation, established at birth in his case and routinely acknowledged by those in society who can claim to "belong." Sad as this is for Don John, it is only somewhat less so for Beatrice, who, as we have noted, is also an alien in the world she inhabits and who in addition must learn to her sorrow that neither the affectation of society's love rituals nor a genuine experience of love itself, on which society is presumably based, can ever entirely redeem an alien from his or her separateness. Messina, at the level that preoccupies us in this play, is a loveless society.

We get a hint of this in the first few lines of the play, in that scene in which Governor Leonato is receiving a messenger from the wars. His first question is "How many gentlemen have you lost in this action?" The messenger's reply is calculated to please the Governor, and it succeeds nicely. "But few of any sort, and none of name," he says, to which Leonato replies sententiously, "A victory is twice itself when the achiever brings home full numbers." One may suppose that few if any in Shakespeare's audience felt the chill in this exchange, but it is hard to believe that Shakespeare himself was not conscious of having planted it there with special deliberation. Mark Twain achieves a similar effect, though with far less subtlety, in the last part of *Huckleberry Finn*. There, one may recall, Huck goes in search of Jim and soon learns that a runaway is being held captive on the Phelps plantation. He arrives at the plantation to find himself confused with someone (it later turns out to be Tom Sawyer) whom the Phelpses have been expecting for several days; and fumbling for a way to explain his delay, he grasps at Mrs. Phelps's "What kep you?—boat get aground?" and briefly tries to develop an explanation from that. When his ignorance of local sandbars proves to be a liability, however, he tries another tack:

"It warn't the grounding—that didn't keep us back but a little. We blowed out a cylinder-head."
"Good gracious! anybody hurt?"
"No'm. Killed a nigger."
"Well, it's lucky; because sometimes people do get hurt."[5]

The effect of this passage is not lost on twentieth-century readers, who recognize immediately that Huck, in framing an answer in terms that the Phelpses will find acceptable, is implicitly condemning the code the Phelpses live by. In the same way the unnamed messenger in *Much Ado* gives Leonato a battle report in socially acceptable terms and thereby suggests to at least some of Shakespeare's contemporaries—and, one may hope, to most of us—the kind of society that will be encountered in Shakespeare's Messina. This brief exchange is enough to tell us that "men of name" will usually have things their own way there and that the unenfranchised—among them bastards and orphans and, in general, women—will do well to live and die inconspicuously.

Once we sense this much, the significance of Don John's action and his insensitivity to Hero's plight can begin to come clear. We should note that in none of Shakespeare's possible sources is there a counterpart for the petty but seemingly malevolent villain that Shakespeare created. In fact, in Matteo Bandello's Novella XXII, one of the most likely sources, the corresponding character, Sir Girondo, is a disappointed suitor who turns Machiavellian as a consequence of his frustrated love and brings the whole messy matter to an end by publicly confessing his guilt.[6] Don John has no such motive. He is simply the bastard who hates a half-brother lucky enough to have been born in wedlock; and only because she happens to be convenient for his purposes does he use Hero as a weapon against that brother—against Claudio, too, in fact, for both of these in the propriety of their breeding are natural targets of his perennial and inextinguishable wrath.

Claudio behaves little better, however: he proffers love to Hero and then ignores her humanity, suspects the worst at the first opportunity, and damns on evidence that he does not even pause to investigate.[7] Regrettably, Messina's society applauds Claudio in this seemingly inconsistent behavior, for Messina recognizes that Claudio's attitude toward womankind is one it shares and considers honorable in a gentleman of breeding. His behavior throughout, in fact, is consistent with the Renaissance principle that love depends upon the "virtue of seeing," which is all that Claudio uses in choosing Hero to be his bride.[8] He simply sees, falls in love (or so he supposes), and without hearing so much as a word from the girl's lips, at least on this occasion, contemplates marriage: "I would scarce trust myself [not to turn husband], though I had sworn the contrary, if Hero would be my wife" (I.i.195-96). He rejects her quite as abruptly, and again on the basis of sight alone. In a world where uncertainties are the rule, Don Juan's firmly based and therefore predictable hostility is almost preferable to an affection as hastily and shakily grounded as Claudio's.[9]

The shakiness of Claudio's affection manifests itself early. Scarcely one hundred lines after his fervent declaration, he is asking Don Pedro, "Hath Leonato any son, my lord?" Don Pedro assures him that Hero is an only child, and Claudio's brief anxiety about money quickly subsides; but we note that instead of relishing the joy of a courtship (something in which he as a Florentine might have enjoyed a clear advantage over a mere lady from Messina), he readily accedes to Don Pedro's offer to provide a proxy wooing. One consequence of this indifference to love's early joys is that he almost falls victim to Don John's first stratagem, which is to insinuate that Don Pedro is wooing for himself. But Don Pedro, before he or anyone else realizes that trouble is imminent, frustrates that stratagem by announcing publicly: "Here, Claudio, I have woo'd in thy name, and fair Hero is won. I have broke with her father, and his good will obtain'd. Name the day of marriage, and God give thee joy!" (II.i.298-301). Claudio seems genuinely pleased (we have no way of knowing what Hero is thinking) and impatiently would marry at once ("Time goes on crutches till love have all his rights"); but on being urged to wait at least a week, he falls to playing at matchmaking with Don Pedro and Leonato so the time "shall not go dully by," as Don Pedro puts it.[10] Hero, who apparently has no choice in the matter, joins somewhat joylessly in the game and for the first time since her betrothal speaks: "I will do any modest office, my lord, to help my cousin to a good husband" (II.i.375-76). Don John, however, is also unwilling to let the time go dully by and devises a second strategem for upsetting the marriage, this time one that can provide excitement for everybody.

His new device is much more elaborate than the first but, in Shakespeare's version of it, clumsily executed. The text of

Much Ado has Borachio use Claudio's name in the assignation he stages with Margaret. This detail, if not someone's careless error, can suggest only that a lustful Hero in continuing to receive illicit lovers has assumed that a casual passerby will think nothing of seeing a strange man at her balcony provided he can be accoutred with the name of her betrothed. Such an interpretation of what Claudio and Don Pedro actually see (Borachio and Margaret in a private balcony scene) is hardly credible to us; but, for all the clumsy device that has led up to it, that interpretation seems to be the one that they make, suggesting more strongly than almost anything else could that they have been prepared from the beginning to find "luxurious" behavior in the innocent girl. We note that Bandello had the young man in his story expect nothing of the sort but let him, on being roundly deceived by the girl's former suitor, arrange to charge the girl discreetly by means of a private messenger. Both Claudio and Don Pedro are ready for blood and eager to discredit Hero if their spying confirms what Don John has alleged:

Claud. If I see any thing to-night why I should not marry her, to-morrow in the congregation, where I should wed, there will I shame her.

D. Pedro. And as I woo'd for thee to obtain her, I will join with thee to disgrace her.   [III.ii.124-27]

In church the next morning they do discredit her, shamelessly and cruelly, so that Don John's spurious censure seems almost kind by comparison: "Thus, pretty lady, / I am sorry for thy much misgovernment" (IV.i.98-99). They remain at the church until Hero swoons and then go off to seek more profitable pursuits. In their eyes the whole business of choosing, wooing, winning, and destroying a young woman has indeed been much ado about nothing.[11]

In the parlance of dramatic analysis the word *climax* is at best a debatable term, but a climax of sorts does occur in the first half of this first scene in Act IV. The traumatic repudiation comes to pass; Claudio, Don Pedro, and Don John leave in a demonstration of righteous indignation; and Hero lies, to all appearances dead, on the church floor. Of those remaining,

Beatrice alone flatly refuses to believe the charges of misconduct; Benedick is at least inclined to disbelieve them, as is Friar Francis. Leonato, however, representing the voice and mind of Messina, declares that his daughter is better off dead: "O Fate! take not away thy heavy hand, / Death is the fairest cover for her shame / That may be wish'd for" (IV.i.115-17). In a longer speech of some twenty-four lines he lays out a good collection of the stock responses for an outraged parent (he regrets that he ever wished for more children, he considers even this one too many, he wishes that he had nurtured some orphan that could not have brought discredit to his blood) and concludes:

> O she is fall'n
> Into a pit of ink, that the wide sea
> Hath drops too few to wash her clean again,
> And salt too little which may season give
> To her foul tainted flesh!
> [IV.i.139-43]

With this speech the issue of the play comes clear: settling it will not be a matter of resolving differences between lawlessness (Don John) and the rest of society but of somehow correcting, or at least challenging, that society's inability to transcend its own arbitrary mores and give elementary comfort where common humanity decrees that compassion take precedence over propriety. The Friar is willing to stake his reputation that this is such an occasion:

> Call me a fool,
> Trust not my reading, nor my observations,
> Which with experimental seal doth warrant
> The tenure of my book; trust not my age,
> My reverence, calling, nor divinity,
> If this sweet lady lie not guiltless here
> Under some biting error.
> [IV.i.164-69]

Moreover, Hero revives to protest her innocence with a stronger voice than she has been able to muster anywhere else in the play: "If I know more of any man alive / Than that which

maiden modesty doth warrant, / Let all my sins lack mercy!"
(IV.i.178-80). Nevertheless, Leonato's humanity continues to
sleep—or at least to nod. Some nagging doubt perhaps accounts for the equanimity with which he enters into the coun-
ter-deception that Friar Francis proposes (that is, to let Hero
remain "dead" for a brief space in the hope that a chance to
reflect on her dying may bring an outraged Claudio to compassion); but even that concession hardly makes palatable his
elaborate display of grief (V.i.3-38), which alarms Antonio, his
genuinely grieving brother. Leonato concludes hypocritically,
"I will be flesh and blood, / For there was never yet philosopher / That could endure the toothache patiently."

The fact remains that no male in Messina challenges the
discrediting of Hero with anything like manly vigor except
Antonio, who declares to Claudio and Don Pedro:

> God knows I lov'd my niece,
> And she is dead, slander'd to death by villains
> That dare as well answer a man indeed
> As I dare take a serpent by the tongue.
> Boys, apes, braggarts, Jacks, milksops!
>
> [V.i.87-91]

By comparison, the Friar's challenge is timid ("There is some
strange misprision in the princes"); Leonato's, non-existent.
Claudio, still confident that he has been dishonored, hears the
news of Hero's death with equanimity and moves forward
immediately to new adventures. It is interesting that the Friar,
in expressing a hope that Claudio will come to reconsider his
action against the girl, puts forth the same Neoplatonic notion
of love that had made it justifiable for Claudio to woo "spiritually" in the first place:

> When he shall hear she died upon his words,
> Th' idea of her life shall sweetly creep
> Into his study of imagination,
> And every lovely organ of her life
> Shall come apparell'd in more precious habit,
> More moving, delicate, and full of life,
> Into the eye and prospect of his soul,
> Than when she liv'd indeed.
>
> [IV.i.223-30]

Lovely as this thought is, it suggests the kind of appreciation of women that left Claudio vulnerable to the clumsiest of deceptions. Had he known his Hero as a person rather than as a pseudo-Platonic ideal, he would most likely have challenged the perpetrators of her slander on the spot. The Friar, apparently unable to conceive of counseling Claudio or correcting him, would have him retrace his steps, once more exercise his faculty of sight, and conceivably repeat the fatal pattern, again with Hero as his object. Sadly, in the end this is not unlike what Claudio does.[12]

Meanwhile, Claudio and Don Pedro, thinking Hero dead and entombed, treat her presumably grieving father and her genuinely grieving uncle with an indifference that borders on disdain; and Claudio, shortly afterwards, even says flippantly of the encounter, "We had lik'd to have had our two noses snapp'd off with two old men without teeth" (V.i.115-16). When Benedick proffers the challenge that Beatrice has imposed upon him, the two gallants brush it aside as a symptom of madness generated by his infatuation with that orphaned lady:

> *D. Pedro.* What a pretty thing man is when he goes in his doublet and hose and leaves off his wit!
> *Claud.* He is then a giant to an ape, but then is an ape a doctor to such a man.   [V.i.199-202]

They both, however, will express grief in conventional hyperboles when Borachio's confession makes it clear that Hero was wrongly accused:

> *D. Pedro.* Runs not this speech like iron through your blood?
> *Claud.* I have drunk poison whiles he utter'd it.   [V.i.244-46]

Yet Claudio maintains his innocence ("sinn'd I not / But in mistaking"), as does Don Pedro: "By my soul, nor I, / And yet, to satisfy this good old man, / I would bend under any heavy weight / That he'll enjoin me to" (V.i.275-78). It turns out that satisfying "this good old man" involves, for both of them, telling Messina what has happened and performing an act of contrition at Hero's tomb; for Claudio it also means marrying Hero's "cousin." Leonato tells him:

Be yet my nephew. My brother hath a daughter,
Almost the copy of my child that's dead,
And she alone is heir to both of us.
Give her the right you should have giv'n her cousin.
And so dies my revenge.

[V.i.288-92]

An easy satisfaction indeed! And the easiness of it nowhere shows more clearly than in the scene where Claudio reads an epitaph and hangs it on Hero's tomb. At the risk of further berating a character whom critics have long considered at least superficially culpable, let us examine this scene, which most pass over quickly or treat as a conventional device for signaling the completion of Claudio's change of heart.[13]

The change, if it has really occurred, is only sign-deep. The verses of the epitaph are admittedly bad, but pardonably so if they are meant simply to represent the awkward versifying of a graceless young man. Yet one imagines that Shakespeare created all the verses in his plays, bad as well as good, with an artist's deliberateness and meant us to heed their quality as well as their substance. In any case, Claudio's feeble lines contrast sharply with other dirgelike expressions in the plays: Ariel's song in *The Tempest* (I.ii.397-405); "Fear no more the heat o' th' sun," which the rough young men in *Cymbeline* are represented as having created in honor of the unspeakable Cloten (IV.ii.258-81); and most important of all, the impromptu exclamation of Romeo at the tomb of a presumably dead Juliet:

O my love, my wife,
Death, that hath suck'd the honey of thy breath,
Hath had no power yet upon thy beauty:
Thou are not conquer'd, beauty's ensign yet
Is crimson in thy lips and in thy cheeks,
And death's pale flag is not advanced there.

[V.iii.91-96)

Claudio's first stanza, the epitaph, says fatuously that Hero has been given "glorious fame" by her death, presumably as a consequence of the epitaph's being hung as a scroll on her tomb. The second stanza, a "solemn hymn" consisting of a prayer to Diana followed by apostrophes to Midnight and to the buried dead round about ("assist our moan"), is a curious combination of clichés, to say the least, and one in questionable taste. After that, the proceedings over, Don Pedro breaks in with a joyous notice of the dawn that calls to mind an earlier and happier scene in *Romeo and Juliet*, in which Romeo announces the morning with

> Look, love, what envious streaks
> Do lace the severing clouds in yonder east.
> Night's candles are burnt out, and jocund day
> Stands tiptoe on the misty mountain tops.
> [III.v.7-10]

Don Pedro does somewhat less well:

> The wolves have preyed; and look, the gentle day,
> Before the wheels of Phoebus, round about
> Dapples the drowsy east with spots of grey.
> [V.iii.25-27]

Nevertheless, a simple declaration that daylight has come is quite enough for Claudio, who promptly puts off his mask of sadness, figuratively dusts off his hands, and announces: "Hymen now with luckier issue speed's / Than this for whom we rend'red up this woe." By the most charitable interpretation Claudio's unspecified "this" refers to the whole situation just passed, but it appears likely to refer to the lifeless body of Hero. Whichever the case may be, in Claudio's mind the girl joins the ranks of the nameless dead alluded to in Act I, who lie where they fall and are buried where they fall. It is no wonder that Beatrice earlier, on seeing Hero discredited by one capable of such insensitivity, should have pressed upon her own newly declared lover the charge "Kill Claudio" (V.i.289); and it scarcely does her lover credit that he complies timidly and inconclusively, letting an initial show of indignation dissolve to inaction. It does Messina no credit whatever that almost all the others in the play accept the death of Hero as a regrettable accident and reserve their anger for Don John.

Beatrice, as noted earlier, is not at the center of the dramatic action that gives the play its shape, but she views the scene of that action more perceptively than anyone else, and she sees that the scene does not generate a movement of its own—that the action of *Much Ado*, in other words, is contrived and manipulated from without, and that the life it presumably manifests and perpetuates is at best a mechanical action, a "much ado about nothing." One should note, further, that such an absence of life does not characterize the action in Bandello's novella, however inferior that work may be to the minor masterpiece that Shakespeare made of it; and one reason is that Bandello seems to have concentrated on presenting in straightforward, honest fashion yet another version of the ancient comic action whereby an aging society meets the challenge of death, emerges victorious, and grows young again. As in countless other romantic versions of that action, Bandello's story tells of a young woman grown eligible for marriage, of suitors for her hand, of her designation of a successful suitor, and of the near-frustration of their marriage because of the jealous machinations of an unsuccessful suitor. The society in Bandello's story is healthy, vital, and renewable. It generates passion and conflict in the normal course of things, and it resolves both of these with the same life by which it has generated them. The result is that Bandello's presentation of a society metamorphosing from youth to age and back to youth again is reassuring to any set of readers that has felt irritation at the aggressive presence of youth and despair at the perennial advance of senility. This is part of its charm. By contrast, Shakespeare's Messina, as we have seen, runs according to formula, mindlessly and without passion, until an intruder with no credentials throws a clog into the works. At that point the machine breaks down and would presumably have remained broken down forever had there not been another outsider waiting in the wings (he does not even signal his presence in Messina's world until midway through the third act) to find the impediment and point to the need for its removal so that the machine can resume its action.

That beneficent intruder in *Much Ado about Nothing*, of course, is Constable Dogberry, who with the aid of Headborough Verges and the other "good men and true" of Mes-

sina's watch identifies the perpetrator of Don John's plot and
brings him to justice, thereby making possible a technical
denouement that the action on its own could never have
achieved. Dogberry's outrageous malapropisms and utter stu-
pidity in general provide occasion for some of the memorable
merriment in this play; but that merriment unfortunately
distracts as well as delights and helps to obscure several points
of importance. First, it hides the fact that the watch is only
nominally a part of the society that has been engaging our
attention. For all practical purposes it is, by its own admission,
a watch that does little if any watching:

> *Dog.* This is your charge: you shall comprehend all vagrom men;
> you are to bid any man stand, in the Prince's name.
> *2. Watch.* How if 'a will not stand?
> *Dog.* Why then take no note of him, but let him go, and presently
> call the rest of the watch together, and thank God you are rid of a
> knave.
> *Verg.* If he will not stand when he is bidden, he is none of the Prince's
> subjects.
> *Dog.* True, and they are to meddle with none but the Prince's
> subjects. You shall also make no noise in the streets; for, for the watch
> to babble and to talk, is most tolerable, and not to be endur'd.
> [*2.*] *Watch.* We will rather sleep than talk, we know what belongs to
> a watch.   [III.iii.24-38]

Less than one hundred lines later, however, two of the men are
overhearing Borachio tell Conrade of the deception that he has
played on Don Pedro and Claudio; and shortly thereafter they
do arrest these two culprits, though partly because they mis-
understand Borachio's innocent observation that fashion is a
deformed thief and wildly conjure up an imagined memory of
a thief named Deformed. Understandably, no one at Leonato's
at first takes the watch seriously; and when Dogberry tries to
report something of the matter to Leonato, the Governor is too
busy with preparations for the wedding to stop to sift out the
grain of sense in Dogberry's nonsensical digressions. At last
the Constable comes close to the point:

> *Dog.* Our watch, sir, have indeed comprehended two aspicious
> persons, and we would have them this morning examin'd before your
> worship.

Leon. Take their examination yourself, and bring it to me. I am now in great haste, as it may appear unto you.

Dog. It shall be suffigance.

Leon. Drink some wine ere you go; fare you well.

[III.v.45-52]

The examination that follows (IV.ii.) is noteworthy mainly because of the superb farce that it contains. It ends with Dogberry's memorable "O that I had been writ down an ass!" and it produces a report that confuses more than it enlightens:

D. Pedro. Officers, what offense have these men done?

Dog. Marry, sir, they have committed false report; moreover they have spoken untruths; secondarily, they are slanders; sixt and lastly, they have belied a lady; thirdly, they have verified unjust things; and to conclude, they are lying knaves. [V.i.213-20]

Don Pedro and Claudio proceed to make sport with this too until Borachio, now prisoner, is moved, as he says, by the report that Hero is dead (and perhaps by the knowledge that Don John has left him in the lurch) and confesses everything: "The lady is dead upon mine and my master's false accusation; and briefly, I desire nothing but the reward of a villain" (V.i.241-44). Clearly, it is Dogberry who has brought this villainy to light; but just as clearly, he has done so by accident rather than by design, and he does not quite understand what he has accomplished. He has, moreover, unwittingly directed Messina to the ony solution of its ills that it can understand: namely, to find the bastard malefactor and make him pay. Nothing that Dogberry says or does casts the slightest shadow of blame on either Claudio or Don Pedro.

To their credit, both Claudio and Don Pedro express regrets at this point and offer to do penance at Leonato's pleasure, but what follows is their perfunctory performance at the tomb that evening and a return to Leonato's house the following morning for another go at a wedding in Messina. The play ends some three scenes and twelve hours after the public confession of the presumably fatal deception, with Claudio unmasking what he thinks to be Hero's cousin only to discover the real Hero behind the veil, and with Benedick gaily resuming his contentious progress with Beatrice toward the altar. Messina has quickly returned to normal, and the status quo has been preserved without recourse to any true metamorphosis. Benedick, now having completely recovered his confidence, ventures to urge Don Pedro to take a wife also, for "there is no staff more reverent than one tipp'd with horn" (V.iv.123-24). His last words (and the last words of the play) are his response to the news that Don John has been captured and returned to Messina: "Think not on him till to-morrow. I'll devise thee brave punishments for him. Strike up, pipers" (V.iv.127-29). And so the story ends.

Elizabethan audiences would have applauded and, perhaps after some reflection, approved this ending. It shows the interloper about to be punished, the lovers united, and the old man happy with it all. Yet this ending also promises considerably less than the ending of *The Taming of the Shrew*, where two of the ladies are at least spirited and resolute in their determination to manipulate the will of their lords and the third, more knowledgeable, is equally resolute in the face of a society that undoubtedly will continue to pose threats to her integrity. Here, however, Hero capitulates completely, apparently happy to resume a march to the altar that days before had almost resulted in her death. Beatrice ventures one final retort, about consenting to marry Benedick because she thought he was dying; but her heart seems not to be in it, and Benedick stops the repartee, such as it is, with a kiss before turning aside to talk with the men. Friar Francis, Antonio, and Dogberry are not among them.[14]

In short, *Much Ado about Nothing* would be sad enough were it simply a play about the last days of high comedy. Unhappily, however, it is also a play in which most of the principal characters of the dying mode never recognize their plight and in which relatively healthy human beings on the periphery do not perceive until too late the contagion in the body they would join. Beatrice alone glimpses what she has been a party to and reacts with her horrified "Kill Claudio." But the young man charged with the killing does not quite hear and certainly does not understand. He timidly and covertly calls Claudio "villain," "coward," and "boy" and then returns to Leonato's garden to practice his writing of bad poetry, confident that nothing will come of his discreet challenges—and nothing does. In the end, we must believe, Beatrice and Benedick are both submerged in the deadly dullness that has already possessed even the best parts of a rigidly graceful and courtly Messina.

Francis Fergusson, one of the most perceptive of our modern critics, in commenting on the last scene and on the play as a whole has urged forbearance. "Everything which Shakespeare meant by *The Comedy of Errors*," he writes, "is immediately perceptible; the comic vision of *Much Ado* will only appear, like the faces which Dante saw in the milky substance of the moon, slowly, and as we learn to trust the fact that it is really there."[15] Some such act of faith is surely necessary. Leo Salingar has found *Much Ado* as fraught with problems as any of the later plays that commonly receive the label of "problem";[16] and one must, perhaps reluctantly, agree with him. There is a weariness in the mirth of this so-called joyous comedy that calls to mind innocent Dogberry's comment on ancient Verges: "As they say, 'When the age is in, the wit is out.' God help us, it is a world to see!" (III.v.34-35). Unfortunately, however, with the exception of Beatrice, the young people of Messina seem to be victims of the same fossilization that has stultified their elders, and the title *Much Ado about Nothing* is as broadly applicable as it is painfully appropriate.

10

As You Like It

As readers may know, Thomas Lodge, "university wit" and a playwright more by necessity than by choice, repeatedly reached for a kind of fame that he thought the theater could never give him. His most successful effort was the *Rosalynde* of 1590, a prose romance based upon *The Tale of Gamelyn*, then still being attributed to Chaucer, and executed in a style occasionally reminiscent of John Lyly's *Euphues*.[1] The popularity of *Rosalynde* outlasted Lodge himself, who died in 1625, and by 1634 the work had gone through eleven editions. Lodge's permanent fame, however, such as it is, probably rests upon *As You Like It*, the play which Shakespeare, six years Lodge's junior and a product of the Stratford Grammar School, made of his novel. In 1600 *As You Like It* was entered on the Stationers' Register as a play "to be staid," an indication that the translation of Lodge's novel to the stage had sufficient promise of continued success to warrant keeping it at least temporarily out of print.

Shakespeare had not done anything quite like *As You Like It* before. He had adapted other prose tales for the theater, notably a prose tale from Gil Polo's *Diana Enamorada* for *The Two Gentlemen of Verona* (though the possibility of an intermediary version cannot be ruled out there) and a novella by Matteo Bandello that became *Much Ado about Nothing*; he had conflated a pair of prose tales for *The Merchant of Venice*, and he had adapted Arthur Brooke's *Romeus and Juliet* into a pathetic tragedy cast in the comic mold. In *As You Like It*, however, he undertook to cast into dramatic form with ostensibly minimal changes a piece of nondramatic literature that was current and extremely popular. It was the sort of translation that takes place more or less regularly nowadays as best-selling novels after a year or two achieve metamorphosis into film. In Shakespeare's time the practice was less well established, and one may wonder what Lodge thought at seeing his nondramatic characters come to life on someone else's stage.

It is possible that he was not altogether pleased. Shakespeare had added several characters, among them Le Beau, Touchstone, Audrey, William, Jacques, Amiens, and the country vicar Sir Oliver Martext; but scholars usually say that none of these is essential to the plot. Helen Gardner exaggerates only slightly when she writes, "These additional characters add nothing at all to the story. If you were to tell it you would leave them out."[2] Shakespeare also made changes in the story, however: he converted the two kings into dukes and made them brothers, thereby providing a parallel to the hostility between Orlando and Oliver (called Rosader and Saladyne in Lodge's version); he reduced Orlando's inheritance to a token gift of one thousand crowns (in Lodge, Rosader actually inherits more than Saladyne); he made Adam Spencer old, almost eighty in fact, and then let him disappear at the close of the second act (perhaps in death, though no one says so, and there is no grieving); and he softened the conclusion by having the usurping duke give up war and become a religious, whereas Lodge has the usurping brother, Torismond, die in one last battle, in which Rosader and Saladyne, now reconciled, fight side by side. All these changes, thus baldly enumerated, signify little; but the difference between Lodge and Shakespeare is nevertheless real and deep.

The novel presents a two-dimensional world of a competent and moderately gifted writer, in which the characters all speak more or less alike and move in disciplined progression through a tapestried realm where court and forest seem to have been constructed out of the same material and colored with the same dyestuffs. The events that take place there derive from relationships that are recognizable reflections of ones we have

known in real life: the love of men for women and women for
men, the rivalry of brothers, and the contrasts between levels
of society in a system that still has traces of feudalism in it.
Lodge's recognizable reflections, however, perpetuate the conventions of pastoral and seldom rise above the level of diverting artifice; they amuse us but they do not demand our belief.
Shakespeare's play, by contrast, presents a world in which
court and country are sharply distinguished and in which both
are believable. The slight element of artificiality that remains
is not so much an aspect of pastoral as it is a fossil residue
peculiar to Lodge's narrative. The conspicuous example, of
course, is the lioness, an incredible detail in any sylvan context
that Shakespeare or his audience might have been familiar
with but here an implicit affirmation of fidelity to the source,
which at least some must have known and come to the theater
to see in dramatic form. Other details that may appear artificial to us did not necessarily appear so to Shakespeare's
contemporaries. The adder, for example, was no mere convention, for adders were still a palpable threat in English and
continental woodlands, and the appearance of one in the play
lent credibility to the scene. Similarly, the palm tree, which
many have treated as an exotic touch deliberately added, was
probably a perfectly normal English willow or one of the other
deciduous trees regularly plundered for branches on Palm
Sunday and throughut the year referred to as "palms."[3] Moreover, *As You Like It* gives almost no warrant for the Watteau-
esque forest that appeared in an early film version with
Laurence Olivier and Elisabeth Bergner. It supports fully, however, the real forest (actually a Scottish one) that graced the
recent British television production of *As You Like It*, starring
Richard Pasco as Jaques.

Critics who recognize the realism of *As You Like It* sometimes account for the difference between Lodge and Shakespeare by pointing to such things as Shakespeare's transformation of Lodge's conventional Coridon into the rustic Corin and his creation of such characters as Touchstone, Audrey,
and William;[4] but the difference is not something that can be
accounted for by citing alterations and additions. The dis-

tinctive thing about *As You Like It* is the conspicuous the-
atricality that characterizes it virtually from beginning to end.
It is as if Shakespeare had set up Lodge's imaginary world on
the stage and then gone about peopling it with actors from the
Chamberlain's Men; and, in fact, this is what he would inevitably have done, given the Elizabethan practice of typecasting
and the custom of allowing some actors, notably those typed
for comic parts, the right to a measure of free improvisation. In
a play like *As You Like It*, where the intrigue counts for relatively little, it was also inevitable that the actors should have
expected to be identifiable as performers and that the playwright should have been more or less content to provide occasion for them to be so.[5] Something of the sort happened in
Warner Brothers' 1936 production of Max Reinhardt's *A Midsummer Night's Dream*, in which the comic actors—Hugh Her-
bert, James Cagney, Joe E. Brown, and Frank McHugh—were
allowed to remain recognizably themselves while delivering
Shakespeare's lines. Trying to identify Shakespeare's actors in
their various roles is at best an inconclusive game, but one can
imagine William Sly in the re-creation of Lodge's Rosader as
the impetuous Orlando. Richard Burbage and Henry Condell
as the two dukes, and perhaps Shakespeare himself as Adam
Spencer. The need to assign a part to the company's older
comic actor, Thomas Pope, could account for the transformation of Coridon into Corin, and the need to accommodate
popular members of the company still unprovided for would
explain the addition of a Touchstone (Will Kemp), Amiens (for
the musical Augustine Phillips), and Jaques (for John Hem-
inge). What is important, however, as has been noted, is the
impression this play gives to audiences of a group of actors
exploring and re-creating a setting and the story that takes
place within it.[6]

From time to time the play gives us signals about this
situation, and our awareness of what is before us vacillates, as
in a recursive drawing, between the figure of the forest and the
normally suppressed background of theater. For example, the
banished Duke Senior, on sending the bumptious Orlando
back into the brush to fetch his ancient charge, reminds us

briefly of the paradox inherent in the artificial but concrete device of theater that is actually before our eyes, with its natural limitations and—because of the sanctions we give it—its almost miraculous capability of capturing and presenting the full range of human experience:

> Thou seest we are not all alone unhappy:
> This wide and universal theatre
> Presents more woeful pageants than the scene
> Wherein we play in.

[II.vii.136-39]

Then without warning we are once more back in the forest, where Jaques reminds us that, conversely, the world itself is a stage "and all the men and women merely players." Nevertheless, throughout the play the theater necessarily remains the ground for our vision and the forest its normal but occasionally suppressed figure.

That is one reason why any discussion about the nature of Shakespeare's forest of Arden will approach futility in proportion as participants in the discussion seek to make their characterizations of it definitive. Commentary on the subject should begin with a frank recognition that all we actually see is a relatively bare stage which only moments before has served as the lawn before the Duke's palace and before that as an orchard at the manor house now owned by Oliver de Boys, and that like these two previous locations the forest is merely designated, not presented. Having acknowledged this much, we should be able to suspend criticism of such things as J. Dover Wilson's characterization of it as a blend of "the delightful scenery of Montemayor, and . . . Shakespeare's memories of the Warwickshire scenery round about his native home."[7] What Wilson was responding to, quite legitimately, was the mixture of signals in *As You Like It*, and he was precise in calling the play "a triumph of dramatic scene painting," though this does not alter the fact that the triumph takes place where all triumphs of dramatic scene painting take place: in the head of the spectator, auditor, or reader. We are shown a Silvius and Phebe in an action reminiscent of pastoral romance, and we are also told that we are in the presence of real sheep and believable rustics. Surprisingly, these two disparate conditions do coalesce for us, but the result is not Lodge's French forest. Neither is it an image of the "golden world," where men may "fleet the time carelessly," such as the wrestler Charles imagines (I.i.114-19), but a place that is to be conceived of as predominantly real, in whatever terms we may conceive as being appropriate to a representation of the particular reality.

In this connection David Young has provided a useful observation in his chapter about the variability of pastoral effects generally in Shakespeare's plays. "What emerges as we read or view *As You Like It*," he says, is a demonstration of "the essential subjectivity of pastoral" and "a growing awareness of the fundamental relativity of human experience."[8] This puts the emphasis where it belongs, on the action that derives from the characters themselves; and it properly calls attention to the "essential subjectivity" of one's initial exposure to the world of nature, especially if such exposure comes relatively late in the maturation of the person being exposed. Whereas the initiate tends to see in the forest only reflections of himself or herself, the more seasoned traveler learns to see the forest objectively. This is the difference between Orlando and Jaques. Duke Senior, one may suppose, stands somewhere in between.

For the fully seasoned traveler, however, there is nothing magical or mysteriously efficacious about the forest, as some, presumably following Northrop Frye, might have it. Frye, in an early essay cited in a previous chapter, relates the forest of Arden to Shakespeare's forests in *The Two Gentlemen of Verona*, *A Midsummer Night's Dream*, and *The Merry Wives of Windsor* and to the pastoral world presented in Act IV of *The Winter's Tale*, the Illyria of *Twelfth Night*, and Prospero's island in *The Tempest*. Frye sees these as examples of what he calls Shakespeare's "green world," which, he says, signals the appearance of the distinctive aspect of Shakespeare's comedy and the mode he chose in preference to the New Comedy mode of Ben Jonson and the Restoration writers. Of this distinctive aspect Frye writes: "This is the drama of folk ritual, of the St. George play and the mummer's play, of the feast of the ass and the Boy

Bishop, and of all the dramatic activity that punctuated the Christian calendar with the rituals of an immemorial paganism. . . . Its theme is once again the triumph of life over the waste land, the death and revival of the year impersonated by figures still human, and once divine as well."[9] Frye has given us a valuable insight here, but accepting that insight should not preclude our recognizing Shakespeare's continuing participation also in the tradition of New Comedy, and it should not mislead us into seeing Shakespeare's forests as being in themselves agents of renewal.

An unfortunate concomitant of Frye's suggestion, once it has become dominant in a reader's mind, is the tendency to focus attention on the relative "plotlessness" of *As You Like It*, which in Anne Barton's view results in a "curious stillness at the heart" of the play.[10] The plot of *As You Like It*, by comparison with that of *Much Ado about Nothing*, is indeed relatively slight. Plot, however, is only one vehicle for action, and the action of this play is still a version—admittedly a complicated version—of the action of Roman comedy, in which a young person usually defies the restraints of authority. In *As You Like It* two young people do the defying, become alienated as a result from the society that gives sanction to the restraints, and then plow through their inherited forest of dead mating conventions to discover a natural mode of effecting the accommodation, one to the other, that will allow them to play their proper part in reconstituting and renewing the society that has temporarily expelled them. Producers of the play would do well to let themselves be guided by a passage from Montaigne's "Of the Cannibales" which was certainly in Shakespeare's mind when he wrote *The Tempest* and most likely there when he wrote *As You Like It* as well: "There is no reason art [in which term Montaigne was including all the products of human invention] should gain the point of honor of our great and puissant mother nature. We have so much by our inventions surcharged the riches and beauties of her works that we have altogether choked her. Yet, whenever her purity shineth she makes our vain and frivolous enterprises wonderfully ashamed."[11]

Surcharging the riches and beauties of nature is in Montaigne's view the universal malady of civilization, and it is a malady that appears to be endemic in Duke Frederick's usurped domain. An inclination to "surcharge" nature's accustomed patterns may be detected at the root of Orlando's restiveness in a situation in which he thinks his natural superiority is doomed to obscurity by the custom of inheritance. It also serves as an excuse for Duke Frederick's uncivil behavior toward his brother. Shakespeare's contemporaries would have given various interpretations of these two examples. A Machiavellian advocate of power probably would have applauded both unruly brothers. A Christian humanist might have condemned both as violators of a natural order revealed in Scripture and in church doctrine and confirmed by reason. A naturalist of Montaigne's persuasions, however, might have come close to taking the position that Shakespeare's plays, at least those from *As You Like It* to *The Tempest*, seem to support. According to this view, the actions of both rebellious brothers, though ethically defensible to different degrees, are motivated by a congeries of "inventions" that has little to do with the realities of life. Frederick and Orlando, like us, are products of a highly sophisticated man-made civilization heavily surcharged with sacred monuments of human presumption and folly; and wisdom for exiles like these can come only as a result of seeing through the façade erected by human ingenuity and recognizing that the natural world, which has survived for centuries without many rational inventions, may provide a better reflection of truth than manor or court and that therefore it deserves at least our respect.This is Jaques' stance throughout the play, and it is the one that Orlando struggles toward and has almost reached as the play comes to an end.

Orlando's approach to that position is the principal corollary of the central action of *As You Like It*, which, as in all Shakespearean comedy, is to satisfy the society's impulse to renewal. Producers and critics have sometimes been inclined to have us think of Rosalind as occupying the center,[12] and Shakespeare might well have given her that position; but forcing her to occupy it in the play that he wrote results in distortion. Granted, Rosalind is the character in the play most apt to catch the modern eye; for Shakespeare has invested her with a power to fascinate which, with or without help from professional interpreters, can easily deflect the attention of an audience or a reader. She may have had the same sort of appeal for the Elizabethan audience, which, as commentators have frequently noted, saw a talented boy actor playing a girl who dresses like a boy and maintains that identity even as she plays at being a girl, ostensibly to show her young man the folly of his affection for her. The resulting performance is wittily ambiguous throughout, dazzlingly so at times; nevertheless, Rosalind's real function in the play, like Portia's in *The Merchant of Venice*, remains that of helping her man move towards maturity as quickly as possible and (in Rosalind's case) when she has fulfilled that function, to bring the play to a close with an epilogue.

Unlike Portia, however, Rosalind is never fully in control. She assumes her male attire at the end of Act I, for the purpose of ensuring safety, she says, though one suspects she is mainly seizing a chance to masquerade. Having encountered Orlando while thus disguised, she continues the deception in order to "cure" him of his lovesickness and manages to deliver herself of a stream of observations, facile for the most part but so charmingly put that they have beguiled some into thinking them truths. In an crucial scene in Act IV she declares:

The poor world is almost six thousand years old, and in all this time there was not any man died in his own person, *videlicet*, in a love-cause. Troilus had his brains dash'd out with a Grecian club, yet he did what he could to die before, and he is one of the patterns of love. Leander, he would have liv'd many a fair year though Hero had turn'd nun, if it had not been for a hot midsummer night . . . But these are all lies: men have died from time to time, and worms have eaten them, but not for love.   [IV.i.94-108]

There is undoubtedly an element of therapeutic common sense in all this, but Orlando regards it as trivial and Rosalind herself will come to think it so when she inadvertently swoons at the sight of her beloved's blood. Eventually, she presses her game to outrageous lengths in a mock marriage, shocking the literal-minded Celia, who comprehends a danger in proceedings of this kind even if Rosalind does not. According to a belief prevalent then and not entirely dead even now, marriage is a sacrament that is performed by the participants themselves, the priest merely solemnizing. Were Rosalind the male youth she is pretending to be, there could be no harm. As it is, in the eyes of heaven—at least theoretically—Orlando and Rosalind are husband and wife at the end of the scene, and Celia is privately incensed at her cousin's recklessness: "You have simply misus'd our sex in your love-prate. We must have your doublet and hose pluck'd over your head, and show the world what the bird hath done to her own nest" (IV.i.201-4). The final scene of the play brings the pair to an acceptance of the state to which Rosalind's irresponsibility has, in the eyes of Celia, already brought them; but the resolution is not entirely Rosalind's doing. As in previous scenes, she responds there to the exigencies of the moment and is at least partly the tool of circumstance.

By contrast, Orlando, though he readily accepts the youth Ganymed's offer of instruction, is more inclined to set his own course. He rejects Jaques' unpalatable wisdom, takes only as much of Rosalind's as he likes, apparently does not let the sessions interfere with his means (IV.i.177-81), and ends them when they begin to grow tedious. We should have imagined he would behave so from our first encounter with him at the manor, where as a "third son" he is rebellious at having to take a role beneath his native endowments. We have reason to believe he reports with a fair degree of accuracy the treatment he has received from his eldest brother, Oliver:

. . . he keeps me rustically at home, or (to speak more properly) stays me here at home unkept; for call you keeping for a gentleman of my birth, that differs not from the stalling of an ox? His horses are bred better, for besides that they are fair with their feeding, they are taught their manage, and to that end riders dearly hir'd; but I (his brother) gain nothing under him but growth, for the which his animals on his dunghills are as much bound to him as I. Besides this nothing that he so plentifully gives me, the something that nature gave me his countenance seems to take from me. He lets me feed with his hinds, bars me

the place of a brother, and as much as in him lies, mines my gentility
with my education.   [I.i.7-21]

Oliver has no reason to call Orlando "a secret and villainous
contriver," and he certainly has no cause to plot his death
(II.iii.16-23); but Orlando clearly has given provocation, and
just as clearly he has intimidated his brother from time to time
with shows of superior strength. He may therefore be at least
partly responsible for Oliver's unlovely behavior in the first
half of the play, which in view of the readiness with which
Oliver changes later on may be regarded as defensive behavior
prompted by fear and a painful awareness of Orlando's penchant for violence.

An unfortunate complement to Orlando's irascibility is his
naiveté, probably a consequence of the limited experience and
education he has received under the domination of his brother.
Both are evident in the wild challenge to Duke Senior's party
in the forest, issued under the assumption that anyone there
must be a savage; and both are manifested during his abortive
attempt to make a place for himself at Duke Frederick's
court—irascibility in his overwhelming defeat of the prize
wrestler Charles, and naiveté in his tasteless response to
Rosalind's offer (in the interest of his safety) to have the match
called off:

... let your fair eyes and gentle wishes go with me to my trial;
wherein if I be foil'd, there is but one sham'd that was never gracious;
if kill'd, but one dead that is willing to be so. I shall do my friends no
wrong, for I have none to lament me; the world no injury, for in it I
have nothing. Only in the world I fill up a place, which may be better
supplied when I have made it empty.   [I.ii.185-93]

Orlando's essential virtue comes to the fore soon after, when
his self-pity gives way to a genuine concern for old Adam, who
accompanies him on his flight into the forest. Even so, his
naiveté, or ignorance, continues for a time. Once disabused
about the savagery of all who live in forests, he jumps to the
conclusion that because courtiers are in Arden it must be as
safe from savagery as the court. Thus he is not prepared when
the adder and the lioness make their appearance and teach

him that even in propitious season Arden can exact her toll of blood; but his encounter with these—a brush with mortality that brings the action to a climax—matures Orlando in more ways than one. From this point on, he says, he "can no longer live by thinking" (V.ii.50).

It should be noted that Orlando does not encounter any of Arden's rustics until his meeting with Silvius and Phebe in Act V. He thinks he has met one in Rosalind, whom he takes to be a country youth with "an accent something finer" than one might expect from "so remov'd a dwelling" (III.ii.341-42), and he continues to think of her so until the moment he sees her revealed as Rosalind indeed in the unpriested wedding ceremony known as the masque of Hymen. Orlando has admitted shortly before this general epiphany that he had earlier noted a resemblance but discounted it in the light of what he took to be evidence to the contrary:

> My lord, the first time that I ever saw him
> Methought he was a brother to your daughter.
> But, my good lord, this boy is forest-born,
> And hath been tutor'd in the rudiments
> Of many desperate studies by his uncle,
> Whom he reports to be a great magician,
> Obscured in the circle of this forest.
> [V.iv.28-34]

He is addressing the banished Duke here, of course, whose laudable skepticism contrasts sharply with Orlando's easy credulity. Apparently the Duke has regarded Orlando's story of a wonder-working magician somewhere in the depths of the forest as a fantastic tale, as indeed it is; but Orlando's belief is nourished by a now fully matured hope which, quite without help from him and without magic of any kind, is about to be fulfilled in another piece of bogus rusticity, the artificiality of which will be underscored by Audrey's bewildered presence at it.

The wedding is properly staged as an impromptu affair, with a courtier dressed in female garb to suggest Hymen. For English audiences (particularly those in Shakespeare's time, when the custom of trothplight still flourished) it proceeds in the context of the same popular but theologically impeccable opinion about marriage that earlier in the play prompted Celia's misgivings about Rosalind's impromptu ceremony: where words are said and vows made, the marriage is valid and binding. To be sure, Jaques had intervened to prevent Audrey's marriage to Touchstone at the hands of the country parson Sir Oliver Martext, sometimes mistakenly charac- terized by critics as a hedge-priest; but the text makes it clear that Jaques' real objections were to Touchstone's dishonorable intentions toward the girl. Moreover, Sir Oliver, however stu- pid he may be, is a genuine priest and voices his indignation that anyone should challenge his credentials: "Ne'er a fan- tastical knave of them all shall flout me out of my calling" (II.iii.106-7). The character Hymen, one should note, takes the validity of the whole proceeding in Act V at face value, recog- nizing the couples one by one and promising a successful marriage to all, including, with a touch of irony, Touchstone and Audrey: "You and you are sure together, / As the winter to foul weather" (V.iv.135-36). Charming as all this is, it has no more necessary relevance to reality than do those eccle- siastical celebrations in the world of town and court where men and women begin their attempts at matrimony with un- qualified vows, in the language of *The Book of Common Prayer* of 1559, "to love and cherish, till death us depart." The masque of Hymen, in short, is simply another manifestation of so- ciety's attempt to symbolize meaningfully something that had long since become frozen into lifeless convention, and it takes its place in the succession of gestures that began with Rosalind's pointless masquerade and Orlando's fumbling dec- oration of the forest with bad poetry. It is at this point that Jaques de Boys breaks in with his reminder of the disaster that might well have occurred if Duke Frederick had carried out his original plan to scour the forest and put his brother to the sword and of the unforeseeable reversal that spared them all that disaster. Suddenly a life that could center on such triv- ialities as courtly wooing and masques of Hymen begins to seem intolerable, and it remains for the genuinely rebellious Jaques to redeem the unions that this masque has presumed to celebrate by relating them to earth and the genuine needs and capabilities of the sexes.

Jaques has not fared well at the hands of scholars and critics. For many he is the epitome of Elizabethan melancholy, for others an inept pessimist, and for still others an inveterate poseur. Obviously, Shakespeare thought it important that someone should sound a series of discordant notes in a play that ostensibly (but not actually) projects a version of Lodge's superficial pastoral scene; and just as obviously he planned his invented character Jaques to perform this function.[13] He prepares us for this aspect of Jaques' role in the first scene of Act II. There the banished Duke begins by delivering a set piece on the glories of the primitive life and then adds, almost as an afterthought, that it is regrettable to have to kill the deer, "the native burghers of this desert city," for food. A pair of unnamed attendant lords observe that Jaques has already moralized extensively on this topic, lamenting particularly over one deer that had been wounded but not killed by the hunter's arrow and declaring that where such as these were concerned the Duke in the forest was an even more heinous usurper than his brother still at court. One modern critic declares this an example of sentimentality,[14] but it is no more sentimental than the Duke's "Sermons in stones, and good in everything" (II.i.17), or Rosalind with her "gallant curtle-axe" and boar spear, or Orlando with his absurd versifying. Jaques is admittedly quick to parody, but the things he parodies are usually patent follies, lies by sanctioned convention, or else practices that only recently have become readily recognizable as reprehensible. So it is with the slaughter of wildlife in the forest, regrettable even when necessary for human survival (more obviously so today perhaps, now that we have well-established slaughter industries to supply our need for protein and our taste for red meat). Jaques makes his appearance in the flesh in Act II, scene v, where we find Amiens diverting the group with another set piece, this time a song, extolling the virtues of life in the wilderness: "Here shall he see / no enemy / But winter and rough weather (II.v.6-8). Jaques importunes him to sing yet another "stanzo" and then turns the delicate but fatuous lyric against the singer with a devastating parody: "If it do come to pass / That any man turn ass," etc.

The most important thing to note about Jaques, however, is that he is appreciably older than the other gentlemen lolling about on the grass, at least old enough to be considered an "old gentleman" by marriage-minded Audrey (V.i.4). He is certainly too old to be a proper foil for Touchstone, as critics would sometimes have him to be; but he is appropriately cast as a counterweight to the conventionally wise Duke, whose readiness to substitute platitude for perceptiveness is conspicuous throughout the play. The Duke is perhaps doing what is expected of a banished duke when he attempts to cheer his fellow exiles by describing their situation in terms reminiscent of a second Eden, but we are perhaps wiser if we listen more closely to Jaques, who not only marks the imminence of death in the Duke's Eden but notes the inevitability of it.

He does this for us in Act II, scene vii, which opens with the Duke's comments on Jaques' habitual contrariness. Suddenly Jaques himself arrives looking uncharacteristically merry. He has just encountered a motley fool in the forest, he says (Touchstone, of course), and apparently Touchstone had responded to his courteous salutation with a standard bit of clownish pessimism:

> . . . he drew a dial from his poke,
> And looking on it, with lack-lustre eye,
> Says very wisely, "It is then a' clock.
> Thus we may see," quoth he, "how the world wags.
> 'Tis but an hour ago since it was nine,
> And after one hour more 'twill be eleven,
> And so from hour to hour, we ripe and ripe,
> And then from hour to hour, we rot and rot,
> And thereby hangs a tale."
>
> [II.vii.20-28]

Touchstone's performance here is not particularly clever, at least as Jaques reports it; but with characteristic hyperbole he says that it set his lungs to crowing and that he laughed for a full hour afterwards. Accurate or not, however, his report should be a tip-off that another courtly party is at large in the forest and, Arden being where it is, that such a party should most likely consist of representatives from Frederick's court; but the Duke does not react to this bit of evidence or, for that matter, to any similar evidence that arises during the five days we are in a position to observe. Thus the appearance of Celia and Rosalind and the news of Frederick's doings brought by Jaques all come as complete surprises to him in the last scene of the play.

Here in this early scene Duke Senior responds only to the witty acrobatics of his melancholy Jaques, who seems to be freshly "full of matter," and tries to cope with the new challenge that he presents (see II.i.67-68), not quite realizing perhaps that what Jaques has given him is a parody of a parody. Some critics have not been fully aware of this either, and one has suggested that Jaques is merely repeating imperceptively Touchstone's parody of his own mode of the melancholic.[15] Jaques knows better, of course, playfully demands the badge of special license that motley can confer, and proposes if granted it to assume motley's therapeutic function in the world. The Duke's response to this is somewhat more serious than the situation requires. "What . . . would I do but good?" Jaques asks, and the Duke replies:

> Most mischievous foul sin, in chiding sin;
> For thou thyself hast been a libertine,
> As sensuous as the brutish sting itself,
> And all th' embossed sores, and headed evils,
> That thou with license of free foot has caught,
> Wouldst thou disgorge into the general world.
> [II.vii.64-69]

We may be grateful that the Duke's remark here recognizes at least obliquely Jaques' advanced years and so prepares the way for the inspired clowning of his set piece on the seven ages of man, with its realistic assessment of the progress of an English bourgeois gentleman from puking infant to dribbling senility, "Sans teeth, sans eyes, sans taste, sans everything" (II.vii.166).[16] Jaques himself is almost ready for the "sixt" age of "lean and slipper'd pantaloon," as his refusal to dance at the end of the play suggests; and his situation thus makes poignant and even a bit frightening the appearance of the now all but speechless Adam, who has told us four scenes earlier:

> At seventeen years many their fortunes seek,
> But at fourscore it is too late a week;
> Yet fortune cannot recompense me better
> Than to die well.

[II.iii.73-76]

"Reminders of mortality flicker everywhere through the language of the play," Anne Barton has written perceptively[17]; and, as she herself implies, a similar observation might be made about all the other comedies, from *The Comedy of Errors* to *The Tempest*. An awareness of mortality, the limitation of human life, is the unarticulated premise of all of Shakespeare's plays, and the epiphany that comes to the alert spectator always includes some degree of that awareness. Here Jaques' function is to articulate for us, if not for his companions in Arden, the invariable condition of the Shakespearean scene; and *As You Like It* is richer for us in proportion as we grasp that part of the significance of his role.

Thus, with awareness of mortality as his premise, Jaques in Acts III and IV directs his corrective wit at the new intruders in Arden before turning back to the good-natured but somewhat fatuous Duke. At best he has only limited success. Orlando, determined to be a courtly lover, resents being told to stop marring the trees with his verses and reacts with a hint of the hostility that has marked his resistance to his older brother (III.ii.253-97); and Rosalind rejects Jaques' implied suggestion that she stop playing games, "be sad and say nothing" (IV.i.8). As we have already noted, he frustrates for the moment Touchstone's attempt to seduce the nut-brown Audrey under a show of marriage: ". . . will you (being a man of your breeding) be married under a bush like a beggar? Get you to church, and have a good priest that can tell you what marriage is. This fellow will but join you together as they join wainscot; then one of you will prove a shrunk panel, and like green timber warp, warp" (III.ii.83-89). Touchstone with his knave's mind reflects that an irregular marriage might suit his purposes better than a proper one, and Audrey comes to think that any

kind of marriage would probably be better than none at all
(V.i.3-4); but they will arrive at Hymen's altar at least fore-
warned, and the consequences, whatever these may be, will be
their own responsibility. No one really listens to Jaques, least
of all the Duke, who goes right on having his men kill the deer.
Jaques' final word on this subject comes in the second scene of
Act IV:

> *Jaq.* Which is he that kill'd the deer?
> *Lord.* Sir, it was I.
> *Jaq.* Let's present him to the Duke like a Roman conqueror, and it
> would do well to set the deer's horns upon his head, for a branch of
> victory.   [IV.ii.1-5]

The song which he commands allows the victor his right to
wear the horns of the slain animal and turns such trophies
predictably into the horns of the cuckold, but apparently no
one takes note of the disrespect. At any rate, Jaques, unlike the
disrespectful Lucio of *Measure for Measure*, is not destined to
live out his days under the Duke's dominion. He has no place in
courtly hierarchies and here as elsewhere dances to his own
tune.

None of this, however, quite prepares us for the stunning
effect of Jaques' entry at the end of the masque, where he
politely usurps the Duke's prerogative and pronounces an honest satirist's benediction on all concerned. Here one is hard put
to understand the charges of cynicism so frequently leveled at
this character.[18] We note that in the end he allows the Duke his
due: "You to your former honor I bequeath, / Your patience and
your virtue well deserves it" (V.iv.186-87). He also clarifies two
matters that Hymen and the Duke with undiscriminating benevolence have left ambiguous. Oliver, in a moment of romantic enthusiasm and still thinking Celia a simple girl of the
forest, has bestowed his entire estate upon Orlando and vowed
to live and die a shepherd (V.ii.11-12). Jaques sensibly recognizes that this will never do and assigns the young man as
follows: "You to your land and love, and great allies" (V.iv.189).
He also recognizes that Touchstone and Audrey have made no
marriage for all their vows. These he commits "to wrangling,
for thy loving voyage / Is but for two months victuall'd." With-

out reservation he allows Orlando "a love that [his] true faith doth merit" and Silvius, who has never wavered in his wholehearted pursuit of the disdainful Phebe, "a long and well-deserved bed." Truth thus has his moment in spite of Hymen and in spite of the Duke, who goes on to promise everybody "true delights," in the best fairy-tale fashion.

As You Like It is not a fairy tale. That much at least is made clear throughout the play, where the unrealities that abound are all of them inventions with which we or our forebears have from time to time surcharged nature. The scaffolding of Lodge's romantic narrative is improbable but not absolutely incompatible with reality, and occasionally it groans under the weight that Shakespeare and his actor-characters, by the simple device of taking it seriously and demanding that we do also, have given it. Among these characters the one with the most insistent voice is, as we have seen, Jaques, who repeatedly debunks received conventions and ultimately insists on the validity of those actions that coalesce to ensure the satisfaction of society's impulse to renewal. It is Jaques, in short, who directs us to see the potential for true comedy in Lodge's *Rosalynde*, and without him the play would be as dated as its source. That the impulse to renewal may actually destroy comedy as well as fulfill it, however, is suggested in the concluding moments when the actor playing Rosalind, now at last legitimately wearing the male clothing of a forest youth, comes forward, as a male, to pronounce the epilogue. "If I were a woman," he says, "I would kiss as many of you as had beards that pleas'd me, complexions that lik'd me, and breaths that I defied not." This expresses truth, too; but it is a truth that is inimical to society as we know it and to the comedy that celebrates it. Perhaps a sober awareness of this particular truth, about the incorrigible animal proclivities of human males and females, was the consideration that prompted Jaques to forgo dancing measures and retire to a hermit's cave.

11

Twelfth Night

Ever since the time of the Romantics, high praise for *Twelfth Night* has been one of the commonplaces of Shakespeare criticism. In our own time Leo Salingar has called it the "crowning achievement in one branch of his art";[1] and J. Dover Wilson, implicitly replying to Samuel Johnson, who complained that the latter half of the play "exhibits no just picture of life,"[2] has gone even farther: "That gem of his comic art, that condensation of life and (for those who know how to taste it rightly) elixir of life," were Wilson's superlatives; then he added, "He could never better this—and he never attempted to. He broke the mold—and passed on."[3] Other commentators have been more specific. Kenneth Muir, by way of introducing his comments on *Twelfth Night*, cites Barrett Wendell's characterization of the play as a masterpiece of recapitulation and goes on to note that it combines, among other things, the device of mistaken identity that has proved so successful in *The Comedy of Errors* (making the look-alike pair brother and sister, however, as in numerous Italian comedies); the use of the disguised heroine as emissary, "from the man she loves to the woman he loves," from *The Two Gentlemen of Verona*; the theme of friendship from *The Merchant of Venice*; the singing fool (a combination of Amiens and Touchstone); a Falstaffian character in Sir Toby; and a half-witted suitor from *The Merry Wives of Windsor*.[4] T.W. Baldwin has demonstrated that all this variety fits harmoniously into a frame that may well have been derived from Terence's *Andria*;[5] and both Salingar and C.L.

Barber have attributed at least part of its unity of tone to a pervasive spirit of saturnalia, Barber adding that the play goes well beyond this in its "exhibition of the use and abuse of social liberty."[6] More recently Carolyn G. Heilbrun has touched briefly but persuasively upon the play as a celebration of androgyny;[7] and Walter N. King, in his introduction to a collection of essays on the play, has provided an able discussion of the subtly changing perspectives that threaten to bring most of its characters to complete bewilderment and frustration but, in the manner of similar perspectives in a metaphysical poem, ultimately find resolution.[8]

What many of these critics have been praising in *Twelfth Night* is the convention of romantic comedy—or rather the romantic version of Italianate comedy—which for Shakespeare's generation served, as it has for most generations since, to reassure audiences about civilized society's ability to renew itself. Joseph Summers, himself an admirer of *Twelfth Night*, finds the resolution of the play and hence its presumably implicit reassurances less than convincing. *Twelfth Night* is the climax of Shakespeare's early achievement, he writes, but at the same time it comes close to proclaiming the limitations of that achievement: "More obvious miracles are needed," he concludes, "for comedy to exist in a world in which evil also exists, not merely incipiently but with power."[9] Summers's reservation here also has to do with the convention of romantic comedy, which he understandably considers inadequate to represent real life. The details of his diagnosis are questionable, but not the insight that has prompted it: in Shakespearean comedy neither the dramatic convention nor the plot—nor even the special occasion if there is one—is ever more than incidentally determinative. Such things point not to the play but to the expectations that we in our habitual inattention to the complex way in which the world really works bring to the play and to other fictions, and in many cases to life itself.

The patterns of comedy that Shakespeare inherited, like patterns in other traditional forms of art, symbolized communal responses that his world still considered natural and valid—in particular, those responses involving the preservation of stability and order in a society which like its constituents was necessarily forever perishing. For the most part, we today are comfortable with those same responses and expect comic art to confirm their adequacy; thus Shakespeare's comedies still give most of us at least part of what we have always expected from comedy generally. Art, however, is not always the complaisant handmaiden of society. It is her nature, especially when endowed with the vitality of someone like Shakespeare, to deny as well as to confirm, to generate new responses to perennially recurring situations, and sometimes in the process to break as many icons as it preserves. As we have seen, even in such early and relatively conventional plays as *The Comedy of Errors* and *The Two Gentlemen of Verona* Shakespeare gave indications of the iconoclastic character that comic dramatic art was to assume under his hand. In *Love's Labor's Lost* and *The Merchant of Venice* he raised questions about human suffering, cruelty, and mortality that writers in fulfilling comedy's responsibility to entertain had traditionally elected to ignore. In *Much Ado about Nothing*, he challenged the propriety of comedy's traditional ending. In *As You Like It* he dared to suggest that the mold itself of comedy might ultimately be irrelevant. In short, hints about the limitations of conventional comedy had been lurking at the fringes of Shakespeare's vision all along, and the situation in *Twelfth Night* was calculated to make audiences uneasy almost from the outset.

To begin with, as Summers notes, there are no parents or their equivalent in *Twelfth Night*, and the young people are therefore free to make their own way. "According to the strictly romantic formula," Summers writes, "the happy ending should be already achieved at the beginning of the play."[10] Just the reverse is true, of course; and the reasons for that, though conspicuous, have apparently not been obvious to the play's admirers. First, Shakespeare at the beginning has provided no visible means of balancing the equation of lover and beloved that he has set before us. Olivia occupies the role of marriageable female in *Twelfth Night*, but she has no suitor that is both acceptable and available to her—no Fenton, no Orlando, no Ferdinand—until the beginning of Act IV, when Sebastian, who she thinks is the Cesario she knows, glides ready and able into her view. She could have Duke Orsino, but she will not. She would have Viola-Cesario, but cannot—for reasons that Viola, Antonio the sea captain, and we alone know. Thus for three acts the Duke pursues Olivia, Olivia pursues Viola, and Viola yearns for the Duke—a merry-go-round chase, a three-way stalemate, that has no prospect of resolution in matches until a fourth person arrives to turn Olivia out of the circle and make it possible for the other two to confront one another as pursuer and pursued.

Second, the absence of parents is not an unmixed blessing for any of the lovers in *Twelfth Night,* but it is an especially unfortunate circumstance for Olivia. In the normal course of a comic action, those filling the role of *senex* have subtle positive functions to perform as well as the more spectacular negative ones; and Olivia's parents and elder brother, all dead as the play begins, would have been expected at least to foster the idea of a good marriage for the girl and more than likely in the end to have come round to her way of thinking about an appropriate candidate. By convention they would have been faulty in their initial judgments about her best interests, but as sponsors distinguished by good will and protective instincts they would have been entitled to seats of honor at the prenuptial feast. As it is, Shakespeare's Olivia stands defenseless in a world that with the death of her brother has suddenly turned threatening. Orsino, whom she does not and apparently cannot love, relentlessly presses his suit, undoubtedly in part because he finds the love-game amusing but also in part because by marriage he would annex Olivia's estate. He has rivals in the latter objective. Commoner Malvolio, taking advantage of a social revolution that has recently made it possible for "the Lady of the Strachy" to marry her yeoman of the wardrobe (II.v.39-40), seeks to rise in the world from steward's quarters to his lady's chamber; and Sir Toby Belch, Olivia's sottish uncle and her next of kin, has presumed to stand *in loco parentis* and promote a suitor of his own.[11] We see no other suitors, but these are quite enough to show the dangerous situation of a landed and wealthy young female in Shakespeare's world, where authority over land and wealth was expected to be vested ultimately in a suitable male. Hence Olivia assumes a mask of grief, not necessarily out of self-love or whimsy (as has been commonly assumed by critics and producers of the play) and perhaps not even out of genuine grief, but out of an urgent need to protect her own interests. Despite her declared intention to mourn for an improbable seven years, the convention of mourning can serve at best as a temporary stay; but that convention is the only protection she has. Into this strained situation Viola enters to become unwittingly a fourth suitor for Olivia's hand—in Olivia's eyes the only suitor, and in the eyes of others, including eventually even Orsino, an impudent interloper to be dealt with contemptuously and with appropriate violence.

One might argue, especially in this last quarter of the twentieth century, that Olivia's need to be rescued by a strong male is to her discredit—that her position is only as parlous as she herself chooses to let it be. So it is; and so can it be considered in the world that Shakespeare creates in his plays, for repeatedly these invite approval for the threatened female who seizes the male role in a male-dominated society and triumphs over the disadvantages that society has imposed on her own sex. The fact remains, however, that Shakespeare lived in and depicted a society in which the woman who does not escape by extraordinary means must settle for being either an ornament or a slave. Moreover, even those who resort to extraordinary means may escape only temporarily—witness Julia, Portia, and Rosalind, all of whom presumably put off their masculine garments and return to live ever after in the subservient role that society has assigned to them. Angry Kate's ironic note, for all we know, was not detected until fairly recently. And Beatrice's concluding remark to Benedick is as follows: "I would not deny you, but by this good day, I yield upon great persuasion, and partly to save your life, for I was told you were in a consumption" (V.iv.94-97). To this, editors since the eighteenth century would have us believe, Benedick replies with a mouth-stopping kiss.[12] Shakespeare, however, apparently gave the quieting to an embarrassed Leonato, who told his irreverent niece, "Peace, I will stop your mouth," and perhaps applied a gesture of a different sort.

In Illyria, consensus about the natural dependency of women seems to be fairly solid. Malvolio is convinced that his mistress is secretly yearning for an appropriate man to take charge, and so when Maria applies the bait to his vanity, he is apt to believe he is that very man. Duke Orsino, denied admittance by the conventions of mourning, continues to make advances through his messengers and tells the last of these, Viola disguised as Cesario, that the problem with Olivia is her woman's inability to comprehend the depth and seriousness of the passion that men may feel:

> Alas, their love [i.e., women's] may be called appetite,
> No motion of the liver, but the palate,
> That suffer surfeit, cloyment, and revolt,
> But mine is all as hungry as the sea,
> And can digest as much. Make no compare
> Between that love a woman can bear me
> And that I owe Olivia.
>
> [II.iv.97-103]

Even Sir Andrew Aguecheek assumes that Olivia is ready for appropriate male advances and recoils in something between indignation and disgust when he spies her making what he believes to be overtures to the Duke's messenger: "No, faith, I'll not stay a jot longer. . . . Marry, I saw your niece do more favors to the Count's servingman than ever she bestow'd upon me. I saw't i' th' orchard" (III.ii.1-7). Sir Toby moves quickly to disabuse him, but Toby is clearly of like mind about women. He resents Olivia's declared state of mourning as a feminine frivolity that interferes with his more serious plans. "What a plague means my niece to take the death of her brother thus?" he fumes to Maria (I.iii.1-2); and in the exchange that follows he details Sir Andrew's qualifications as a lover and thereby further reveals his obtuseness where Olivia's predilections are concerned. Fortunately for her, Sir Toby's implementation of his plans is as inefficient as his judgments about women are erroneous. The proposed duel between Sir Andrew and Cesario backfires upon the head, literally, of its perpetrator, though one should recognize here that but for the lucky presence of Sebastian on the scene to take the challenge intended for Cesario, that duel and the action of the play might have ended quite differently. Unseen by all these watchful males, however, is a clever Olivia driven to extraordinary means of her own, who will abandon proprieties and confound definitions by pursuing forthrightly and then marrying on the spot a young man of no station whatever.

In more ways than one Viola is a counterpart to Olivia. She too is parentless; she has also lost a brother, or thinks she has; and she has put on a pretense for essentially the same reason as Olivia—to protect herself against such predators as may be at large in the presumably civilized world of Illyria. The device Viola has chosen, however, has placed her in an awkward situation. No sooner has she put on male attire and enlisted in the Duke's service than she falls in love with her master, who requires her to advance his cause with a lady manifestly amenable to being woed by someone—though not by the Duke, either directly or indirectly.

This improbable situation is the source for several aspects of the play that have charmed modern audiences—most of these being touches of pathos rather than of comedy. Viola's best speeches are cases in point. For example, she tells Olivia at their first meeting that if she were Duke Orsino she would

> Make me a willow cabin at your gate,
> And call upon my soul within the house;
> Write loyal cantons of contemned love,
> And sing them loud even in the dead of night;
> Hallow your name to the reverberate hills,
> And make the babbling gossip of the air
> Cry out "Olivia!"
>
> [I.v.268-74]

Her language here speaks of a more intense experience than brief infatuation would warrant. Some critics have postulated a justification for it in Marsilian-Platonist terms,[13] but one is probably nearer the spirit of the play to see it as something quaintly amusing, the mysterious attraction of a scarcely grown moth for an unresponsive star. Nevertheless, Viola's argument here has the power of a nascent but very real love for the Duke; and the same bittersweet passion of young love informs the account she gives to him of the depth of women's affection as demonstrated by the unspoken adoration of her "father's daughter":

> . . . she never told her love
> But let concealment like a worm in th' bud
> Feed on her damask cheek; she pin'd in thought,
> And with a green and yellow melancholy
> She sate like Patience on a monument,
> Smiling at grief.
>
> [II.iv.110-15]

Because she is apt to feel such stirrings as no longer trouble the Duke, which indeed the Duke for all his declarations about masculine love can no longer even recall, Viola moves in company with Euphrasia-Bellario of Beaumont and Fletcher's *Philaster* (1608-10), the determined Helena of *All's Well That Ends Well*, and the Imogen of *Cymbeline*. Like these, Viola is genuinely and, to speak literally, hopelessly in love; but the special irony of the situation that develops in Act I is that Olivia is no less genuinely in love and in her misapplied affection exhibits to Viola precisely the kind of intense feeling that Viola chides her for not rendering to the Duke.

If we were not dealing with characters whom Shakespeare has endowed with flesh and blood, we might say that Viola is the love-in-idleness in this second play that Shakespeare wrote about "midsummer madness" (III.iv.56). Before her coming, there was no genuine love in Illyria. Her arrival there set all in motion, activating Olivia's suitors to an intensity that had previously seemed unwarranted and, more important, pushing the hitherto diffident Olivia out from behind her façade of grief to discover possibilities in the world that she had not dreamed of. Her newly found love, though it has some of the aspects of the ultimately divine fixation that Marsilio Ficino, Castiglione, and countless sonneteers have written about, is no more Neoplatonic than Viola's equally sudden love for the

Duke. One might better say that the love manifested by these two women has an agapeic quality in that it prompts one of them, denied of her station and even of her sex, to offer services and devotion to a duke who barely notices her as anything more than a servant, and prompts the other, a lady of acknowledged station, to spurn suitors at all appropriate levels—duke, knight, and competent steward—to throw herself shamelessly upon a page boy.

Where Olivia is concerned, however, it is important to note that Shakespeare in presenting her initial awakening to the universal call of the flesh depicts it as an unconscious appreciation of that androgynous ideal which is normally conceived in youth and subsequently suppressed in adulthood, here beautifully portrayed by Viola as woman-man and reinforced subliminally for the Elizabethan audience by the boy-actors who were portraying both female characters on the stage. Regardless of how one tries to explain this love, there is much in it that remains inexplicable; and Shakespeare's portrayal continues to succeed with readers and audiences undoubtedly in part because most people subconsciously want something like it to be true and are delighted when Shakespeare's art can bring their wishes to a semblance of reality. Unfortunately, our latter-day conventions, translated into expectations, encourage us to discredit the genuine and innocent warmth present here and in similar situations in other Shakespearean plays and thus prevent our acknowledgment of emotional tremors which even now we hasten to dismiss as inchoate feelings, childish preludes to adult emotions that are presumably more stable and lasting, and in any case more respectable.

Nevertheless, regardless of how seriously one takes the suggestions of agapeic or androgynous attachments in *Twelfth Night*, one should never lose sight of the heterosexual grounding that is essential to the comic resolution achieved in the play. All the lovers here ultimately demand for satisfaction the physical possession of a member of the opposite sex. Olivia could not have been happy with Viola indefinitely, for all the beauty of Viola's face and form; and Orsino, attuned to practical considerations, finds it possible to disregard Viola's charms until he recognizes that they are as feminine in fact as they appear to be. Moreover, sexual attraction is all that really matters. Rank apparently has nothing to do with love and loving in *Twelfth Night*. In spite of the outrage Toby expresses at the thought of a steward's aspiring to take the hand of his niece, he does not hesitate to marry Maria, Olivia's diminutive gentlewoman ("the youngest wren of nine"), whom he mockingly dubs Penthesilea and repeatedly calls "wench." Olivia herself has no compunction about marrying someone she takes to be a serving-man; and even after the unveiling in Act V neither she nor the Duke gains any substantial knowledge about the pedigree of the twins they are linking permanently to their fortunes. One looks in vain here for some hint of what is clearly set forth in Barnaby Riche's *Apolonius and Silla*: that the two were actually children of another illustrious duke, Pontus of Cyprus, and worthy to mate with nobility anywhere.[15] In short, practical and even spiritual motives for love ultimately give way in Shakespeare's *Twelfth Night* to elemental sex, and thus the ancient order of society as understood by commentators—political, ecclesiastical, and otherwise—painfully maintained over the centuries and presumably divinely ordained, is here challenged by the basic animal impulses that are the reason, often unacknowledged, why society is essentially not an institution at all but a process.

This reduction of comedy in *Twelfth Night* to the ground of its being intensifies an ironic dimension in the gulling of Malvolio that is often overlooked in modern readings and productions, which persist in ignoring the complex effects of the play. To begin with, Malvolio is not a mere appendage to the plot; nor is he the insensitive killjoy and social climber that Sir Toby sees or the "time pleaser" Maria would have him be. As one critic has observed, Malvolio's part is structurally at the center of the plot and his gulling is symbolic of the challenge to order that persists throughout the play.[15] There is truth in both observations. The setting of Shakespeare's comedies, regardless of designation, is invariably English; and as Shakespeare and his contemporaries knew, the ranks of the English gentry included more than a few families that had achieved their status relatively recently. Lady Olivia's all but defunct family has the marks of being one of these; at the very least, Sir Toby, the one surviving elder member of the family, still has the class-consciousness of the newly arrived and the tavern manners of a serving-man. Malvolio, by contrast, has the marks of a belated aspirant, quite as class-conscious as Toby but awkwardly so, and as zealously committed as any newly arrived neophyte to the preservation of order, precedence, and propriety. Charles Lamb's view of him is not currently popular, but it is closer to the truth and infinitely preferable to the farcical Malvolio that simpers and prances on some stages. Consider this passage from Lamb's essay:

His quality is at the best unlovely, but neither buffoon nor contemptible. His bearing is lofty, a little above his station, but probably not much above his deserts. . . . We must not confound him with the eternal old, low steward of comedy. He is master of the household to a great Princess, a dignity probably conferred upon him for other respects than age or length of service. . . . His rebuke to the knight, and his sottish revelers, is sensible and spirited; and when we take into consideration the unprotected condition of his mistress, and the strict regard with which her state of real or dissembled mourning would draw the eyes of the world upon her house affairs, Malvolio might feel the honor of the family in some sort in his keeping; as it appears not that Olivia had any more brothers, or kinsmen, to look to it—for Sir Toby had dropped all such nice respects at the buttery hatch.[16]

This is a Malvolio who makes the tactical error of forthrightly confronting one who is technically his superior for indulging in a form of gaiety that has in it no real love of life (Maria calls it "caterwauling") and certainly no consideration for others, and thus finds himself both rebuked by that superior and caught in a mill devised by a fellow servant (again Maria) who also aspires to a higher station no less than he, though with far less warrant. Malvolio is right to regard all of his tormentors with contempt. Maria's ingenuity probably makes her the best of the lot. Sir Toby is a bore as well as a boor. Fabian is an insensitive serving-man, whom Malvolio has properly rebuked for staging a bear-baiting on the estate (II.v.7-11), Feste is at best (except for the actual gulling scene) a second-rate clown, and Sir Andrew is a fool. Fabian observes at the end that their mischief has been such as "may rather pluck on laughter than revenge, / If that the injuries be justly weigh'd / That have on both sides pass'd"; but Fabian the bear-baiter is hardly one to give a reliable opinion. Malvolio may be deficient in humor, and he is certainly naive; but he has injured no one, and he has every cause to be angry. Moreover, the gulling that destroys him destroys the last conscious defender of the graceful world to which he would aspire.

Mark Van Doren, who also considered Malvolio central to *Twelfth Night*, concluded his essay on the play with the following sentence: "The drama is between his [Malvolio's] mind and the music of old manners."[17] This is true, but perhaps not quite in the way Van Doren intended. For Van Doren the important thing about the play was its courtly decor, lyrics that could be set to appealing music, carefree roistering belowstairs, expressions of romantic love followed by appropriate matings. Considered solely in the light of these things, *Twelfth Night* appears to be a triumph of sophistication and wit and a reaffirmation of the values of conventional Italianate comedy. Actually it is nothing of the sort.

As has already been noted, *Twelfth Night* presents a world in which the opportunity for undertaking a comic action and pursuing it to the conventional conclusion has collapsed. Control of the social unit that occupies the center of our attention, Lady Olivia's estate, has passed for the moment to that lady's keeping; and because she is young, female, and unprotected, the wolves are circling. Wit characteristic of the old order is still present: for all her pretense of grief, Olivia has a large measure of it, and Viola brings in still more; but in the empty corridors where these two meet, its sparkle has more poignancy than brilliance. Music is still present, at least on the periphery of the main action, but music in *Twelfth Night* no longer symbolizes the harmony and order that comedy would achieve or restore. Of the two memorable lyrics in the play, the one that celebrates young love in its immediacy, "O mistress mine," is caterwauled by the aging Sir Toby and company. The other is a lament for a dead love that cannot be revived: "Come away, come away, Death." A number of older critics—F.G. Fleay, Richmond Noble, and J. Dover Wilson—suggested that this sophisticated piece of melancholy replaced the "old and antique song" that the text calls for (II.iv.3) when Robert Armin, a clown with a trained voice, performed the singing function originally intended for a singing boy who would play the part of Viola posing as a eunuch (I.ii.62). S.L. Bethell, after summarizing the whole argument, pointed out sensibly that it is sufficient the song be "romantically suggestive of antiquity," as indeed it is.[18] Orsino in asking for the song notes that it differs sharply from the "light airs and recollected terms / Of these brisk and giddy-paced times" (II.iv.5-6) and thus makes the point of the play: that the old times are beyond recall; the old order is dead. He speaks with more truth than he knows or would like to believe. No amount of music can bring back the world in which courtship of the kind he would pursue can exist. Maria knows this. Olivia shows by her actions that she knows it too. Viola, but for her infatuation with Orsino and her loyalty to him, would know it sooner than she does. Malvolio, who has been outside the magic circle all his life, does not know it and thus is apt to be tricked by a spurious invitation to join in the (to him) unfamiliar dance. Still inexperienced in spite of his years, he has no way of recognizing that the show of courtly manners he is urged to assume can only be an inadvertent parody and a reaffirmation of his incompetence to participate in a game that people are no longer playing. His incorrigible loneliness is merely accentuated by the folly that a heartless anarchy has thrust upon him.

A production of *Twelfth Night* at Stratford-upon-Avon some years ago solved the problem of Malvolio by playing him for laughs and reducing him to little more than a stick figure with the diminished humanity of a Keystone Cop from the early cinema. The gulling thus became a harmless trick perpetrated on one who had neither dignity nor the capacity to feel. What was left in that production, however, was hardly the graceful apotheosis of Italianate comedy for which Shakespeare "broke the mold—and passed on." Even Shakespeare's language, which was largely uncut, was insufficient to prevent the general charges by London critics of prosiness and farce; the balance had been disrupted, and the illusion dispelled. The glitter was tinsel.[19] One production, of course, proves nothing about a Shakespeare play; but *Twelfth Night* may best be regarded as an elaborate *trompe l'oeil*. Superficially it resembles Italianate comedy, but actually it is the apotheosis of a development that Shakespeare had been anticipating ever since he portrayed the French ladies at the court of Navarre. It is already a part of the era in which a Helena and a Mariana would resort to bed tricks to snare reluctant males, an Imogen put off her sex to go after a husband who had rejected her, a Hermione retire for sixteen years, freeze a kingdom, and take her man at the end by a trick, and an innocent and uninstructed Miranda out-woo and out-argue a prince who most likely would have preferred a casual seduction. Dr. Johnson was understandably disturbed by the ending of *Twelfth Night*, but he was wrong to say that it exhibits no just picture of life. Like most of his contemporaries, he was guided by expectations that are essentially inapplicable to this play except by way of ironic contrast. For him it exhibited no picture of life that he could comfortably accept, but one suspects he saw well enough what was there.

12

Troilus and Cressida

Some years ago R.A. Foakes wrote, "There are almost as many opinions about the nature of Shakespeare's *Troilus and Cressida* as there are critics; and each critic can fortify his argument by referring to the inability of the play's first editors to see eye to eye about it."[1] The printers of the quarto (1609) had referred to it in their epistle to the reader as "passing full of the palm comical," yet the editors of the Folio placed it among the tragedies and called it, as had the quarto, a "History." This smacks of indifference more than bewilderment. The play clearly lacks the focus of what we normally think of as a tragedy, though the Folio designation has had serious advocates among modern scholars.[2] A better case can be made for calling the play satire, especially if by the term one means a serious criticism of life.[3] Nevertheless, *Troilus and Cressida* displays and puts emphasis on a fair amount of the stuff that Elizabethans expected to find in a comedy, most modern categorizers have let it pass as a comedy, and that term will serve as well as any so long as we avoid trying to make an issue of it. Whatever the category, the play stands at a crucial juncture in the development of Shakespeare's treatment of the comic theme.

It might be more accurate to say that the play stands at a crucial juncture in the development of Shakespeare's exploration of the world from a comic perspective, because themes and subject matter are at best glasses through which we expect to see—and if the comedy is successful, presumably do see—

the grounds for our own reassurances and continuing peace of mind. Shalkespeare's comedies up to this point have all assumed *a priori* the presence of such grounds; regardless of the troubling ambiguities that we encounter along the way in these earlier plays, we are never allowed for long to doubt that the values of love and honor are ultimately verifiable and that we may reasonably expect to find them in the patterned actions of custom, notably courtship and the exchanges of friendship. Some readers might make an exception for *Love's Labor's Lost,* but we should keep in mind that the male characters in that play have committed themselves to specious patterns, and even to those only superficially, so that in the course of things real life properly finds these gentlemen wanting. The ladies in *Love's Labor's Lost* are not deceived, and through them we see that the values we want to believe in are everpresent and can be found by the simple in heart and the sincere. In almost every play considered thus far there is some guidepost to denote the existence of a cosmic order that justifies our quests and our hopes, and in most there is also the formal pattern of comedy to raise and ultimately satisfy our expectations. In *Troilus and Cressida* however, such markers are missing. It is as if Shakespeare had suddenly plunged us into the real world and challenged us to find for ourselves the verification of those consoling fictions of our childhood. The comforters have disappeared, and the spirit of satire—though not merely what usually passes for satire—has taken their place.

To be sure, the play contains an abundance of conventional satire—barbed criticism of manners and mores, specific personages, and perhaps rival theaters—but its critical knife probes for more basic things than these and touches some of the fundamental assumptions of Elizabethan life. Consider, for example, Ulysses' famous speech on degree, often cited as the best statement of the principle of order in which people of that time believed and by which they justified their most cherished institutions of governance, secular as well as ecclesiastical:

> The heavens themselves, the planets, and this centre
> Observe degree, priority, and place,

Insisture, course, proportion, season, form,
Office, and custom, in all line of order;
And therefore is the glorious planet Sol
In noble eminence enthron'd and spher'd
Amidst the other; whose med'cinable eye
Corrects the ill aspects of planets evil,
And posts, like the commandment of a king,
Sans check, to good and bad.

[I.iii.85-94]

Ulysses is offering here an explanation of the Greeks' failure to conquer Troy; and Nestor, who is supposed to represent official Greek wisdom in such matters, gives approval even before Ulysses gets to the point of his argument. Agamemnon predictably follows suit, although only minutes before he had enjoyed Nestor's equally firm approval of his own very different explanation. It soon develops, however, that Ulysses is not arguing from conviction. His objective has never been to repair a damaged order in the Greek chain of command but simply to return the power of Achilles and his Myrmidons to the Greek effort, and he proceeds to reveal that he would achieve that end by appealing to Achilles' pride, the very quality that presumably has made the defected hero violate the principle of degree in the first place. A bit later in the play, Hector, in trying to persuade the Trojans to put an end to the conflict by surrendering Helen, appeals to the same principle of order:

Nature craves
All dues be rend'red to their owners: now,
What debt in all humanity
Than wife is to the husband?

. . . .

If Helen then be wife to Sparta's king,
As it is known she is, these moral laws
Of nature and of nations speak aloud
To have her back return'd. Thus to persist
In doing wrong extenuates not wrong,
But makes it much more heavy.

[II.ii.173-88]

Unlike Ulysses, Hector here obviously means what he says. In his view, women are lower in Nature's scale than men, and wives by natural law belong to their husbands; thus he is for giving Helen back forthwith. Hector recognizes, however, that he can never persuade his brothers to pay the price of submitting to order (or, perhaps one should say, of acting to bring that order into being):

> Hector's opinion
> Is this in way of truth; yet ne'ertheless,
> My spritely brethren, I propend to you
> In resolution to keep Helen still,
> For 'tis a cause that hath no mean dependence
> Upon our joint and several dignities.
>
> [II.ii.188-93]

Thus he defers to their limitations and lets the law of the jungle prevail.

Ironically, Shakespeare's Achilles, longer than anyone else in the play, holds fast to the illusion that a principle of order exists. Homer had explained Achilles' absence from the fighting by citing Agamemnon's peremptory seizure of his paramour Chryseis. Shakespeare could easily have used this detail from Chapman's translation of the *Iliad*, but instead he elected to take another, reported in both John Lydgate's *Troy-Book* and William Caxton's *Recuyell of the Historyes of Troye:* that Achilles, *after* killing Hector, fell in love with Polyexna, Hector's sister, and promised thereafter to stay out of the fighting. In both Lydgate and Caxton, Achilles' return is the occasion for his killing of Trolius; Shakespeare made it the occasion for his killing of Hector. In the play, therefore, Achilles—for all the arrogance imputed to him by Ulysses (I.iii.142-84)—abstains from fighting for one reason only:

> My sweet Patroclus, I am thwarted quite
> From my great purpose in to-morrow's battle.
> Here is a letter from Queen Hecuba,
> A token from her daughter, my fair love,
> Both taxing me and gaging me to keep
> An oath that I have sworn. I will not break it.
> Fall Greeks, fall fame, honor or go or stay.

My major vow lies here, this I'll obey.

[V.i.37-44]

Keeping an oath, even temporarily, implies a respect for the order by which the oath is sworn; and Ulysses, who swears by nothing, tries to break his friend's resolve, first by staging an elaborate snub and then by pressing upon him the argument that all the world is fickle where values (again a concomitant of order) are concerned:

> . . . beauty, wit,
> High birth, vigor of bone, desert in service,
> Love, friendship, charity, are subjects all
> To envious and calumniating Time.
> One touch of nature makes the whole world kin,
> That all with one consent praise new-born gawds,
> Though they are made and moulded of things past,
> And [give] to dust, that is a little gilt,
> More laud than gilt o'erdusted.
>
> [III.iii.171-79]

When that effort fails, Ulysses taunts Achilles with his presumably foolish constancy:

> And all the Greekish girls shall tripping sing
> "Great Hector's sister did Achilles win,
> But our great Ajax bravely beat down him."
> Farewell, my lord; I as your lover speak:
> The fool slides o'er the ice that you should break.
>
> [III.iii.211-15]

Achilles is deeply disturbed, and after extended verbal exchanges with his friend Patroclus and with Thersites he leaves to make preparations for entertaining the visiting Hector in his tent. As he turns to go, we hear him murmur, almost to himself, "My mind is troubled, like a fountain stirr'd; / And I myself see not the bottom of it" (III.iii.308-9).

The decay of order which provides the context for *Troilus and Cressida* has a demoralizing effect on Greeks and Trojans alike. This becomes increasingly evident as cherished institutions on both sides begin to sicken and crumble. Even courtesy and honor falter, though publicly both sides continue to honor truces, more or less, and to negotiate exchanges. When in the next act (IV.v) the noble Hector does in fact stand before him, Achilles, realizing that honoring a private obligation has caused him to let his reputation be "gored," comes close to capitulating to the growing chaos within him. He manages to preserve something resembling composure until Patroclus is slain; then he lets the storm of anger overwhelm him. Similarly, in Act V the young Troilus, though standing in the presence of the same Hector, allows chagrin and anger (in his case, the result of disillusionment with love) to wipe away his façade of *gentilesse*. It happens that Andromache and Cassandra, apprehensive because of their premonitions, have been doing their best to persuade Hector not to fight on this day and have even sent for King Priam to help them; but their persuading comes to nothing when Troilus, eager for fight, enters in full armor and Hector takes the occasion to turn aside their soliciting to do some persuading of his own:

> No, faith, young Troilus, doff thy harness, youth,
> I am to-day i' th' vein of chivalry.
> Let grow thy sinews till their knots be strong,
> And tempt not yet the brushes of the war.
> Unarm thee, go, and doubt thou not, brave boy,
> I'll stand to-day for thee and me and Troy.
>
> [V.iii.31-36]

But Troilus turns on his brother with a sarcasm that might be counted arrogance in any other set of circumstances. The exchange continues:

> *Tro.* Brother, you have a vice of mercy in you,
> Which better fits a lion than a man.
> *Hect.* What vice is that? Good Troilus, chide me for it.
> *Tro.* When many times the captive Grecian falls,
> Even in the fan and wind of your fair sword,
> You bid them rise and live.
> *Hect.* O, 'tis fair play.
> *Tro.* Fool's play, by heaven, Hector.
> *Hect.* How now? how now?
> *Tro.* For th' love of all the gods,
> Let's leave the hermit pity with our mother,
> And when we have our armors buckled on,

The venom'd vengeance ride upon our swords,
Spur them to ruthful work, rein them from ruth
   Hect. Fie, savage, fie!
   Tro.   Hector, then 'tis wars.

                                [V.iii.31-49]

"That's the way with wars" is the gist of what Troilus says here, and he is right. The disregard of fair play in warfare will shortly result in the death of Hector and all the hope of Troy—and, in his last instant of consciousness, Hector's own all-but-faded hope of chivalry in a world that he has almost come to see as meaningless.

This, of course, is no way to end a comedy, which must celebrate the orderly continuity of things and do so with at least a show of joy; and the only reason we can even halfway expect this play to be a comedy is that Shakespeare has given the action of the young lovers prominence in it and, in temporary disregard of the known end of that action, has treated it in such a way as to invite us to expect a comic resolution. Thus our foreknowledge of what that ending must be provides an ironic ground for the courtship that Shakespeare sets before us and further adds to the impression of satire that the play has conveyed to many readers and viewers. We recall that in two previous plays Shakespeare had alluded to the Cressida that his audience knew best, one that was at first a clever whore and afterward a beggar and a leper—Robert Henryson's version of the character rather than Chaucer's.[4] Here Shakespeare presents a Cressida that is distinctively his own, one graced with charm and a sincerity that too often has been overlooked. The irony of Cressida's situation is one of the genuinely moving things in this anomalous play, and it stands clear (or should do so) in the trothplight scene, where it merges with other ironies both within the play and without—and some of these reach out to involve us all. There at the climax of the play young Troilus proclaims his eternal loyalty with an extravagance matched only by that of an even younger Romeo:

> True swains in love shall in the world to come
> Approve their truth by Troilus. When their rhymes,
> Full of protest, of oath and big compare,

> Wants similes, truth tir'd with iteration,
> As true as steel, as plantage to the moon,
> As sun to day, as turtle to her mate,
> As iron to adamant, as earth to th' centre,
> [Yet] after all comprisons of truth
> (As truth's authentic author to be cited)
> "As true as Troilus" shall crown up the verse,
> And sanctify the numbers.
>
> [III.ii.173-83]

Cressida responds with a similar piece of extravagance cast in the form of a vow:

> If I be false, or swerve a hair from truth,
> When time is old [and] hath forgot itself,
> When water-drops have worn the stones of Troy,
> And blind oblivion swallow'd cities up,
> And mighty states characterless are grated
> To dusty nothing, yet let memory,
> From false to false among false maids in love,
> Upbraid my falsehood! When th' have said as false
> As air, as water, wind, or sandy earth,
> As fox to lamb, or wolf to heifer's calf,
> Pard to the hind, or step-dame to her son,
> Yea, let them say, to stick the heart of falsehood,
> "As false as Cressid."
>
> [III.ii.184-96]

The contrast between these two protestations is sometimes overlooked. Careless auditors in Shakespeare's theater could, and probably did, hear in them the unambiguous substance they had anticipated. In their minds Troilus, almost by definition, was a lover who would indeed prove true, and thus the images of cosmic stability by which he had affirmed his loyalty were shortly to be validated in shows of genuine grief and outrage. By contrast, Cressida, the occasion for that grief, was nothing more to them than another successor to Mother Eve, the perennial betrayer of man's trust—"as false / As air, as water, wind, or sandy earth." Yet surely the more perceptive spectators in Shakespear's audience had begun to recognize by this point in the play that Troilus was proving, both in his mindless infatuation and in his childish view of the issues of the war, to be scarcely superior to his brother Paris, whereas Cressida, whatever she may have been heretofore, was in this present affair with Troilus at worst a cautious lover and at best a deeply committed one. Troilus declares his constancy one with the stability of the sun and the earth, but the stability of these in 1602 was very much in doubt. Cressida's declaration is preferable. Even in view of the "betrayal" to which her vow of constancy is doomed, her fallibility at worst is one with the certain incertitudes by which under the moon all normal human beings live—air, water, wind, and sandy earth. In any case, in the ecstatic union that Shakespeare has given these two lovers destined to separate after their one night together, we see a doubt cast upon the hope that all his previous comedies have generated. These lovers are no better but no worse than those proper young lords and ladies upon whose formal marriage society based its hope of renewal. Pandarus concludes his impromptu proceedings with a cynical but prophetic "If ever you prove false to one another, . . . let all constant men be Troiluses, all false women Cressidas, and all brokers-between Pandars!" (III.ii:199-204), and then adds, as soon as the lovers are out of hearing, "Cupid grant all tongue-tied maidens here / Bed, chamber, Pandar to provide this gear!" One suspects that he has truth on his side and that his present wish for the ladies of the audience characterizes much that has long passed for comic action, in and out of the theater, Shakespeare's theater included.

We can, if we wish, take the story of Troilus and Cressida as the presentation of a special case in the transient circumstances of war, which traditionally has been hard on lovers and their dreams of the future; but honesty compels us to admit that even Shakespeare's earliest comedies are marked by touches of intransigent reality: the shadow of death that tempers the merriment of *The Comedy of Errors* and *Love's Labor's Lost*, the unresolved case of Shylock in *The Merchant of Venice*, the unreconciled Don John and Malvolio of *Much Ado about Nothing* and *Twelfth Night*, respectively, and the inescapably aged Falstaff of *The Merry Wives of Windsor*. But in all these plays young love has at least its momentary triumph, and on the strength of that we can take courage and look to the life ahead.

Troilus and Cressida, by contrast, offers no life ahead to look forward to. There we are witnesses both to the lovers' mating game and to the stances they assume in the hard morning light that follows the consummation and we see, if we had not seen before, that some of the impediments that make the marriage of true love a rarity are ingrained in lovers themselves. For this is the play in which Shakespeare brought romantic comedy to the test of human life and declared implicitly that that kind of comedy, as he and his contemporaries understood it, would have to begin making assaults upon the realities of the human condition if it was to survive. It was precisely Shakespeare's own step in this direction that gave character and strength to his next two comedies, *Measure for Measure* and *All's Well That Ends Well*, plays which have left audiences shaking their heads from that day to this.

He might have moved farther in that direction in *Troilus and Cressida* had not the likelihood of spectator foreknowledge stood in his way; even so, he moved far enough to leave several generations of critics behind. Few commentators have been prepared to recognize the extent to which in this play Shakespeare reversed the values traditionally assigned to the principal characters and made Troilus solely responsible, not for the collapse of his liaison with Cressida (that was doomed in any case), but for the failure of the love that gave it a tentative substance. Current wisdom is still in general agreement with Anne Barton that Troilus is at worst idealistic and naïve, that Cressida is at best a coquette, and that the play points towards "a position of profound skepticism" which is contradicted and corrected only by Shakespeare's orderly control over his materials.[5] One may acknowledge at least the partial truth of the third of these assertions without conceding the truth of the first two. Shakespeare's Cressida is a coquette made, not born; and *naïve* and *idealistic* are inaccurate terms for Troilus's consistently destructive misunderstanding of the requirements of human relationships. Barton finds it reprehensible in him that he idealizes only the sensual aspects of his love and never once mentions marriage to Cressida; but considering the courtly tradition which Chaucer unforgettably impressed upon the story, one should consider neither of these things a mark against him. One notes that the attachment of Tristan and Iseult similarly consisted of idealized sensuality and probably would not have involved a contemplation of marriage even if circumstances had not spared the lovers the need of considering such a bourgeois option.

The play begins with a scene in which Troilus urges a tactically reluctant Pandarus to deliver Cressida to him. The young man is barely old enough to go to war, being, if we may believe Pandarus (I.ii.110-14), still unable to grow a beard and by his own admission uncomfortable at the thought that his brother Hector or his father may discover his infatuation (I.i. 36). Predictably, when Pandarus feeds him a series of banalities comparable to those resorted to by Orlando and Benedick in earlier comedies, Troilus is deeply moved:

> I tell thee I am mad
> In Cressid's love; thou answer'st she is fair,
> Pourest in the open ulcer of my heart
> Her eyes, her hair, her cheek, her gait, her voice,
> Handlest in thy discourse, O, that her hand,
> In whose comparison all whites are ink
> Writing their own reproach; to whose soft seizure
> The cygnet's down is harsh, and spirit of sense
> Hard as the palm of ploughman. This thou tell'st me,
> As true thou tell'st me, when I say I love her.
> [I.i.51-60]

Acceptance of these clichés says more about Troilus's inexperience than about his lack of sincerity; but the language of his own devising, delivered in soliloquy as soon as Pandarus leaves the scene, gives us an insight into the way his mind runs:

> I cannot come to Cressid but by Pandar,
> And he's as teachy to be woo'd to woo,
> As she is stubborn-chaste against all suit.
> Tell me, Apollo, for thy Daphne's love,
> What Cressid is, what Pandar, and what we:
> Her bed is India, there she lies, a pearl;

> Between our Ilium and where she [resides],
> Let it be call'd the wild and wand'ring flood,
> Ourself the merchant, and this sailing Pandar
> Our doubtful hope, our convoy, and our bark.
>
> [I.i.95-104]

Apollo, Daphne, pearl, exotic India—all these have excellent
resonances, but they are framed in a metaphor of merchandis-
ing that casts Troilus in the role of merchant and Cressida,
though a pearl of price, in that of chattel. This, rather than
sensuality, is the situation that Troilus idealizes at the beginning, and we recognize that lovers in comedy have been at this
point before. Fenton, we may recall, at his point of turning in
The Merry Wives of Windsor confessed that he had begun in a
similar state of insensitivity:

> . . . thy father's wealth
> Was the first motive that I woo'd thee, Anne;
> Yet wooing thee, I found thee of more value
> Than stamps in gold, or sums in sealed bags;
> And 'tis the very riches of thyself
> That now I aim at.
>
> [III.iv.13-18]

Troilus might have undergone the same development, with or
without marriage in view; but in Shakespeare's depiction of
him he undergoes no development at all. He remains the merchant and continues to see Cressida as the pearl that he holds
briefly in his hand and to which, by that moment of possession,
he claims permanent title. If the selfless relationship between
Hector and Andromache means anything to him, we have no
evidence of it. His pattern is the action of Paris: to take at will
and to find value and honor solely in the keeping.

This attitude dominates the Trojan council in Act II, scene ii,
where Troilus, seconded heatedly but flimsily by Paris, prevails over the wisdom of Hector. The Greeks have offered to call
off the war and forget other damages if the Trojans will return
Helen. Hector, as we have seen, argues for acceptance, noting
that the Greeks, in this matter at least, have "the moral laws of
nature and of nations" on their side. He points out that Helen
has no intrinsic value and is "not worth what she doth cost /

The keeping." Troilus counters with an assertion that values are subjective affairs ("What's aught but as 'tis valued?") and, when Hector calmly but quickly demolishes him with superior logic, stubbornly proceeds to maintain his position with a series of analogies—buying, selling, and, this time, stealing too—and appeals to the honor of the marketplace, which, like that of the jungle, depends upon maintaining one's will at all costs:

> We turn not back the silks upon the merchant
> When we have soiled them, nor the remainder viands
> We do not throw in unrespective sieve,
> Because we now are full.
>
> . . . .
>
> Is she worth keeping? Why, she is a pearl,
> Whose price hath launch'd above a thousand ships,
> And turn'd crown'd kings to merchants.
>
> . . . .
>
>   O theft most base,
> That we have stol'n what we do fear to keep!
>   [II.ii.69-72;81-83;92-93]

Hector charitably proclaims Troilus's argument "superficial," but he knows the way of the world when he hears it and, outnumbered, concedes the debate.

This concession, as Hector probably knows, is in effect his death, and in any case it is less to his discredit than some readers have averred. Hector is no Puritan or Platonist, someone to insist upon his ideal as an ultimate reality, a truth to be maintained at all costs. He does believe in perfection, but like the Aristotelian he presumably is (II.ii.166-67), he sees it as existing only *in potentia* in the imperfect world about him. What he urges upon his "spritely brethren" in Act II is the ideal which according to his lights is their best destiny and which they obviously are capable of implementing or achieving provided they have the will to try. Troilus and Paris, however, repudiate the older man's ideal and choose to follow one of their own; and thus Hector falls back upon the one absolute he recognizes, selfless love between human beings, and puts affection for his brothers above a care to maintain a genuine philosophical insight, even though he believes that insight can provide a nobler and a safer guide than the facile honor they would so passionately defend. His own capacity for unselfish love, which does not diminish throughout, is the one lovely thing in the play and our one justification for optimism about the world that it presents. Hector is not the only one in the play to look squarely at the ethically bankrupt world of *Troilus and Cressida;* Ulysses and Thersites do also. But unlike these others, Hector manages to love in spite of what he sees, and what he sees is a spectacle more disheartening than any previously presented in an English comedy. That comedy had always presented evil, to be sure, but it was manageable evil, a mischievous intruder, an inhuman civil law, a passing affliction in an otherwise good character, a stone in the shoe, something to be ferreted out, confronted, and disposed of. Were it not for this kind of evil, comedy had usually been at pains to say, the world might be able to survive its changes with a minimum of human inconvenience and discomfort. The flaws we see in the world of *Troilus and Cressida,* however, are so deeply ingrained as to be conclusively fatal, and the disturbing thing about it all is that this is precisely the world we ask comedy to help us at least briefly to ignore.

The ménage of Paris and Helen, which we see at close range when Pandarus calls to explain Troilus's expected absence at supper, is a conspicuous part of what disturbs us; and Shakespeare presents it as an image of the world that Troilus is about to enter, not as a contrast to it. This interpretation of the situation comes into focus when Pandarus, prevailed upon for a song, complies with one that descries bawdily the sexual performance of lovers. Helen, as one might expect, is delighted, and the following exchange ensues:

Helen. In love, i' faith, to the very tip of the nose.
Par. He eats nothing but doves, love, and that breeds hot blood, and hot blood begets hot thoughts, and hot thoughts beget hot deeds, and hot deeds is love.
Pan. Is this the generation of love—hot blood, hot thoughts, and hot deeds? Why, they are vipers. Is love a generation of vipers? Sweet lord, who's a-field to-day?

Par. Hector, Deiphobus, Helenus, Antenor, and all the gallantry of
Troy. I would fain have arm'd to-day, but my Nell would not have it so.
How chance my brother Troilus went not?

Helen. He hangs the lip at something. You know all, Lord Pandarus.

Pan. Not I, honey-sweet queen. I long to hear how they sped to-day.

[III.i.127-42]

Paris's description of the generation of love is only minimally
diverting to begin with, but it becomes much less funny as
Pandarus qualifies it with his chilling biblical echo in "generation of vipers" (See Luke iii.7) and his professed indifference to
erotic escapades when the life-and-death matter of returning
warriors comes up. We note that Paris and Troilus, who argued
to maintain the war in order to keep Helen and protect their
Trojan honor, have neither of them gone to battle this day.
While others have fought the war which they insisted on continuing, their thoughts have been on lovemaking; and under
the circumstances, making love rather than war is for them
somewhat less than laudable.

Troilus, we learn immediately, is almost beside himself with
anticipation of delights to come, walking up and down before
Cressida's door and muttering an astonishing combination of
figures:

> . . . I stalk about her door
> Like to a strange soul upon the Stygian banks
> Staying for waftage. [To Pandarus] O, be thou my Charon
> And give me swift transportance to these fields
> Where I may wallow in the lily-beds
> Propos'd for the deserver! O gentle Pandar,
> From Cupid's shoulder pluck his painted wings,
> And fly with me to Cressid!

[III.ii.8-15]

Death is a common enough Elizabethan metaphor for sexual
consummation, but it is not usually accompanied by references to Charon and the River Styx and a trip to the Elysian
fields. Pandarus is more matter-of-fact: "Walk here i' th' orchard," he says, "I'll bring her straight." But Troilus continues:

> I am giddy; expectation whirls me round;
> Th' imaginary relish is so sweet

> That it enchants my sense; what will it be,
> When that the wat'ry palates taste indeed
> Love's thrice-repured nectar? Death, I fear me,
> Sounding destruction, or some joy too fine,
> Too subtile, potent, tun'd too sharp in sweetness
> For the capcity of my ruder powers.
> I fear it much, and I do fear besides
> That I shall lose distinction in my joys,
> As doth a battle, when they charge on heaps
> The enemy flying.
>
> [III.ii.18-29]

Death again, and this time mortality rather than a pagan Paradise. Pandarus returns to say that Cressida is on her way, and he urges the young man to be witty; but Troilus is so overcome with the thought of impending pleasure that he can do little more than pile up banalities, culminating in protestations of his eternal steadfastness. Cressida is more straightforward:

> Who shall be true to us.
> When we are so unsecret to ourselves?
> But though I lov'd you well, I woo'd you not,
> And yet, good faith, I wish'd myself a man,
> Or that we women had men's privilege
> Of speaking first.
>
> [III.ii.124-29]

As we have seen, this disparity between Troilus's tone and Cressida's continues in the oaths they swear in what amounts to a ceremony of trothplight—Troilus swearing grandly that he will be as steadfast as the universe itself and Cressida declaring, as though Troilus had not spoken at all, that if she ever proves unfaithful, she will allow herself to be called more blameworthy than air, water, wind, or sandy earth.

There is no doubt about what Shakespeare's Cressida has been in time immediately past. Virtually unsponsored in Troy since the defection of her father, she has submitted to the control of her uncle, who does not hesitate to use her favors to advance himself with people of position such as Troilus. In Act I, scene ii, she stands, first with her servant Alexander and then with both Alexander and Pandarus, and like the courtesan she has recently become surveys critically the procession of warriors returning from the battlefield. Her failure to recogize such worthies as Antenor and Helenus (and perhaps others as well) speaks to her inexperience, but she has enough experience in her new profession to make effective repartee. When Pandarus tells her she is so unpredictable that "a man knows not at what ward [that is, position of defense] you lie," she replies:

> *Cres.* Upon my back, to defend my belly, upon my wit, to defend my wiles, upon my secrecy, to defend mine honesty, my mask, to defend my beauty, and you, to defend all these; and at all these wards I lie, at a thousand watches.
> *Pan.* Say one of your watches.
> *Cres.* Nay, I'll watch you for that; and that's one of the chiefest of them too. If I cannot ward what I would not have hit, I can watch you for telling how I took the blow—unless it swell past hiding, and then it's past watching.   [I.ii.260-70]

Critics thus have often found it easy to label Cressida a whore, perhaps a young and still sentimental one, but a whore nevertheless; and they characterize her capitulation to the assembled Greeks in Act IV and to Diomedes in Act V as a reversion to type. This view of Cressida does an injustice to the subtlety of Shakespeare's presentation of her and distorts the meaning of the play.

Cressida in Shakespeare's version is a whore newly made, and she plots in advance her strategy with the Troilus whom Pandarus would force upon her (I.ii.282-95). Yet when Troilus later asks, "Why was my Cressid then so hard to win?" she replies with remarkable candor:

> Hard to seem won; but I was won, my lord,
> With the first glance that ever—pardon me,
> If I confess much, you will play the tyrant.
> I love you now, but till now not so much
> But I might master it. In faith I lie,
> My thoughts were like unbridled children grown
> Too headstrong for their mother. See, we fools!
> Why have I blabb'd? Who shall be true to us,

When we are so unsecret to ourselves?
[III.ii.117-25]

She hears Troilus's world-without-end promises, wants to
credit them, we may believe, and goes willingly, eagerly to bed.
The next morning she protests his leave-taking with all the
sincerity of a Juliet. "Night has been too brief," she says, and
then adds:

> Prithee tarry.
> You men will never tarry.
> O foolish Cressid! I might have still held off,
> And then you would have tarried.
>
> [IV.ii.15-18]

This pleasant exchange is interrupted by the unexpected arrival of Aeneas, who reports that Paris, Deiphobus, and the Greek
Diomedes are waiting outside, come to make an exchange of
Cressida for the captive Antenor. Cressida, Aeneas says, must
be given over to Diomedes within the hour. Troilus's immediate
response to this news is revealing:

> *Tro.*   Is it so concluded?
> *Aene.* By Priam and the general state of Troy.
> They are at hand and ready to effect it.
>   *Tro.* How my achievements mock me!
> I will go meet them; and, my Lord Aeneas,
> We met by chance, you did not find me here.
>
> [IV.ii.66-71]

Clearly his distress here is minimal. He has simply been to bed
with a beautiful woman whom he has acquired and taken for
his whore. His first concern is that his efforts have come suddenly to nothing; his second, that he has been caught by someone like Aeneas in a slightly embarrassing situation. Cressida's
response is altogether different but equally revealing. Her first
words are, "O you immortal gods! I will not go!" And when
Pandarus says she must, she wails:

> I will not, uncle. I have forgot my father,
> I know no touch of consanguinity;
> No kin, no love, no blood, no soul so near me
> As the sweet Troilus. O you gods divine,
> Make Cressida's name the very crown of falsehood,

If ever she leave Troilus! Time, force, and death
Do to this body what extremes you can;
But the strong base and building of my love
Is as the very centre of the earth,
Drawing all things to it. I'll go in and weep.
[IV.ii.96-105]

There is no coquetry in this speech, no dissembling of any kind. One imagines that a true courtesan would have looked forward to any exchange promising such a rich field as the Grecian camp. Yet Cressida concludes: "Tear my bright hair, and scratch my praised cheeks, / Crack my clear voice with sobs, and break my heart, / With sounding Troilus. I will not go from Troy" (IV.ii.107-9).

At the actual moment of leave-taking Troilus puts on a good show. To Paris, who has known about the previous evening's assignation from the beginning, he speaks "poetically" of delivering Cressida to Diomedes' hand much as a priest might lay his own heart upon the altar (IV.iii.5-9); but Cressida herself has no fine speeches to make. Her lines are little more than pained cries: "O Troilus, Troilus! . . . Have the gods envy? . . . And is it true that I must go from Troy? . . . What, and from Troilus too? . . . Is't possible?" (IV.iv.13-32). As she approaches hysteria, Troilus moves to console her. His words continue in the same high vein, but his real stance leaks through them and she sees what he has taken her for. Twice he qualifies his speeches with "Be thou but true of heart" and "But yet be true"; and Cressida is shocked into an agonized "What wicked deem is this?" (IV.iv.59). Troilus's explanation, that he is simply using an expression, that "the Grecian youths are full of quality," and that "sometimes we are devils to ourselves," alarms her even more. That either of them should not be true has not entered her mind, but now she justifiably fears that Troilus himself may not be, and, as his troubling questions and innuendos continue, she asks, straightforwardly as always, "My lord, will you be true?" His response to this is devastating to her but for reasons that he himself does not see:

Who, I? Alas, it is my vice, my fault:
Whiles others fish with craft for great opinion,

> I with great truth catch mere simplicity;
> Whilst some with cunning gild their copper crowns,
> With truth and plainness I do wear mine bare.
> Fear not my truth: the moral of my wit
> Is "plain and true"; there's all the reach of it.
>
> [IV.iv.102-8]

This is more of the Troilus whose steadfastness is one with that of the universe, and it puts his faithfulness beyond challenge, and beyond credibility. From this point on, Cressida has no reason to believe that she can ever be taken as anything but a whore. Troilus's speech turns in the middle to Diomedes, who now enters with Paris, Aeneas, Deiphobus, and Antenor:

> Welcome, Sir Diomed! Here is the lady
> Which for Antenor we deliver you.
> At the port, lord, I'll give her to thy hand,
> And by the way possess thee what she is.
> Entreat her fair, and, by my soul, fair Greek,
> If e'er thou stand at mercy of my sword,
> Name Cressid, and thy life shall be as safe
> As Priam is in Ilion.
>
> [IV.iv.109-16]

Diomedes' response is to make a cavalier advance to the girl standing before him. The gesture prompts Troilus to make threats, and this in turn leads Diomedes to say that in any case he will do as he pleases. The brief exchange here between these two smacks of talk over the transfer of a horse, when one participant chooses to regard the transaction as the conclusion of a binding trade and the other sees it as a temporary loan; but barter or banter, it tells Cressida that the outcome can be of no material difference to her. Either way she is merchandisable flesh. Troilus breaks off the discussion and turns once more to her with: "Lady, give me your hand, and as we walk, / To our own selves bend we our needful talk" (IV.iv.138-39). But there is really nothing more to say, and Cressida in this scene utters no further word in our hearing.

When we next see her (IV.v), Cressida is meeting the Greeks and kissing them all in turn except Menelaus, whom she scorns wittily as a cuckold. Ulysses, who has already had his kiss, is apparently irritated by the squelch given to his fellow Greek, and re-enters the list to put Cressida in her place by scorning a second kiss that she seems quite prepared to give. Diomedes quickly hustles her off the scene at this point as Nestor observes, "A woman of quick sense." He is probably referring to her quick wit, but Ulysses takes "sense" to mean sensuality; at any rate, he is not prepared here to concede that she has any merit at all:

> Fie, fie upon her!
> There's language in her eye, her cheek, her lip!
> Nay, her foot speaks; her wanton spirits look out
> At every joint and motive of her body.
> O, these encounters, so glib of tongue,
> That give a coasting welcome ere it comes,
> And wide unclasp the tables of their thoughts
> To every ticklish reader! set them down
> For sluttish spoils of opportunity,
> And daughters of the game.
>
> [IV.v.54-63]

Ulysses' judgment here, like his speech on degree, has worn well, and more critics than should have done have taken it as the play's judgment on Cressida. It is clearly Troilus's judgment after he has spied on Cressida at Calchas's tent: "O Cressid! O false Cressid! false, false, false! / Let all untruths stand by thy stained name, / And they'll seem glorious" (V.ii.178-80). Ulysses, to whom she was principally an impertinent Trojan flirt, has tried to calm the indignant Troilus: "What hath she done, Prince, that can soil our mothers?" But Troilus in his purblind vanity has worshiped not Cressida but the projection of an imagined purity in himself and made Cressida's physical beauty a correlative for a dream that bears no relation to any aspect of warm-blooded humanity, Cressida's or anyone else's:

> This she? no, this is Diomed's Cressida.
> If beauty have a soul, this is not she;
> If souls guide vows, if vows be sanctimonies,
> If sanctimony be the gods' delight,
> If there be any rule in unity itself,

This was not she. O madness of discourse,
That cause sets up with and against itself!
Bi-fold authority, where reason can revolt
Without perdition, and loss assume all reason
Without revolt. This is, and is not, Cressid!
                                    [V.ii.137-46]

Troilus here is still half in his collapsing dream-world, from the complete dissolution of which will spring the destructive anger that sends him at last back to the battlefield. Meanwhile, the play has revealed a Cressida who is capable of loving selflessly, who for one brief night has managed to believe she has found a man who can share a commitment with her, but who learns upon awaking from that night that his commitment is no deeper than that of other men like Paris, Aeneas, and Diomedes, and, seeing that he offers almost no resistance to the order to let her go, decides in her disillusionment to play the cards that life has dealt her. Troilus's disillusionment follows as a consequence of her decision, but his discomfiture should not be the occasion for our own. Our sympathies belong with Cressida, whose fate forces us to look upon the world as it is, and her despair marks a crisis for comedy and the end of romantic resolutions such as we found in *Twelfth Night*, *As You Like It*, and *Much Ado about Nothing*.

Admittedly, the fable of *Troilus and Cressida*, unlike that of *Romeo and Juliet* (which Shakespeare also allowed to run its noncomic course), was prevented by a well-established tradition from reaching a happy conclusion. A conventional Menandrian solution to things was simply not to be made out of these materials. Nevertheless, Shakespeare's initial treatment of them was such as to encourage the hope that the spirit of comedy might be evoked if both lovers should prove capable of rising to the point of selfless commitment that romantic comedy requires. At the least, such a commitment would have permitted the pair to retire to some pantheon with all those other capable but unlucky lovers (for example, Romeo and Juliet) who would surely have given renewal to their worlds had not the impediments been overwhelming. Here, however, the impediment is Troilus himself, who turns out to be one with Paris and Pandarus, denizens of a world in which sex is a matter of intense pleasure associated with women and where women are valued primarily as means to that end. Cressida apparently had already decided that something like this attitude was true of all men until Troilus's declarations of a nobler attachment caused her to hope briefly that there might be a kind of transcendental love, approachable through bodies but not restricted to them. The regrettable thing is that she could not have known someone like Hector. One is almost tempted to add Achilles here, for Achilles demonstrates throughout most of the play that he can make a meaningful commitment to another human being and maintain it even to the point of submerging his superior talents as a warrior. In the end Achilles goes to war out of anger rather than pride. The death of his beloved Patroclus, presumably at Hector's hand (Achilles calls him a "boy-queller"), replaces honest soldiering in his mind with a compulsion to murder. He disparages Hector's show of courtesy on the battlefield (V.v.13-21) and then orders his Myrmidons to hack the unarmed Trojan to death just as the day's fighting comes to an end. Yet if Troilus is responsible for Cressida's disillusionment, he is ultimately at least indirectly responsible for Achilles' fall from graciousness also.

The chain of events by which this comes about begins with the damage inflicted on Troilus's pride as he stands with Ulysses in the dark outside Calchas's tent. That damage prompts him to return to fighting the next day with the primary purpose of killing Diomedes. Hector, as we have seen, is under unusual pressure to refrain this one day from the fighting. As Priam sums it up:

> Thy wife hath dreamt, thy mother hath had visions.
> Cassandra doth foresee, and I myself
> Am like a prophet suddenly enrapt
> To tell thee that this day is ominous:
> Therefore come back.
>
> [V.iii.63-67]

Hector does not give in to their entreaties and goes forth to meet his death; but the factor that stiffens his resistance to the advice of the wiser members of his household is the spectacle of irrational fierceness in his younger brother Troilus, who (as noted earlier) bursts into the midst of the family's urging and with the intensity of his distress, or hysteria, convinces Hector that the youth needs watching. It is the extraordinary fury of the subsequent fighting that brings about the death of Patroclus at Hector's hand and sends Achilles also, at first unarmed, into the midst of the fighting. And through it all one remembers Hector's wish to end the war, Troilus's impassioned but specious arguments for continuing, and the older man's tolerant concession.

One critic has observed that the meaning of the play is manifest in a detail that Shakespeare borrowed from Lydgate: Hector's slaying of the Greek in "sumptuous" armor, "most putrefied core, so fair without" (V.vi.27-31).[6] Certainly, part of the meaning is there. Hector is simply following an ancient custom of combat in killing and claiming the armor of a Greek warrior who crosses his path. The bravery of the armor constitutes an automatic challenge, and there is nothing reprehensible, at least so far as the context of this play is concerned, in Hector's pursuing the man, regardless of whether or not the man was trying to run away.[7] The point of the incident is that the man inside the armor does not measure up to the glory of his packaging; and that much is true of almost every aspect of this play: Troilus's devotion, Achilles' honor, Cressida's beauty, the Greeks' valor, and the Trojans' sophistication. In short, there are no perfections in *Troilus and Cressida*, and there will be none in any of Shakespeare's comedies to follow, whether we call them problem plays or romances. Comedy henceforth in Shakespeare's practice of it will find its love and devotion in a world where unadulterated truth and beauty are illusions and where the viewer or reader is constrained to accept a human approximation of these ideals in something like charity and forgiveness.

13

All's Well That Ends Well
and Measure for Measure

The previous chapter referred to *Troilus and Cressida* as an anomalous play. The term is a useful one for all three of the comedies that Shakespeare wrote between 1602 and 1604—*Troilus and Cressida*, *All's Well That Ends Well*, and *Measure for Measure*—if only because it has the advantage of being non-committal. From time to time critics have given these plays such epithets as "dark comedies," "problem comedies," "problem plays," and even "tragicomedies"; but such terms tend to obscure more than they reveal. Whatever one calls Shakespeare's middle plays, they address themselves to the basic function of comedy, which is to reassure the reader or spectator that the processes by which society renews itself are still valid in all but extraordinary circumstances.

Troilus and Cressida, of course, does so only negatively. As we have seen, it misses being a fully realized comedy only partly because in it an exchange of prisoners separates the lovers. The real impediment to comedy in the play is the unfortunate collection of attitudes that determines the behavior of Troilus, who, despite his status, never ceases to think like a merchant. In selfishness the callow young prince almost matches the sensual Paris, and he appropriately unites with Paris to frustrate their brother Hector's futile attempt to take a first step in the direction of renewal for the beleaguered city of Troy. A marriage between Troilus and Cressida, were that possible, would promise no more renewal for the city than Paris's liaison with Helen, for all hope of Trojan renewal vanishes with Hector's capitulation (at the conclusion of the Trojan council in Act II) to the childish insistence of his younger brothers to continue the war. Yet even in that part of *Troilus and Cressida* the norm and furniture of comedy remain, to measure, ghostlike, the futility of the courtship that follows and to condemn the savage Greek vengefulness that finally brings to an end the dreams of a society which has already long since lost its means of survival. Nevertheless, this play, however it is categorized, shares with *All's Well That Ends Well* and *Measure for Measure* a quality that distinguishes all three plays from the ten preceding comedies: that is, they take nothing for granted—not the validity of established social institutions, nor the psychology of human beings, nor even the physical and moral order of the universe—but instead confront the human situation without preconceptions, as preternaturally sophisticated children might confront it, or visitors from another planet. They compel us thereby to contemplate the actions we see in a manner described by one of the unnamed lords in Act IV of *All's Well That Ends Well:* "The web of our life is a mingled yarn, good and ill together: our virtues would be proud, if our faults whipt them not, and our crimes would despair, if they were not cherish'd by our virtues" (IV.iii.71-74). That is, these middle comedies present what appears to be an indiscriminate mixture, and with them the hope of a conclusive sorting out—light from dark, good from evil, justice from injustice—vanishes, never to return. Understandably, the sting of disappointment tempts us from time to time to quarantine the plays in question with special labels; and having done that, we are thus prone to go on overlooking the fact that these are not abnormal comedies requiring our apologies but merely comedies with an enhanced relevance to the lives most people lead.

In *All's Well That Ends Well* and *Measure for Measure* we can begin to see, if *Much Ado about Nothing* has not already enlightened us, that traditional comedy—including to some extent, Shakespeare's earlier plays—has always tended to run along relatively safe paths, with values clearly marked for us and all the turns protected against unforeseen contingencies. Here, by contrast, our vehicles are forced to strike out across open country, through forests and bogs, and over rocky terrain, without benefit of road or map. It is no wonder, therefore, that they arrive at the prescribed destination with marks of the passage still showing. The vehicles of comedy are formally the same as before: romantic variants of Menandrian comedy or New Comedy with a generous selection of familiar conventions, themes, and devices. But whereas Shakespeare's earlier comedies had run, at least ostensibly, upon the assumption of a universal hierarchical principle that manifested itself in all the orders of creation—cosmic, political, social, and familial— and was seldom successfully challenged, here that assumption dissolves in the face of a decisive challenge that is both fundamental and successful and not only changes the direction of comedy but foreshadows changes in society itself.

The most important change involves the place of woman in the world. In previous Menandrian comedy woman had occupied a place in the human hierarchy which gave her the status of chattel. We have seen traces of that status for women in Adriana of *The Comedy of Errors* and in the marriages in *The Taming of the Shrew* and *Much Ado about Nothing*. Frequently, however, in the romantic variant of Menandrian comedy, which is the natural consequence of the semi-apotheosis of woman in Christian tradition, woman does begin to gain a qualified humanity. In such plays the male does not merely seek to *acquire* the woman; he seeks to gain her acceptance of him. This means courtship and sometimes a playful deification, after which the woman may or may not revert to the status of chattel. In Shakespeare's version of romantic comedy, as noted earlier, the woman regularly resists any such reversion and sometimes even strains towards achieving equality with the male.

Troilus and Cressida is at base a conflict between these two views of woman, and that realization gives us a way of dealing with the problem of interpretation encountered by readers who insist on reading the play with traditional versions of the story in mind. Shakespeare's Troilus sees Cressida as a woman to be won after the manner of romantic comedy, but for him the wooing is little more than a charade. Having won, he assumes that he has achieved the rights of ownership. He assumes, moreover, that Cressida understands what he has achieved; and he is partly right. Cressida has never doubted that she lives in a society capable of allowing her to become chattel, but for a brief moment she has thought Troilus a man capable of regarding her as something more. When by morning light she sees that he is no different from all the others, she once more accepts her status as merchandise, this time with a decision to exploit her situation in the only way remaining that will allow her a modicum of self-determination. Thus the romantic comic action of *Troilus and Cressida,* which by rights should have led to some kind of renewal, only serves to turn Cressida into a permanent whore, and in so doing it makes explicit the criticism of romantic comedy that was adumbrated in both *The Taming of the Shrew* and *Much Ado about Nothing.* By the end of the fourth act of *Troilus and Cressida* we see that young love, courtship, and marriage in themselves guarantee nothing. The society that is willing to tolerate frivolous idealizations of the mating game and declines to look at the consequences of its marriages may well be a society that has always been quite content to deny full humanity to half of its population.

Not all critics will agree. Officially, marriage between a man and a woman was considered a sacrament in Shakespeare's time, as it had been throughout much of Europe for more than a thousand years; and as a sacrament marriage was expected to purge the physical bonding of the couple, at least for the moment of setting forth, of some of the flaws and inequities that natural flesh is heir to. The statement in *The Book of Common Prayer* of 1559 is clear about the meaning of holy matrimony; it is

an honorable estate, instituted of God in paradise at the time of man's innocency, signifying unto us the mystical union, that is betwixt Christ and his Church: which holy estate Christ adorned and beautified with his presence and first miracle that he wrought in Cana of Galilee, and is commended of Saint Paul to be honorable among all

men, and therefore is not to be enterprised nor taken in hand unad-
visedly, lightly, or wantonly, to satisfy men's carnal lusts and ap-
petites, but reverently, discreetly, advisedly, soberly, and in the fear of
God.[1]

This is what all Elizabethan couples heard at the altar,
whether they heeded it or not, from parish church to St. Paul's;
and by those words they were reminded of the key position that
Elizabethan society accorded marriage as an institution.
Some have argued that Shakespeare's plays give it equally high
marks. For example, Leo Salingar insists that love as an initia-
tion to marriage "is the central, unifying theme that runs
through all [Shakespeare's] comedies and romances,"[2] and he
elaborates as follows:

Shakespeare makes no use in his purely comic plays of a love-intrigue
outside marriage [this, of course, rules out *Troilus and Cressida*]. . . . Love in his comedies always leads towards marriage, marriage in accordance with the Elizabethan ideal of a free choice of
suitable partners and mutual love and trust (subject to the husband's
authority). This is the ideal Shakespeare upholds in his sonnets, and
similarly in *The Shrew* and *The Merry Wives*, despite their light-heart-
ed tone and their kinship with farce. . . . His comedies, then, are essentially celebrations of marriage, which he presents in a social as
well as a personal aspect. . . . In his last tragic-comedies or romances
. . . marriage appears as the resolution of the broader tensions, as the
type or focus of harmony in society as a whole.[3]

Salingar's generalizations seem reasonable enough at first
reading, but they become suspiciously easy as we take into
account the ambiguities that determine the character of even
the simplest of Shakespeare's comedies. Marriage, actual or in
prospect, certainly plays a key role in most of them: it is the
culmination of the mating game, the ceremonial occasion for
awarding prizes and punishment, if any, and the epiphany of
the dramatic action. One may imagine that the ordinary, unre-
flective Elizabethan derived satisfaction merely from seeing a
portrayal of marriage on the stage, as some moderns still do,
and made no distinction between the marriages portrayed in
Shakespeare's comedies and those portrayed in any other comedies. But Shakespeare's plays, if we take them seriously and

listen as well as look, seldom provide unmixed satisfaction. Virtually all the marriages we find there, when he allows us more than a passing glance at them, are troubled with uncertainties, suspicion, jealousy, or deep misunderstanding and suggest anything but harmony. Moreover, one may question whether the ideal of marriage as an institution based on "free choice of suitable partners and mutual love and trust (subject to the husband's authority)" is something that a careful reading of these plays will allow one to discover as a norm. It probably represents fairly enough the norm that a Petruchio or a Benedick would settle for, but it is hardly Kate's norm or Beatrice's; and it is nothing like the ideal marriage of Sonnet 116 (if that is what Salingar had in mind), which has to do with intellects rather than bodies and is, in any case, tantalizingly ambiguous.

The ideal for marriage that does emerge from these plays is best thought of as a process rather than as a status to be achieved with any finality, a relationship between equals involving constant renewal and abnegation of self on both sides. This is what the Princess of France and her ladies in *Love's Labor's Lost* attempted with only limited success to convey to the philosophical young lovers of Navarre, and it is the lesson that women teach their men in all the comedies that Shakespeare wrote after *Troilus and Cressida*. The clearest example is in the first of these, *All's Well That Ends Well,* in which all five acts are devoted to the attempts by Helena, a sometimes misunderstood young woman, to prepare Bertram, the young man of her choice, for a union that will be more than a marriage in name only.

The process begins in the first scene of the play, in which Shakespeare presents the principals in their initial isolation and, in Bertram's case, unawareness. Bertram is the supreme example of callow youth in Shakespeare, surpassing in his naiveté such innocents as Romeo, Orlando, Troilus, and Ferdinand. Though his father is only recently dead and his mother obviously will be painfully bereft by his going to Paris, he shows no feeling at all about leaving Rossillion except a childish eagerness to get on with his first opportunity to venture into the sophisticated world. Completely self-centered, he cannot perceive either Helena's genuine affection for him or the shallowness of Parolles's friendship; and he is so ill informed about the circumstances of the life he is preparing to enter that he does not even know of the "notorious" terminal illness of the King of France, who has now become his guardian (I.i.32-36). By contrast, Helena is sufficiently mature emotionally to know what love is, and she bestows it selflessly on both Bertram and his mother. In addition, she has honored her dead father by acquiring and perpetuating his skills and will shortly risk the reputation of both father and skills, to say nothing of her own life, in an attempt to save the King. She also hopes, vainly as it turns out, to rescue Bertram from his solipsism by the same maneuver; but her salvation of Bertram will require another kind of risk, which differs in no essential way from the risk that any woman must take when on her own initiative she submits physically to a man, be he lover or husband. To cope with that situation she will need to resort to the worldly wisdom offered gratuitously by Parolles, who knows nothing about love but understands some of the consequences of harboring inhibitions about sex. "Virginity is peevish, proud, idle, made of self-love, which is the most inhibited sin in the canon," he tells her. "Keep it not, you cannot choose but lose by it. Out with't!" (I.i.144-46).

Nevertheless, at the beginning of the play both Helena and Bertram stand alone, separated as much by immaturity as by status. The Countess stands alone also, but she has the wisdom to know that her role is simply to be open to the young people's advances, when and if they make requests for help. Hence, she simply waits for the young people to activate the situation and turn it into a movement in the direction of comedy. This happens soon after the beginning of the play, as Helena comes to the realization that human love is most often engendered not by some kind of miraculous visitation or intervention but by simple human initiative:

> Our remedies oft in ourselves do lie,
> Which we ascribe to heaven. The fated sky

Gives us free scope, only doth backward pull
Our slow designs when we ourselves are dull.

. . . .

Impossible be strange attempts to those
That weigh their pains in sense, and do suppose
What hath been cannot be.

[I.i.216-19;224-26]

From this point on, it is possible for the young people in the play to move forward and fulfill in Rossillion the function of all comedy, which is to cheat the absolute demands of a death that has already taken (in this case) their fathers and now lays claim to the life of the province as well.

Two special problems have preoccupied critics of this play: the aggressiveness of Helena and the apparent unworthiness of Bertram—both of which characteristics were required by the time-honored pattern of the story.[4] In any case, the first of these should not have troubled students of Shakespeare's comedies. Helena's assumption of a role usually assigned to the male simply perpetuates a Shakespearean pattern already well established by plays in which the woman is the strong member of the evolving partnership. One thinks immediately of Julia in *the Two Gentlemen of Verona*, the tactful but aggressive Princess in *Love's Labor's Lost*, Portia in *The Merchant of Venice*, Rosalind in *As You Like It*, and Viola in *Twelfth Night*; and to these one should certainly add Katherina and Beatrice, who are at least as spirited as the males they finally allow to dominate them. Here in *All's Well That Ends Well* we have a woman who quickly proves superior to her man in both professional skill and diplomacy: she intrudes in a field normally reserved for males, successfully bends even the ruler of that field to her will, and through him takes her man by fiat. To the King's irritation and the astonishment of those standing about, Bertram resists marriage to Helena with a persistence that amounts almost to disrespect and with a snobbishness that may have disturbed early audiences as much as it disturbs us ("A poor physician's daughter my wife! Disdain / Rather corrupt me ever!"); yet we must acknowledge an element of justice in his plea to the King at this point: "I shall beseech your Highness, / In such a business, give me leave to use / The help of mine own eyes" (II.iii.106-8). We should acknowledge, too, that there is something more than an element of justice in his resentment at having had no say in a decision which affects not only his own future but that of Rossillion and its people as well. Moreover, many would argue that Helena shows a lack of sensitivity in not recognizing earlier that any marriage forced upon Bertram here can be little more than an empty formality. Be that as it may, Bertram's dismissal of Helena without a kiss at the end of Act II shows that the marriage she has achieved is not a renewal but a disaster, for herself (if not for him), for the Countess, and for Rossillion. Having thus wrought so much damage by an aggressiveness that for some even now passes as unladylike, Helena has no choice but to continue on a similar course and hope that eventually she can bring the marriage that has been no marriage to consummation and produce the heir which the Countess and her subjects have every right to expect. Even without Bertram's letter and its impossible challenge ("show me a child begotten of thy body that I am heir to" [III.ii.58-59]), something like the bed trick has at this point become inevitable.

Under the Christian dispensation, marriage sanctifies the bed, and thus Helena, being legally married to the man she sleeps with, technically incurs no blame when she replaces Diana Capilet in Bertram's embraces. Nevertheless, both ethics and common sense remind us that Helena is cooperating in what for Bertram appears to be an act of adultery; in addition, she is bedding with a man who despises her and is lustfully enjoying her body only because he does not realize whose body it is. These considerations have troubled some who otherwise find Helena ethically faultless, but scholarship has offered a way out with the reminder that the story of Giletta of Narbon, whether borrowed directly or indirectly from Boccaccio, has its roots in folklore and fairy tale, where the lady in performing the impossible tasks laid upon her by her reluctant husband remains spotless throughout and in successfully completing her action always wins the man's love.[5] Thus a fair number of readers have been content to say that *All's Well That Ends Well* invites the kind of reception one would give to a folk tale and at the end, to adapt a phrase from Anne Barton's introduction, "floats off into a poignant, but attenuated, world of unbelief."[6]

Complementary interpretations have come from several quarters, two of which may be noted here. Muriel C. Bradbrook finds the play a failure because in it "Shakespeare was trying to write a moral play," and he "was not happy when he was theorizing." Yet in spite of his intentions, Bradbrook believes, Shakespeare managed somehow to portray Helena with a convincing but almost miraculous redemptive love, an element which refused to be accommodated to the story materials he had before him and to the stiff types with which otherwise he was peopling his play.[7] G. Wilson Knight, taking a somewhat different tack, calls *All's Well* a religious morality, and develops at great length the thesis that the purity and power of Helena's love qualify her for a kind of "Renaissance sainthood."[8] Both of these interpretations, however, like those which explain the apparent inconsistencies of the play as due simply to the fossilized remains of fairy tale and folklore, remove *All's Well* from the mainstream of comedy and suggest that its important values are extradramatic or else that, considered as a whole, it has value principally as fantasy.

The hesitation to see *All's Well* as comedy may be relieved by several considerations, all of which involve recognizing that here Shakespeare was doing nothing more remarkable than moving firmly along a path that was to some extent discernible in even his earliest work. First, we note that *All's Well*, more positively than its immediate predecessor, *Troilus and Cressida*, moves the design and action of comedy squarely into the world of human affairs. The Countess, Parolles, Lafew, and Lavatch, all Shakespeare's additions to the story and all recognizable importations from the world we know, tell us clearly where we are; and their presence conditions our reading of the two unfledged principals, Helena with her single-minded devotion for Bertram and Bertram with his adolescent yearning to be a manly warrior. Second, the story of this play, as Barton notes, inverts the pattern of Menandrian comedy, in which guardians usually try to prevent rather than encourage the marriage of their young men to women of lesser status.[9] The significant effect of this inversion, again, is to bring the comic pattern into line with patterns of Elizabethan life, in which, one imagines, parents (like their modern counterparts) tended wherever possible to cooperate with young adults in such matters. The great impediment to meaningful marriage has always been the characters of the prospective partners themselves—here, immaturity on both sides: Helena naively supposing that a marriage ceremony will automatically mark the beginning of a real union, and Bertram still so much an adolescent in his adult world that he cannot begin to see what his principal role in that world must be. Nevertheless, the function of comedy in this play remains the same as elsewhere: to make possible a renewal of life in the community and thereby to ensure its continuation.

The third consideration has to do with the main business of the play after Act II, which must serve to bring about the fulfillment of the action of comedy; and that business is simply the education of Bertram, which in a real sense involves the education of Helena as well. Initially Helena knows that the mystery of sex provides the ground for all human relations (her exchange with Parolles in Act I shows that), but she has had no need to put her knowledge to the test, much less an inclination to explore further, before entering a publicly recognized relationship with her chosen partner. Bertram, by contrast, knows less about sex and is less in awe of it. For him it is not so much a mystery as an untried physical experience that his friends tell him is the prerogative of every vigorous and healthy male. Helena's task, therefore, is to find a means to bring Bertram into a real and permanent marriage; and the beauty of the action by which she accomplishes her task consists not so much in an adumbration of sainthood as in the simple readiness with which she moves out to rejoin her beloved at a level where he is capable of participating and generously becomes his mistress before she is truly his wife. Nevertheless, in that selfless motion, as truly an agapeic gesture as anything else in Shakespeare, she does in fact adumbrate sainthood and point to the extended dimension that Shakespeare's plays after *Troilus and Cressida* made possible for Menandrian comedy.

A note should be added here about Bertram, whom Dr.

Johnson in a memorable passage condemned out of hand: "I cannot reconcile my heart to Bertram; a man noble without generosity, and young without truth; who marries Helena as a coward, and leaves her as a profligate: when she is dead by his unkindness, sneaks home to a second marriage, is accused by a woman whom he has wronged, defends himself by falsehood, and is dismissed to happiness."[10] In most romantic comedies the young lovers are relatively blameless figures and, in any case, more sinned against than sinning. Shakespeare in bringing comedy to earth foreshadowed the departure of the *senex* and placed full responsibility where it ultimately is in any valid marriage, on the lovers themselves. With that shift of emphasis it was no longer possible to take courtship for granted—as Ben Jonson does, for example, in *Every Man in His Humor*—or to treat it as a formal game. Hereafter, the playwright increasingly would be expected to show courtship as the adjustment of couples to one another preliminary to the ceremonial act. At that point and only there could the existential achievement of true marriage begin. In that fullest sense of marriage, we should note, Leontes and Hermione are not married at the beginning of *The Winter's Tale*, nor are Posthumus and Imogen at the beginning of *Cymbeline*. Bertram resembles the male partners of both of these pairs in that he not only stands in need of enlightenment but has no awareness of his own ignorance. He is different only in that he is positively averse to the union that has been forced upon him, and in that respect he may be the most virtuous of the three. Helena speaks truly when she replies to the King with " 'Tis but the shadow of a wife you see, / The name, and not the thing" (V.iii.307-8), and Bertram proves that he is at last ready to begin a marriage when on seeing the ring and hearing Helena read from his letter the terms he himself has imposed, he exclaims: "If she, my liege, can make me know this clearly, / I'll love her dearly, ever, ever dearly" (V.iii.315-16). Thus at last is the wedding complete and the true marriage under way. Bertram has been lucky. By the sacrifice of a devoted woman he has been brought to the point where he can begin to deserve her love; and by his final wholehearted acceptance of the union that initially was forced upon him he has guaranteed renewal for Rossillion. It is no wonder that Lafew mumbles "Mine eyes smell onions" and asks Parolles for the loan of his handkerchief.

Measure for Measure, the last of the three comedies that are anomalous only if we choose to make them so, continues the examination of marriage. Duke Vincentio, whom critics have variously condemned as a manipulator and exalted as someone with godlike prescience, stands at the center, but not merely as puppeteer. He is perhaps best thought of as our point of knowing in the play. We share his perplexity at the beginning, his enlightenment as the play proceeds, and his satisfaction at the end. The desperate situation in Vienna that confronts the Duke is at least partly the consequence of his failure to understand human nature. He has recognized that flesh will be flesh regardless of strict laws against fornication; but in quietly trying to make allowances for human frailty, he has underestimated undisciplined humanity's capability for self-destruction through indulgence. Now, saddened by a better understanding, he sees no hope for his demoralized city unless he can institute a rigorous enforcement of the law, and to achieve that end he has taken the extraordinary course of deputizing a man whose credibility has not yet been eroded by an identification with leniency. Angelo, his choice for the newly created post, is one who has never broken the statute against fornication. Moreover, the man has a private chapter in his history which suggests to the Duke, who knows the circumstances in that chapter (I.i.28-29; III.i.208-30) and subsequently decides to make special use of them, that he will be impervious to sentimental appeals and steadfast in preserving the letter of the law. In that perception the Duke is not deceived; but he does not count on Angelo's vulnerability, and his own, to the extraordinary attractiveness of an Isabella, whose erotic beauty burns with such intensity that it initiates the action of the play and determines the progress of that action to a conclusion.

The other principals in *Measure for Measure*, save one, are either (like the Duke) not yet fully initiated in relations with the opposite sex or else indifferent to the mores whereby official Vienna and Christendom in general have integrated sex with the rest of the social system. Claudio and Juliet, in love and deeply committed to one another, have simply conducted themselves as husband and wife without observing public solemnities, and therefore under the law they are guilty of fornication. Their indifference to law is of the benign kind, however, and most readers are reluctant to blame them; but since the law is being challenged and Juliet's pregnancy makes their guilt under it obvious, Angelo has applied the law as written and condemned Claudio to death. Lucio's indifference to the law is of another order entirely. He too has got a woman with child; but being cleverer than Claudio and deft in avoiding commitment to another human being, he has avoided detection and so walks through most of the play a free man. Angelo differs from Lucio only in that he cannot be condemned under the law. He was once affianced to the lady Mariana by formal trothplight, which she thought of as a marriage. Apparently he never took advantage of her complaisance; but when her brother perished in a shipwreck—and with him her expected dowry—Angelo dissolved the arrangements as nothing more than a broken contract, leaving Mariana in her own eyes no better than a widow. Claudio's sister, Isabella, though considerably less experienced than the Duke in mundane matters, like him has found the world about her intolerable. As a novice of the sisterhood of Saint Clare, she has announced her intention to leave the world forever, and she returns only to plead for her brother's life.

Thus the first three acts of the play give us five principals, all deficient in some way: Duke Vincentio in the resolution to deal with the facts of life, Isabella in the courage to face those facts, Claudio in self-discipline, and Angelo in the compassion that can redeem erotic love and make law tolerable. Lucio's behavior exhibits the deficiencies of both Claudio and Angelo, compounded with a licentiousness that has tempted some critics to describe him as satanic.[10] In any case, he embodies the disease from which the Duke is fleeing, and thus he appropriately takes upon himself the role of the disguised Duke's adversary, a "burr" to be endured until the Duke can muster the resolution to expose him and deal with him. Lucio's saving grace, which rescues him from total villainy, is his grain of affection for Claudio and his willingness to bring news of Claudio's arrest to Isabella and urge her to intercede on her brother's behalf.

The remaining principal, Mariana, who does not appear until the first scene of Act IV, provides the potential resolution of all the deficiencies (except those of the incorrigible Lucio) by the simple act of submitting to her former betrothed, who, like Bertram in *All's Well That Ends Well*, thinks he is fornicating with another. By this act she consummates a marriage in which her own *caritas* (which we weakly translate "charity") may have a chance to redeem Angelo from the mask of rectitude he has hitherto worn and in his own mind identified with virtue. Like Isabella's physical beauty, Mariana's love is one of the constants in the play, a quality given rather than achieved through through the action, and in this case a quality uncovered only in the last moments in her words to the Duke and Isabella:

> I hope you will not mock me with a husband!
> . . . .
> I crave no other, nor no better man.
> . . . .
> Sweet Isabel, do yet but kneel by me.
> Hold up your hands, say nothing; I'll speak all.
> They say most men are moulded out of faults.
> And for the most, become much more the better
> For being a little bad; so may my husband.
> (V.i.417;426;437-41)

Mariana's unconditional forgiveness here of the man who has shamed her cracks the image of rectitude that even to this point has blinded Isabella to the true nature of virtue, and it moves Isabella herself to words of forgiveness:

> I partly think
> A due sincerity governed his deeds,
> Till he did look on me. Since it is so,

Let him not die.

[V.i.445-48]

Mariana's performance here also encourages novice Isabella to abandon her plan to return to the sisterhood of Saint Clare, which in any case has never been presented in the play as an appealing alternative to anything. Thus Isabella is free to receive the advances that she inadvertently has prompted in the diffident Duke. Mariana's influence extends even further. Her selfless surrender to Angelo has presented a pattern of surrender by analogy with which unions of truly committed lovers like Claudio and Juliet may hereafter be justified regardless of law and by which even the union of a Lucio and his "punk" may be regarded as having some slight chance of redeeming the defector. At least, redeeming Lucio, should that turn out to be possible, is preferable to whipping him publicly and then hanging him.

It should be noted that the comic action of *Measure for Measure* does not promise redemption for Vienna, merely survival. The Lucios who populate that city are far too clever for magistrates to eradicate or to reform; and the hope for the community, which is the hope of comedy everywhere, lies in the possibility that a residual charity in some human beings may be appealed to and that men and women may on occasion give up their charades and accept one another in the kind of love—Mariana's love—of which the human race at its best is capable. Only then has the community a chance of continuing as a civic organism in relative stability and peace. The achievement of this play in the succession of Shakespeare's comedies, however, is the completion of the revolution initiated in *Troilus and Cressida*, in which a female character, traditionally debased, is presented as taking the lead—futilely, it turns out—in establishing a genuine union between man and woman. That the woman there is unaware of her role and that the man is unworthy of the destination to which she attempts to lead him are irrelevancies. The prospect of true union, the only relationship that merits the term "marriage," is nevertheless hinted at in that unusual play, and it receives further definition and articulation in Helena's education of Bertram in *All's Well That*

Ends Well and Mariana's confession at the end of *Measure for Measure*. Thus in Shakespeare's presentation of the marital relationship, the woman will continue to lead, and she will do so by uncovering the redemptive potential in the submissive role that society has forced upon her. This is not to say that Shakespeare is at pains to justify woman's role in Elizabethan society, but rather that in *all* roles, female and male, involving marriage he shows the importance of a love characterized by giving, commitment, and dedication, or agape. In successful marriages the sex act, regardless of what games and formalities may have preceded it, becomes the initial point of testing whether what is to follow will be a matter of taking or of giving; and since that act is almost never wholly one thing or the other, it must on each occasion be followed by at least an attitude of forgiveness on both sides, and mutual acceptance in charity. Everything else that happens in comedy is anticipatory of this transaction between human beings; and thus even in comedies where we see the pair before the altar and hear their vows, the exchanges that constitute the reality of marriage are still to come, sometimes much later.

As we have already seen, several of Shakespeare's early comedies anticipate this insight. Sometimes they do so negatively, as in the marriages between Bianca and Lucentio and the nameless widow and Hortensio in *The Taming of the Shrew* and, sadly, in all the marriages of *Much Ado about Nothing*, suggesting that the anticipated formal marriages there may well be the "nothing" referred to in the title. Sometimes they do so obliquely, as in the general disorder that attends all the attempts at pairing off in the first four acts of *A Midsummer Night's Dream* and in young Hermia's prissy refusal to lie beside Lysander: "Lie further off, in humane modesty; / Such separation as may well be said / Becomes a virtuous bachelor and a maid" (II.ii.57-59). And sometimes the anticipation of this insight into the nature of human love becomes almost explicit, as in the Princess's refusal at the end of *Love's Labor's Lost* to make a hasty marriage, and her requirement, seconded by her attendant ladies, that the four suitors learn self-denial in one way or another before embarking upon the "world-without-end" process that is marriage. Indeed, none of the early comedies is wholly without a hint of what is to come, both in the middle comedies and in those later plays that some critics persist in calling romances.

Even in the shadowy form of *Pericles* we can detect a marriage that is "proved," first by the siring of a child and then by a life of mutual dedication which is rewarded when the child, grown to maturity, can return to reconstitute and, more accurately, complete the marriage that—however well intentioned—began in passion and ignorance. The same is true of *The Winter's Tale*, in which a presumably established union founders because the male partner, though the father of one child and shortly to become the father of another, has never really comprehended the meaning of marriage. His recovery (acceptance) of the child he tried to kill signifies his triumph over self and his readiness to complete the marriage that was interrupted years before. *Cymbeline* shows another marriage that is not yet a real marriage, rocked by distrust on both sides and achieved fully at the end only because both partners have surrendered their claims and their identities and moved together in a spirit of forgiveness.[12] Finally, *The Tempest*, soon to be discussed at length, returns almost to the traditional formula of New Comedy to deal with the enlightenment of the *senex*, Prospero, who fears to let his daughter go, seeks to protect her virgin-knot, almost diverts his chosen son-in-law from his proper pursuit as a suitor, and in his preoccupation with matters not properly his concern almost fails to protect himself from a murderous assault by three fools.[13] He comes to his senses at the end with a recognition that young people must be trusted to find their own way to marriage, orthodox or not, if the world is to continue in perpetual renewal as a living comedy. This, however, is only one of the insights to be stressed in Shakespeare's last comedies, which reach out beyond the pair or pairs of lovers and beyond the community to apply the action of comedy to a universe that, unlike Dante's, was well on its way to becoming once more totally secular.

14

Cymbeline and *The Winter's Tale*

Chronological lists of Shakespeare's plays frequently show four plays after 1607 as comedies: *Pericles, Cymbeline, The Winter's Tale,* and *The Tempest.* Of these, *Pericles* did not appear in the First Folio, and *Cymbeline* was listed there among the tragedies. *The Winter's Tale* and *The Tempest,* however, were included among the comedies. Modern editors sometimes call all four plays "romances," and the popular new *Riverside Shakespeare* so classifies them. Strictly speaking, of course, only *Pericles,* a dramatization of two versions of the tale of Apollonius of Tyre, which was derived ultimately from a Greek novel or romance, qualifies for that designation; but *Pericles* does display characteristics that are prominent in the three plays following and, as the editors of an older *Riverside* wrote in their introduction to that play, "seems to foretell the new directions in which [Shakespeare] was soon unmistakably to move."[1] Carol Gesner, who has made the most extensive study of the matter, seems to be in full agreement and goes so far in her book as to call all four of the last comedies, "Shakespeare's Greek Romances."[2] One could hardly object to the application of that epithet, provided all users could or would emulate Gesner's precision; but unfortunately, for the general reader and even for some Shakespeare scholars the term "romance" still carries lingering connotations of escapist literature. With the exception of *Pericles,* however, all these plays also meet fully the criteria of comedy set forth at the beginning of this study, and they function as comedy—though admittedly with a solemnity of tone uncharacteristic of Shakespeare's earlier comedies, including the comedies of the so-called "dark period." Thus, this chapter and the one following will omit any consideration of *Pericles* and will focus on the final three plays, which seem to have been written almost together, in the space of two years (1610-11), with no other plays of any kind intervening.

In view of their solemnity, however, and the suggestions of Greek romance throughout, it is not surprising that some recent critics have seized upon the label "tragicomedy" for these plays, noting among other things the approximate coincidence of *Pericles* with John Fletcher's *Faithful Shepherdess* and *Cymbeline* with Beaumont and Fletcher's *Philaster*, the intricacy of the plotting (most notably in *Cymbeline*), the unpredictability of the characters (for example, Posthumus and Leontes), and the pervasive atmosphere of evil.[3] Nevertheless, there are important differences. Tragicomedy after the manner of Beaumont and Fletcher and their successors is marked by lively touches of passion, "set pieces" included ostensibly for the primary purpose of eliciting audience response, a characteristically complicated denouement in which there is frequently a sudden veering towards tragedy, a subsequent avoidance of total calamity (though some of the characters may sustain injuries), and a touch of pathos at the end. Moreover, tragicomedy, at least that of Beaumont and Fletcher, is noteworthy for its natural syntax and an absence of inversions and unusual phraseology.[4] By contrast, Shakespeare's last plays have no touches of passion or pieces sufficiently distinctive to mark them as different from his earlier comedies; with the possible exception of *Pericles*, which is indisputably a romance, there are no tricky denouements of the Beaumont and Fletcher kind; and the language, at least in *Cymbeline* and *The Winter's Tale*, continues to exhibit the knotty constructions and sometimes tortuous logic of *All's Well That Ends Well* and *Measure for Measure*. In short, as was noted in the first chapter of this study, the term "tragicomedy," inviting as it does an association with plays that are radically different in conception and degree of seriousness, obscures more about these plays than it reveals. Admittedly, all four of the last plays present a mixture of what we sometimes call tragic and comic effects; but if such a mixture is the criterion for applying the designation "tragicomedy," we should have to include among the tragicomedies *The Comedy of Errors, The Merchant of Venice, Love's Labor's Lost, Much Ado about Nothing,* and *Twelfth Night,* to say nothing of *All's Well That Ends Well* and *Measure for Measure.*[5] In fact, *Pericles,* with its exotic setting and its unorthodox mixture of appeals to our sensibilities, more nearly than any of Shakespeare's other plays merits exclusive classification as tragicomedy.

This chapter and the one following will be devoted to the final three plays, which are first of all comedies, regardless of whatever else they may have been called, and which represent a final stage in the evolution of Shakespearean comedy. Attention in this chapter will be concentrated on two things which the three plays have in common: first, the familiar pattern of romantic comedy, with its conflict between lovers and elders and a resolution that involves the renewal of society; and second, the presence in each of a very different kind of context, which invites the viewer or reader to see the central action as participating by analogy in a much larger movement of international, or more properly intercultural, significance.

The comic action of *Cymbeline* is spread over the entire play. Shakespeare adapted it from the Ninth Story of the Second Day of Boccaccio's *Decameron,* adding touches from the anonymous *The Rare Triumphs of Love and Fortune,* published in 1589, and, to localize and extend the context, from Holinshed's *Chronicles.*[6] The action develops from two situations. The first is a modified version of the situation of romantic comedy generally: an elderly parent opposes the marriage of two young people, who with the aid of a resourceful servant and other supporters nevertheless manage to remain married. In *Cymbeline,* this situation has been exploited fully by the time the first act begins. The young woman, Imogen, is a princess, sole heir to the kingdom; and because her young man, Posthumus, though respectable, is not of royal blood, the king,

Cymbeline, has taken decisive steps to dissolve the marriage. Thus from the beginning the problem for the protagonists is one of confirming and restoring to recognized status a union surreptitiously but legitimately made. Here the *Decameron* story provides a second situation that occupies our attention for the rest of the play, or almost the whole of five acts: the testing of the estranged couple's resolve to maintain their marriage. The import of this part of the action is that the marriage of Posthumus and Imogen, for all its legitimacy, is not really made, "body and soul," until the closing scene.

By the testimony of unchallengeable witnesses introduced in the first moments of the play, both young people are models of grace and decorum, and their love is thought to be without flaw. Both, however, are as naive as they are well intentioned. Sentenced by Cymbeline to banishment, Posthumus pridefully glories in the steadfastness of their attachment; yet no sooner has he arrived in Italy than he allows himself to be drawn into a foolish wager and subsequently is roundly deceived. Imogen, equally untutored in the ways of the world, on learning of her husband's defection, can only surmise that he has been misled by some Roman courtesan (III.iv.122). Thus are the two perfect lovers estranged, for causes that a modicum of sophistication might have rendered ineffectual; and before a reconciliation takes place, they have each surrendered their identity, which includes for Posthumus his nationality; they have each dealt with the presumed fact of their spouse's death; and they have each, in different fashion, come to terms with the inevitability of their own. Moreover, Posthumus, presumably the mirror of gentlemanly composure, is to be disconcerted so completely by the trial he undergoes that he almost delivers a fatal blow to an innocent page, who is actually Imogen in disguise. By this gesture he is both reunited with his wife and and given a sobering indication of the capacity for rash action that throughout the play has lurked beneath the surface of his disciplined masculinity. Imogen, we note, was probably ready for marriage at the beginning of the play, but only here, minutes from the ending, is Posthumus fully ready to assume the role of husband.

In sharp contrast to *Cymbeline*, *The Winter's Tale* has a comic action that seems to be subsidiary to its main action, which is a near domestic tragedy that envelops the comedy like a matrix. Even so, the traditional pattern of comedy could hardly have a neater exemplar than the one that fills the last two acts (actually slightly more than the last half) of this remarkable play. Sixteen years have elapsed since the end of Act III, and we find a wealthy shepherd of the kingdom of Bohemia making preparations for a sheep-shearing festival in which a young woman who is presumably his daughter will officiate as queen of the feast. Actually, as we know, this young woman is the lost Perdita, Princess of Sicilia; and we consider it altogether appropriate, therefore, that the king's son Florizel should come courting, followed closely by his father in disguise, the *senex* of the piece, who at first seems to approve. In the course of the festivities the King, Polixenes, learns that his son is unwilling to risk telling him of the secret attachment; consequently, in a fit of pique he reveals his identity and forbids the marriage. The young couple are thus left with no choice but to elope. With the help of a faithful friend, who happens to be a refugee from Sicilia and has a "woman's longing" to return there (IV.iv.667), they flee unwittingly to the young woman's true home, where, once their identities have been discovered, they become the means of resolving an impasse that has frustrated that kingdom for the intervening sixteen years. In the end, boy and girl are united, the elders reconciled, and, but for two dead who may not be recovered, all is prosperity and happiness.

The action of *The Tempest*, which will be dealt with at length in the next chapter, is ostensibly that of romantic comedy from beginning to end, with one significant difference. Here the *senex* stands at the focus of the action, actually manipulates the meeting of the lovers, and seeks to direct their affair to its conclusion, which he, the lovers themselves, and we the audience all see as a desirable one. The conflict that gives the play its interest, therefore, is necessarily quite different from the kind we expect to see in romantic comedy. The *senex* gives only token opposition, and the lovers develop no differences that seriously threaten to keep them apart. Instead, the conflict in

The Tempest is essentially that of tragedy—namely, it is an internal conflict in the *senex* himself, who must deal with a crisis in his own psyche while the love affair between the two young people moves forward smoothly and effectively on its own momentum without parental help or hindrance.

The radically different thing about these last comedies, however, is that all three seriously and specifically call our attention to an analogous and much wider context for the action that exhibits its own conflict and resolution as the play proceeds. They make no pretense at giving us something with the universal applicability of a divine comedy, but they do give us comedy that was fraught with clear implications for Shakespeare's audiences more than three hundred years ago and is only slightly less relevant for audiences and readers today. Thus it is a kind of comedy which, as has been suggested earlier, might with justice be called international or intercultural.

The first two plays present their wider conflict as opposing forces which can be reflected in the polarities that at first work to separate boy and girl and eventually work to reunite them. *Cymbeline* introduces its larger conflict about midway through the play as the Roman Caius Lucius appears before King Cymbeline to demand a resumption of the annual tribute of three thousand pounds "by thee, lately . . . left untender'd" (III.i.9-10). Unknown to the King, his banished son-in-law, Posthumus, in exile in Italy, has unwisely entered upon a wager that has prompted the Roman Jachimo to make an assault upon Imogen, still Posthumus's wife and Britain's heir apparent. Thus the opposition between Britain and her continental allly is even sharper than it appears to be on the surface. Moreover, that opposition intensifies as Cymbeline's new Queen and her son, Cloten, undertake to insult the ambassador and between them, Cymbeline being unwisely deferential to their sensibilities, precipitate a war between Britain and Rome. This conflict provides the formula for the second half of the action, which eventually brings Posthumus and Imogen together again, removes the King's objections to their marriage, and effects a comic resolution to the whole affair.

Linking the two conflicts in *Cymbeline,* it should be noted, is Shakespeare's doing; for according to Holinshed, Guiderius, not Cymbeline, was the king responsible for Britain's break with Rome.[7] Holinshed also reports, however, that "the Saviour of the world our Lord Jesus Christ the onlie sonne of God was borne of a virgine, about the 23 yeare of the reigne of this Kymbeline";[8] and Northrop Frye, equating that event with a return of the "green world" or golden age which he finds to be a concomitant of much of Shakespearean comedy, suggests that here Shakespeare has allowed that world to triumph over the iron one represented by the historical conflict between the two nations, thus providing "the halcyon peace with which the play concludes."[9] If so, the triumph must have been one that Shakespeare enjoyed privately, for the birth of Christ takes place beyond the awareness of any of the characters in the play, and the play contains no reference to it, oblique or otherwise. Some form of providence, however, is certainly implied in the resolution of all the conflicts and difficulties. Jupiter intervenes in a dream in Act V to set Posthumus on a happier course than he has been able to chart for himself, leaving as a token a very tangible tablet or book; and the soothsayer, in the next to last speech in the play, declares, "The fingers of the pow'rs above do tune / The harmony of his peace" (V.v.466-67). In any case, the reconciliation of husband and wife here has been achieved at least partly as a consequence of a breach of faith in the Western world, which has been healed after a bloody war with an extraordinary concession by a grateful victor, Britain, to pay "wonted tribute" to an adversary favored by the gods. Needless to say, this reconciliation with Roman Europe of a magnanimous Britain advanced to national maturity is wholly Shakespeare's invention, though an engaging one, and it dominates the ending. G. Wilson Knight understandably thought it proper to regard *Cymbeline* "mainly as an historical play,"[10] supporting thereby the emphasis in King Cymbeline's concluding lines:

> Laud we the gods,
> And let our crooked smokes climb to their nostrils
> From our blest altars. Publish as this peace
> To all our subjects. Set we forward. Let

A Roman and a British ensign wave
Friendly together. So through Lud's-Town march,
And in the temple of great Jupiter
Our peace we'll ratify; seal it with feasts.
Set on there! Never was a war did cease
(Ere bloody hands were wash'd) with such a peace.
[V.v.476-85]

The wider context suggested by the action of *The Winter's Tale* is covertly hinted at throughout the play, but it does not come clearly into view until Act IV, in the pastoral comedy that replaces and ultimately transforms the dismal domestic tragedy of the first three acts. In that comedy, as I argued elsewhere some years ago, the pattern of comic action becomes identifiable with the great divorce between Christendom and the world of Judaism; and by virtue of that pattern, the rest of the play invites us to look forward to an eventual reconciliation of the two worlds in charity and forgiveness.[11] My explanation offended some and irritated others, several of whom balked at the term "allegory," which I had used, perhaps unwisely, in the sense that Dante gave it rather than in the limited modern sense of a correspondence between sign and value.[12] A somewhat better term than "allegory," though perhaps equally risky, is "analogy," a term which Francis Fergusson borrowed from Thomist realism to illustrate the idea of action in his dramatic criticism.[13] St. Thomas Aquinas had used it to explain the relationship between Creator and creation, and Dante, following Aquinas, extended the application to a literary fable. Earlier Christian writers had made similar use of a more Platonic realism in the typological interpretation of ancient texts, especially those texts included in the Old Testament; and St. Augustine in *The City of God* had neatly summed up the whole matter for predecessors and successors alike in a single memorable sentence, "The world like a field is filled with the odour of Christ's name," the incarnate Christ being in his view (as in the view of most Catholic writers) the visible and tangible manifestation of an ineffable reality, God the Father.[14]

The relationship between the comic action of Shakespeare's

Winter's Tale (undeniably a piece of imaginative fiction) and the larger action involving both the hostility between the ancient cultures of Judaism and Christianity and the Christian expectation of a reconciliation between those cultures is a relationship that would have been recognized more readily by Shakespeare's audiences than it is by modern audiences; but it is nevertheless there and a part of the total meaning of the play. The connection hinges on an exchange that takes place in Act IV between Polixenes, the King of Bohemia, come in disguise to spy upon his son's surreptitious courting, and the maid Perdita, queen of the sheep-shearing feast. Perdita has been explaining to the older man that her garden contains no gilly-flowers or pinks, hybrids which she thinks of as "Nature's bastards": "For I have heard it said, / There is an art which in their piedness shares / With great creating Nature" (IV.iv. 86-88). Apparently she has at some time heard, and deplored, Shylock's argument (or its equivalent) in support of usury—that the patriarch Jacob with impunity practiced a similar form of creativity in producing a new breed of sheep *(The Merchant of Venice,* I.iii.71-90). What she has not heard—or at least not accepted—is Antonio's response to Shylock: "This was a venture, sir, that Jacob serv'd for. / A thing not in his power to bring to pass, / But sway'd and fashion'd by the hand of heaven" (I.iii.91-93).

This is essentially the argument of the man who will be her father-in-law—with nature, of course, substituted for heaven as agent:

> . . . Nature is made better by no mean
> But nature makes that mean; so over that art
> Which you say adds to Nature, is an art
> That Nature makes.
>
> [IV.iv.89-92]

Then Polixenes adds, for Perdita's special benefit though she does not understand, an application of his argument that will support her marriage to his son as prince of the realm:

> You see, sweet maid, we marry
> A gentler scion to the wildest stock,

> And make conceive a bark of baser kind
> By bud of nobler race. This is an art
> Which does mend Nature—change it rather; but
> The art itself is Nature.
>
> [V,iv.92-97]

In Polixenes' mind, of course, Perdita is the "bark of baser kind" destined to be made to conceive by the "bud of nobler race," his son Florizel; but unknown to him Perdita is a princess of Sicilia, and from that kingdom's point of view, which the action of the play subsequently validates, the "wildest stock" corresponds to the royal house of Bohemia and the "gentler scion" to Perdita. The point to be noted here is that Polixenes' metaphor, as any knowledgeable auditor, Catholic or Protestant, alert to the inevitable outcome of a comic action would have interpreted it, makes a happy parallel with the metaphor that the apostle Paul used in the eleventh chapter of Romans, that of grafting a wild olive tree to a good one. Paul's metaphor, moreover, is one that would have been familiar to most seventeenth-century English Christians, living as they did in an intellectual climate increasingly permeated by millenial expectations. Shakespeare was certainly familiar with it; and in that parallel Perdita and her mother Hermione stand for the good tree, Leontes for the branch broken off, and Florizel for the wild olive destined to be grafted to a new and richer life.

Paul had been exhorting the Romans to remember that his Gospel was for everybody, including the Jews, and that eventually Jew and Gentile should be one again. The relevant passage (Romans xi.13-26) in the popular Geneva version of the Bible runs as follows:

For in that I speake to you Gentiles, inasmuche as I am the Apostle of the Gentiles, I magnifie mine office, to try if by any meanes I might provoke them of my flesh to followe them, and might save some of them. For if the casting away of them be the reconciling of the worlde, what shal the receiving be, but life from the dead? . . . And thogh some of the branches be broken of, and thou [the Romans] being a wilde olive tre, wast graft in for them, and made partaker of the roote, and fatnesse of the olive tre, Boast not thy self against the branches: and if thou boast thy self, thou bearest not the roote, but the roote thee. Thou wilt say then, The branches are broken of, that I might be grafte in. Wel: through unbelefe they are broken of, and thou standest by faith: be not hie minded, but feare. . . . For if God spared not the natural branches [the Jews], take hede, lest he also spare not thee. . . . And thei also, if thei abide not stil in unbelefe, shalbe graffed in: for God is able to graffe them in againe. For if thou wast cut out of the olive tre, which was wild by nature, and wast graffed contrary to nature in a right olive tre, how muche more shal they that are by nature, be graffed in their owne olive tre? For I wolde not, brethren, that ye shulde be ignorant of this secret (lest ye shulde be arrogant in your selves) that partely obstinacie is come to Israel, until the fulnes of the Gentiles be come in. And so all Israel shalbe saved.

A sceptic may ask whether Shakespeare intended such a parallel; but whatever the answer, one cannot escape the fact that Shakespeare himself contrived it. Robert Greene's *Pandosto*, the principal source for this play, has nothing like it. (Indeed, *Pandosto* moves in an entirely different direction from *The Winter's Tale* and ends in despair and suicide.) Moreover, it should be noted that Shakespeare changed the name "Pandosto" to "Leontes," a name long suggestive of Judah and hence Israel (Genesis 49.9), and created a stern adviser with the even more suggestive name of Paulina to guide his King Leontes to a general restoration. These things can hardly have failed to prompt in at least some millennium-minded Jacobeans thoughts of a larger transcendence than the one depicted in a semi-imaginary kingdom. At any rate, the invitation to see an extension of the action of comedy in *The Winter's Tale* as intimating an ultimate reunion of East and West is there and is no less marked than was a similar invitation in *Cymbeline*, with its explicit and studiously contrived interpolation of a reconciliation between Britain and Rome.

The extended context of *The Tempest* involves the meeting of the Old World (Europe) and the New (America). An implicit suggestion to this effect probably undergirds every attempt to see Prospero's island as Bermuda; but there is more to it than that, as I hope will be clear in the following chapter, which deals exclusively with *The Tempest*. To anticipate briefly, before the play begins there has been an abortive attempt by a New World savage (Caliban) to mate with a European heiress.

The father of the heiress, Prospero, has frustrated this attempt and proceeded with plans to provide a more appropriate spouse for his daughter. In the end he has had the satisfaction of seeing her return to Italy with the young man of her choice (and his own). The play, however, has not skirted the fact that Prospero came uninvited to the island and that whether he likes it or not he has incurred some responsibility for the hopes and aspirations inadvertently raised thereby in the native inhabitant. An important part of the resolution of the play, therefore, is Prospero's belated recognition of the "burden" he has incurred. If this seems distasteful to some as smacking of the attitudes of imperialism, so be it. The notion of civilization's responsibility stems from a polarity represented in the play, and it was a matter that had begun to be of concern to Shakespeare's contemporaries. Shakespeare at least confronts the issue. He should not be held altogether accountable for what subsequent generations have made of it.

In this play, as in the two preceding ones, Shakespeare took comedy not out of the world (as the term "romance" sometimes implies) but into it, with a vigor and an imaginative daring unequaled by any other playwright of his time or since. He was not a prophet, nor did he necessarily assume the stance of one. As a dramatic poet his function was only to explore potentials. Britain's international supremacy has come and gone since Shakespeare's time; Rome has long since ceased to be a power. Christianity and Judaism are not reconciled, and some Europeans still think of non-Europeans as retarded children. The glory of these three plays is that they present the dream of comedy and through that dream a series of dreams of harmony discoverable in specific situations in the world that Shakespeare knew, which is also the world we know. That glory can be ours to enjoy, provided we are willing to share Shakespeare's dreams. Otherwise these plays, the apotheosis of his comic art, like any other masterworks we may presume to trivialize with reductive categories, may become our judges.

15

The Tempest

Until the beginning of this century much of the criticism of *The Tempest* focused on the character of Prospero, a surrogate for Shakespeare, it was alleged, who at the end of the play abandoned book and pen and made his farewell to the world. Other important matters thus tended to remain in a hazy limbo of fantasy, and even today there is no clear consensus about some of them. Several of these neglected matters are of sufficient importance to this study to warrant preliminary consideration. One of these is the geographical situation of the island, a subject about which there is still considerable disagreement. Another is the significance of the shape of classical comedy still clearly discernible behind the exotic veil that Shakespeare has cast over it. Still another is what might be called the ontology of the play: the role of magic in it, the supernatural beings, and the physical nature of the island itself.

If it is mistaken to insist absolutely that the locus of *The Tempest* is an island in or near the waters of the New World, it is equally mistaken to insist that Prospero's island is in the Mediterranean, somewhere between Tunis and Naples. Even a critic like Northrop Frye, who feels that *The Tempest* "really has nothing to do with the New World," acknowledges that the play borrows numerous details from popular accounts of expeditions to Virginia and of Sir Thomas Gates' shipwreck on Bermuda in 1609.[1] This seems to be the view of Hallett Smith,[2] and of Frank Kermode, who, while observing that Shakespeare "is at pains to establish his island in the Old World," nevertheless adds that "the relations of the play to the literature of voyaging remain of the greatest interest and usefulness."[3] Geoffrey Bullough has printed all the relevant portions of this material from the voyagers,[4] and D.G. James in his book on the play has made a lively chapter of it.[5] In brief, the details are there in the play; they suggest an Atlantic island rather than any island that we know of in the Mediterranean. Moreover, Ariel says that he has hid the King's ship with its sleeping crew in a narrow harbor of what he calls the "still vex'd Ber-moothes" (I.ii.229), which could hardly be taken to mean that he has removed them halfway across the Atlantic. Still, Pros-pero's whole world abounds in mysteries, and all we can be absolutely certain of is that with his child Miranda he reached the island under some kind of providential protection (I.ii.62-63;158-59)—near-miraculous protection, considering the improvised vessel in which the two were cast away—and that his passage was at least as extraordinary as that of King Alonso's party twelve years later, and quite as unmappable. Whatever the island is, it proclaims itself characteristic of the New World and specifically of the Bermudas, "otherwise called the Ile of Divels,"[6] and it invites comparison with the island on which Sir Thomas Gates was shipwrecked in 1609.

Another clue to an Atlantic setting is Gonzalo's description in Act II of the utopia he would establish, taken almost ver-batim from John Florio's translation of Montaigne's essay on the New World and its presumably savage inhabitants. Cal-iban, whose name is an anagram for Montaigne's (or Florio's) *cannibal,* is not an American Indian in our sense of the term (though in Shakespeare's day and for many years thereafter Indians were often supposed to have come to the New World from some part of the Old), but he has a native's rights, and his presence there is certainly more appropriate for a place called "the Ile of Divels" than is Prospero's. This gives us one more reason to believe that the island is meant to have an Atlantic setting, and thus even more reason to entertain the view that Shakespeare in his later years felt an impulse to project his comic action on something like a universal stage: first, on a theater of conflict between England and the rest of Christendom, then on one between the Christian world and the Judaic Orient, and finally on the meeting of Christendom and that brave new world of untamed and untrammeled wilderness inhabited by "salvages" of uncertain origin and disposition. In any case, among the bewildering array of human values that *The Tempest* implicitly addresses are those that emerge to be examined and perhaps challenged whenever disparate groups of the human family confront one another in repeated or protracted encounters.

The values that emerge from the imposition of a classical pattern for comedy are also conspicuous in *The Tempest*. It is a commonplace that Roman comedy assumed a society of slaves and masters and that the Renaissance dramatist thus found it necessary to translate the Roman contrast of social conditions into a contrast of hierarchical social categories. However, in a valuable essay Bernard Knox points out that in *The Tempest* Shakespeare did not need to translate the Roman form but could and did use it literally.[7] Prospero, for all his Renaissance garments, is both a classical *senex* (an irritable old man with a marriageable daughter) and a master of real slaves (Ariel and Caliban). Moreover, Airel and Caliban are recognizable versions of the two kinds of slave one finds in Plautus: respectively, the intelligent slave, who helps to solve his master's problem and subsequently gains his freedom, and the bad-tempered slave, who curses, gets drunk, and behaves indecently. "*The Tempest* is as original as *The Comedy of Errors* is imitative," Knox writes, "and yet they are the beginning and end of the same road."[8] The difference is that in *The Comedy of Errors* Shakespeare was able for the most part to leave both the characters and their context intact. Here in *The Tempest* he moves the ancient machinery to a new and presumably primitive world where the conventions are exposed in their naked inhumanity, and thus he tentatively raises the question of what sophisticated Europe should do about unexploited savages in the newly discovered paradise to the west. As readers have done with Shylock and Malvolio, at least in the not too distant past, we may try to compel these extraordinary characters to behave like stereotypes and belie their relevance; but *The*

Tempest, honestly and fully faced, will not let us off so easily. It compels us once more to acknowledge the validity of the truism that we incur an obligation whenever we touch the life of another whom for the moment we have presumed to regard as inferior.

Still another aspect of *The Tempest* needs to be kept in mind throughout any reading that aims at comprehensiveness. Knox, in leading into his discussion of Shakespeare's use of classical formulas calls to mind a production by the Yale Dramatic Association in which *The Tempest* was treated as science fiction. "The point was well taken," Knox writes; "Shakespeare has in fact done what the modern science-fictioneers do—substituted for the normal laws of the operation of matter a new set of laws invented for the occasion."[9] Had it been germane to his purpose, Knox might have noted that the set of laws in *The Tempest* was not that of the emerging empirical science that we with our hindsight identify as the significant development of the seventeenth century, but something which was intellectually more interesting at that time— namely, a reinterpretation in Neoplatonic terms of the established system of order. The details of that reinterpretation were set forth ably by W.C. Curry nearly half a century ago in his *Shakespeare's Philosophical Patterns.*[10] They are fascinating in their own right, and they clarify a number of things about the play; but the importance of Shakespeare's recourse to the Neoplatonic system is that he thereby established Prospero in the role of benevolent magician and ostensibly gave him something approaching unlimited power. Thus what we have in Shakespeare's late adaptation of Roman comedy is a *senex* with special advantages that no Plautine *senex* ever dreamed of. Prospero can order the production of eclipses, storms like the one at the beginning of the play, and, according to his boast, even the resurrection of the dead. In short, he is a *senex* who is fully prepared to have his will with the destiny of a marriageable daughter, and have it he does. Thus, in sharp contrast to Roman comedy, *The Tempest* exhibits a special kind of *senex* who stands at the center of his play and commands our interest before all else.

This mixture of accounts by contemporary voyagers, conventions of classical comedy, and Jacobean science fiction is unique in the Shakespeare canon and unique in the annals of English drama. Nevertheless, two of the constituent elements—the formal pattern of classical comedy and the equally formal system of Neoplatonic sacerdotal science—combine to make an almost explicit affirmation of the hierarchical principle that for two thousand years had served to define both the structure of human society and the structure of the physical universe which society reflected. Moreover, the impression of classical orderliness which these elements give to the play is further enhanced as we note that the action proceeds to its conclusion within formal comedy's prescribed one revolution of the sun; except for the opening scene aboard the ship and the time that must be allowed subsequently for getting people from ship to shore, the play behaves like hundreds of other well-ordered plays from Menander to Molière, covering less than four hours from the beginning of Prospero's conversation with Miranda in Act I, scene ii, to the end of the final scene at Prospero's cell. In spite of appearances, order prevails in *The Tempest*. The ancient principle of hierarchy persists—master and slave, king and subject, higher powers and lower—here in this wilderness just as it did in civilized Italy; and once we perceive this much, we realize that we are still operating in the world of Plato, Aristotle, and Aquinas, under the protection of rules that apparently retain their force regardless of the remoteness of the setting or the savagery of its inhabitants.

Furthermore, the rules for Prospero's island include a supernatural realm which might have been normal in a work by someone like Spenser but which is visible and operative in a way that is unusual for a play by Shakespeare. Of course, some of his earlier comedies give us suggestions of such a realm. In the midst of *The Comedy of Errors*, for example, where for the most part the action proceeds with all the dogged formality of an indifferent mechanical clock, a bewildered Antipholus of Syracuse suddenly invites us to consider the possibility that spirits and witchcraft have invaded the material world; but there, of course, we know better. In *A Midsummer Night's*

Dream, the supernatural world is real enough, but it intersects only occasionally with the world of human beings, after the magical night all the human beings doubt that such things have really happened. A comparable intersection takes place with the invasion of ghosts and a god in Act V of *Cymbeline;* but this, in spite of the palpable tablet left with Posthumus, has no practical effect on the outcome of the plot.

In *The Tempest*, by contrast, the visible universe is patently controlled by a hierarchy of powers, to which Prospero—like his predecessor, Sycorax—has limited access. It is customary to say that Prospero is far superior in every respect to Sycorax; and Caliban would seem to support this view, for in one aside he mutters: "I must obey. His art is of such pow'r, / It would control my dam's god, Setebos, / And make a vassal of him" (I.ii.372-74). Caliban, however, was scarcely more than a whelp when his mother died, and Prospero's is the only power he has known—and felt—during all his years of percipience. It is possible to believe that Prospero, regardless of his moral superiority to the "blue-ey'd hag," is not appreciably more powerful than she was. Apparently Sycorax too had found the spirit Ariel useful, but when angered by his refusal to obey her, she could summon superior powers to imprison him in a pine tree. Prospero on occasion could threaten to do the same (I.ii.294-96), but he freed the spirit from his pine-tree prison and thus earned his gratitude. Since then, presumably by virtue of moral superiority, he has commanded, rebuked, and sometimes threatened his spirit slave (to use a phrase reflective of service-weary Ariel's view of the situation), all the while taking pains to issue only orders that the slave can and will obey; for it is clear that Prospero would be hard put to do without him. Throughout the play Ariel is presented as essential to Prospero's effectiveness, a fact that is crucial to any comprehensive interpretation. The master, for all his learning, is mortal and human and, as we shall see, fallible.

The island itself, moreover, regardless of where we place it or what we call it, is a normal island; it has nothing distinctively magical about it. Producers have often erred here, making their setting for *The Tempest* resemble whatever conception of fairyland happened to be current and fashionable at the time; but all the miraculous things that happen on Prospero's island happen because of spirits who presumably could operate just as effectively anywhere else. Caliban may "sometimes hear a thousand twangling instruments . . . and sometime voices" (III.ii.137-38), but this is either because of spirits Prospero has commanded or perhaps because of a strain of innocence (a primitivistic view one occasionally encounters in criticism) not yet entirely obscured in him. Either way, whatever Caliban hears on this island he could just as plausibly have heard anywhere else on the globe, given appropriate circumstances. In short, the place is best thought of naturalistically and best represented in that way, as far as theatrical resources will permit. Gonzalo and Adrian see it as a pleasant island, green and inviting, a place where one might conceivably want to live and set up a miniature commonwealth. So do Stephano and Trinculo, once the threat of thunderstorm has passed. Caliban apparently likes the place and would live nowhere else, and clearly Prospero and Miranda have not fared badly there. It is, if one may be allowed to make reasonable deductions, a wind-kissed island, in a temperate climate, set in the midst of a normally hospitable sea—a place that critics, scholars, and general readers alike have continued, understandably, to think of as Bermuda. To this haven the witch Sycorax came and on it gave birth to her child, who was there, an orphan, to greet and, as far as he could, help Prospero when the right Duke of Milan arrived with the habits and ignorance of an advanced civilization still upon him.

Caliban has been variously interpreted by critics, but he is obviously low on the scale of human and near human creatures. Mark Van Doren has given an interesting summary of his characteristics: beastliness, an incapacity for human virtue but a capacity for responding to beauty, and a knowledge of physical nature (he knows all the berries, springs, and rocks of the island and has taught them to Prospero).[11] Van Doren describes him, moreover, as possessing "a mind bemired in fact, an imagination beslimed with particulars," a creature without any "capacity for abstraction."[12] Leaving out the pejorative implications of "bemired" and "beslimed," all this is probably true; but none of it marks Caliban as being bad so much as it marks him as being different. The bastard son of a witch and some kind of demon (Curry speculates that the father was an aquatic demon),[13] Caliban stands just outside the normal human hierarchy. He becomes evil only when somebody like Prospero tries to make a regular human being out of him; and as the play opens, that process has already produced its predictable effect. Prospero wakes Miranda from a nap—one enforced by him, it would appear—with the suggestion that they visit "Caliban my slave, who never / Yields us kind answer" (I.ii.307-9). Miranda responds that the creature is a "villain" she does not "love to look on"; but Prospero reminds her that "they cannot miss him" (that is, they cannot do without him): "He does make our fire, / Fetch in our wood, and serves in offices / That profit us" / (I.ii.311-13). In the encounter immediately following, the substance of what has gone on in the preceding twelve years comes out in the space of a few lines: Prospero's initial acts of benevolence, Caliban's response with his invaluable services as a guide, and then the unfortunate attempt to play at sex with Miranda, which resulted in his being confined to a solitary rock unless needed for gathering fuel or doing other acts of menial labor.

Admittedly, Caliban is not blameless. His assault on Miranda, regardless of what form it may have taken, could not be tolerated; but he is also not without right on his side, and Prospero must answer for instituting strictly punitive measures as a permanent order of their relationship. Miranda's gratuitous rebuke of Caliban at this point is simply unconscionable:

> Abhorred slave,
> Which any print of goodness will not take,
> Being capable of all ill! I pitied thee,
> Took pains to make thee speak, taught thee each hour
> One thing or other. When thou didst not, savage,
> Know thine own meaning, but wouldst gabble like
> A thing most brutish, I endow'd thy purposes
> With words that made them known. But thy vild race

(Though thou didst learn) had that in't which good natures
Could not abide to be with; therefore wast thou
Deservedly confin'd into this rock,
Who hadst deserv'd more than a prison.

[I.ii.351-62]

The argument (originally Dryden's) that this speech should be
Prospero's has had a long currency precisely because the ideas
in it are Prospero's; but what that argument fails to take into
account is the way children, savage or civilized, learn language. It was Miranda's natural role to be Caliban's tutor as
well as his playmate, and she was far more apt in either of these
offices than Prospero could ever have been. Her subsequent
abhorrence of Caliban, however, is not a natural attitude but
one clearly fostered by her father, who, we suspect, in rational
moments must have seen very well the logic in the monster's
shrewd observation, "I am all the subjects that you have, /
Which first was mine own king" (I.ii.341-42), to say nothing of
the primitive justice lurking behind his observation that, un-
checked, he might have peopled the island with Calibans. The
context of this play is Jacobean England, but the mentality of
its human principals is that of colonizing Englishmen, in
Shakespeare's time and later, who often failed to distinguish
between the arbitrary mores they had inherited from their
predecessors and the inclinations and attitudes that nature
had bequeathed equally to them and the rest of humankind.

Yet it is imperious Prospero and not Caliban who is the focus
of attention in this play; and Prospero's imperial project provides the vehicle for the main threads of the action. That
project has two major objectives. The first is to return to his
dukedom with the succession of Miranda assured by her betrothal to Ferdinand, heir to the throne of Naples (we must
keep in mind that Prospero has no son in a world that still
prefers males as rulers). The second is to seek the repentance of
those who have wronged him—specifically, his brother Antonio; Alonso, the present King of Naples, in time past his
"enemy inveterate"; and Alonso's brother, Sebastian, Antonio's
chief abettor. The point is sometimes made that Prospero begins by seeking the punishment rather than the repentance of

these three but has a change of heart as a consequence of Ariel's prompting in Act V;[14] but this interpretation is at variance with the text, which has Ariel saying in Act III:

> . . . you three
> From Milan did supplant good Prospero,
> Expos'd unto the sea (which hath requit it)
> Him, and his innocent child; for which foul deed
> The pow'rs, delaying (not forgetting), have
> Incens'd the seas and shores—yea, all the creatures,
> Against your peace. Thee of thy son, Alonso,
> They have bereft; and do pronounce by me
> Ling'ring perdition (worse than any death
> Can be at once) shall step by step attend
> You and your ways, whose wraths to guard you from—
> Which here, in this most desolate isle, else falls
> Upon your heads—is nothing but heart's sorrow,
> And a clear life ensuing.
>
> [III.iii.69-82]

Ariel's statement here, which Prospero approves (III.ii:85-86), does not differ materially from Prospero's own, presumably repentant, words in Act V:

> Though with their high wrongs I am strook to th' quick,
> Yet, with my nobler reason, 'gainst my fury
> Do I take part. The rarer action is
> In virtue than in vengeance. They being penitent,
> The sole drift of my purpose doth extend
> Not a frown further. Go, release them, Ariel.
> My charms I'll break, their senses I'll restore,
> And they shall be themselves.
>
> [V.i.25-32]

There is no suggestion here that Prospero has *repented* of seeking vengeance, or, for that matter, has ever sought to avenge. At various times during the past twelve years he has in moments of "fury" nursed thoughts of punishing his oppressors, but clearly he has never moved in that direction, and the noteworthy phrase in his lines is "They being penitent." Nevertheless, in these lines he has also slipped into an admission of his limitation. Ariel has reported that the three culprits are "distracted" (V.i.12), but Prospero has no other evidence or knowledge of what has been going on in their minds. He is simply prepared to assume that they are penitent and drop the whole matter. Thus we are not altogether surprised at the end of the scene to find that only one of these men has had a change of heart and that the other two seem likely to prove incorrigible. This perhaps pardonable failure, however, is not the only blemish in the romantic portrait of Prospero as righteous miracle-worker and surrogate for Shakespeare that, as has been noted, was common in criticism at the turn of the century.

To begin with, Prospero was the architect of his own usurpation. Being, he proudly tells Miranda, "for the liberal arts without a parallel," he had appointed Antonio to take upon himself the responsibilities of government and so blindly created the situation that tempted his temptable brother:

> He being thus lorded,
> Not only with what my revenue yielded,
> But what my power might else exact—like one
> Who having into truth, by telling of it,
> Made such a sinner of his own memory
> To credit his own lie—he did believe
> He was indeed the Duke, out o' th' substitution
> And executing th' outward face of royalty
> With all prerogative.
>
> [I.ii.97-105]

One may well wonder which is the more remarkable here, the arrogance of the administrator turned scholar, or his naiveté in continuing to cherish, and tell, a patently self-serving explanation of his high-minded abdication and the debacle that followed.

The same arrogance shows itself in Prospero's treatment of subordinates. As has already been intimated, his treatment of Caliban is a clear example, for there his inability to perceive and begin to understand what is human in the abortive monster bespeaks an inability to recognize what humanity in general is. He loves Miranda, but he consistently underestimates the girl; and in their first scene together, he treats her with something less than honesty, chiding her for a sleepiness she does not manifest and then cavalierly putting her to sleep when it suits his convenience to have her out of the way.[15] With Ferdinand he is brusque to the point of rudeness; and although he later gives his reasons, we may suspect that he is brusque, or imperious, at least partly out of habit. With Ariel his manner borders on the threatening; and Knox would see traces here, as in Prospero's behavior to all the others, of the irascible *senex*.[16] That explanation probably has some validity; but some of this harsh behavior suggests a deep-seated uneasiness, particularly where Ariel is concerned.

Prospero simply has no excuse for dealing harshly with Ariel. Granted, he freed the spirit from the cloven pine in which Sycorax had left him; but for that act of charity Ariel has served Prospero and served him well for a full twelve years— this in spite of Prospero's acknowledged promise to let him off a year early for good service, as Ariel reminds him:

> Remember I have done thee worthy service,
> Told thee no lies, made thee no mistakings, serv'd
> Without grudge or grumblings. Thou didst promise
> To bate me a full year.
>
> [I.ii.247-50]

It may be argued that the powers above, whatever they are (Prospero's generic term here is "bountiful Fortune"), have decreed that the time for Prospero's triumph must be now, on this day, certainly not later and perhaps not earlier. He tells Miranda:

> Know thus far forth:
> By accident most strange, bountiful Fortune
> (Now my dear lady) hath mine enemies
> Brought to this shore; and by my prescience
> I find my zenith doth depend upon
> A most auspicious star, whose influence
> If now I court not, but omit, my fortune
> Will ever after droop.
>
> [I.ii.177-84]

Furthermore, the time for the betrothal of Miranda, who is scarcely fifteen years old, surely cannot have been much earlier than the immediate present of the play. Nevertheless, the point to keep in mind is that Prospero has come to this island unprepared, magic or no magic, to meet his situation without the daily help of someone like Caliban and without the aid and support of a spirit like Ariel. Now the recurrent restlessness that characterizes his behavior on this crucial day seems to betray a fear that even with Ariel's help he may not meet the deadline imposed by his auspicious star. Early in the afternoon he asks Ariel, come to report completion of the shipwreck, the time of day, and Ariel replies casually that it is "past the mid season," to which Prospero responds, "At least two glasses. The time 'twixt six and now / Must by us both be spent most preciously" (I.ii.240-41). Some lines later, after he has indignantly rejected Ariel's reminder of the unkept promise, he suggests that they may need an additional two days to complete the work in hand (I.ii.298-99); and an hour or so after that, having seen Ferdinand and Miranda pledge their hearts and hands to one another, he returns to his "book" to prepare for "business" that he must perform in the two hours remaining (III.i.92-96), perhaps referring to the masque which he suggests to Ariel that the young people "expect" of him (IV.i.41-42), though we have no evidence that they expect anything of the sort. The urgent need for a masque exhorting the lovers to premarital continence is a consideration that has arisen solely in Prospero's anxious and agitated mind.

His anxiety reaches a climax when he interrupts the masque to race off and frustrate the attempt by Caliban and company upon his life; but when he returns from that unplanned activity, he has all but run out of time. Clothed now in his full magic regalia, he confronts Ariel and engages in the following exchange:

> *Pros.* Now does my project gather to a head:
> My charms crack not; my spirits obey; and Time
> Goes upright with his carriage. How's the day?
>   *Air.* On the sixt hour, at which time, my lord,
> You said our work should cease.
>
> [V.i.1-5]

"I did say so," Prospero replies, "when first I rais'd the tempest"; and then he changes the subject. His embarrassment, if such it is, is understandable. At this point he has really completed nothing. He has succeeded in betrothing Miranda and Ferdinand and has given them a few minutes of counseling, but contrary to all his expressed better judgments he has left them half-instructed and unchaperoned—a point implicitly and charmingly alluded to when, as he suddenly reveals the pair to a distraught Alonso, we hear Miranda's voice, "Sweet lord, you play me false" (V.i.172), and note that they are innocently playing at chess. Prospero with Ariel's help has contrived the circumstances, but the young couple have made their own eyes and advances, have promised without prompting, and have refrained from unsanctioned indulgence when no one was by to prevent them.

Prospero has done little more to the minds and hearts of those villains he would bring to repentance. King Alonso alone has been moved to repentance by the day's events (III.iii.95-102); but Antonio and Sebastian, rendered immobile in their villainy when Ariel froze them in the line-grove guarding Prospero's cell, remain villainous at the end of the play. Throughout the remainder of Act V Prospero continues to make promises to Ariel, but he never fully delivers. At line 87 he says, "Thou shalt ere long be free"; and at line 241 he says as much again; but at the end of the play he is still promising. To Alonso he says: "I'll deliver all, / And promise you calm seas, auspicious gales, / And sail so expeditious, that shall catch / Your royal fleet far off" / (V.i.314-17). Then to his spirit servant he adds: "My Ariel chick, / That is thy charge. Then to the elements / Be free, and fare thou well!" / (V.i.317-19). Thus he commands Ariel to overtake and rejoin the royal fleet in its passage from Tunis to Italy! Apparently Prospero's estimate of two days in addition to the twelve years was not entirely wide of the mark.

Even so, in reacting against sentimental overvaluation of Prospero's power one should not play the critical pendulum. Prospero is a powerful, if limited, magician; and he does command the respect of Ariel and the ministers who work under Ariel's direction. He is also in touch with the higher power—providence, fortune, or whatever one may choose to call it—

that governs his own destiny; and he has been quick to make good use of occasions as that power has presented them—for example, when he took advantage of the expedition to Tunis to bring the whole wedding party to his island. Moreover, he has been able to do things like this, which are quite beyond the power of ordinary mortals and even of a Sycorax, because of his remarkable moral stature. The lesser powers recognize that stature and cooperate so far as his intentions are consistent with the operations that have been delegated to them. As far as we know, Prospero, unlike Sycorax, has never commanded anything that offends their sense of propriety, and hence they have never disobeyed him; but Prospero, like everyone else, is flawed with pride, and in the course of the day's activity his pride almost beings him to disaster—not because it leads him to a crisis but because it blinds him to crises naturally inherent in the events he would bring to pass. Fortunately, the same moral stature that has brought him a measure of success in his magical operations does enable him, on the brink of disaster, to recognize his creaturely limitations.

Predictably, as in any play that proceeds as an exploration of the possibilities inherent in a given situation, we come to see most of these limitations before Prospero himself does. We recognize, for example, that he has not been able to save himself and his child from death (providence and Gonzalo did that) or from banishment. In twelve years he has not been able to return to Milan or to make a gesture toward that end. He has tried but failed to transform Caliban's nonhuman nature, which he therefore sees as purely evil; and before the day is over it becomes clear that he will not succeed in changing the nature of his enemies either, for even Alonso, as has been noted, changes more in response to a belief that his son is dead rather than as a consequence of anything like moral suasion on Prospero's part. Prospero's own recognition of these things is what prompts his renunciation of magical power. Nothing that Ariel says to him in their brief exchange at the beginning of Act V could have prompted such an unexpected change of heart, for Ariel has noted merely that the innocent members of the party, frozen immobile along with the guilty, are deeply distressed.

This simple observation, however, that Adrian, Francisco, and the good old Lord Gonzalo are suffering equally with the guilty, touches Prospero deeply and adds a decisive weight to the burden of awareness that has been growing all day. Thus when Ariel leaves the scene briefly to bring in the six victims, he speaks quietly to himself, as if addressing the elves, demi-puppets, and other "weak ministers" who have participated in his miracles, and concludes with the announcement:

> . . . this rough magic
> I here abjure; and when I have requir'd
> Some heavenly music (which even now I do)
> To work mine end upon their senses that
> This airy charm is for, I'll break my staff,
> Bury it certain fadoms in the earth,
> And deeper than ever did plummet sound
> I'll drown my book.
>
> [V.i.50-57]

But he abjures considerably more than magic.

From the beginning of the play Prospero has been assuming a role that is beyond the capacity of any mortal, even that of a mortal endowed with magical powers, to execute with inpunity. Marriage, as has been noted throughout, is not merely something that gives satisfaction to a marriageable couple; it is the assurance of continuity for a family and for the community of which that family is a part. In an authoritarian system—for example, that of medieval feudalism—the elders ensure continuity in a mechanical fashion simply by mating the proposed continuators arbitrarily, sometimes in their infancy, and hoping that human vitality will emerge in due course and assert itself to make the continuation something more than mechanical. Even in such situations, however, vital continuation can occur only at the cost of something. For life to go on, a sacrifice must occur. The old ones must somehow be expended; a king must die before subjects can shout "Long live the king!" Prospero, in blithe disregard of this principle, has tried to make himself the prime mover of a comic action—not merely to rectify the misdirection caused by a piece of twelve-year-old mischief, but to inaugurate a new course of life for an

Italy united on a Milan-Naples axis, one that will replace the corrupt Alonso, Sebastian, and Antonio with the youthful Ferdinand and Miranda. What Prospero learns in his manipulation of nature at this level is that the operation must mean replacing himself as well; for regardless of his power and his benevolence, Prospero is still Prospero and not God. He becomes, in other words, the equivalent of a tragic figure, none the less poignant for having achieved his knowledge in a context that remains comic (as, by contrast, the context of Lear does not) and for having tasted death before it comes to him.

Prospero's advance to enlightenment is the source of tension that this ambivalent play can, when properly presented, produce in readers and viewers alike. The comic movement of the two lovers toward a betrothal is as natural and easy as the course of true love can ever hope to be; but it is counterpointed here with the tragic movement of Prospero as *senex*, something that is always implicit in comedy but seldom more than faintly visible or felt. The tension abates momentarily as the lovers plight their troth and Prospero watches with satisfaction, privately observing: "So glad of this as they I cannot be; / Who are surpris'd withal; but my rejoicing / At nothing can be more" / (III.i.92-94). The tension resumes, however, almost as soon as he steps forward to bless their union:

> Then, as my gift, and thine own acquisition
> Worthily purchas'd, take my daughter. But
> If thou dost break her virgin-knot before
> All sanctimonious ceremonies may
> With full and holy rite be minist'red,
> No sweet aspersions shall the heavens let fall
> To make this contract grow; but barren hate,
> Sour-ey'd disdain, and discord shall bestrew
> The union of your bed with weeds so loathly
> That you shall hate it both. Therefore take heed,
> As Hymen's lamps shall light you.
>
> [IV.i.13-23]

The tension seems to intensify slightly as Ferdinand interrupts the masque to exclaim that with a miracle-worker like Prospero for a father he could be happy to live on the island forever:

"Let me live here ever; / So rare and wond'red father and a wise / Makes this place Paradise" / (IV.i.122-24). No mention at all is made of Miranda, unless some copies of the Folio are correct (as is dubious) in printing "wife" for "wise." Prospero interrupts his rhapsodizing with:

> Sweet now, silence!
> Juno and Ceres whisper seriously;
> There's something else to do. Hush and be mute,
> Or else our spell is marr'd.
>
> [IV.i.124-27]

Prospero's uneasiness approaches violence as he suddenly remembers the design of Caliban and confederates upon his life and breaks the spell, forcing the dancers reluctantly to disperse. Ferdinand and Miranda are dismayed, both at the peremptory cancellation of the performance and at the older man's inexplicable anger. The point, which ought to be obvious to us who know of the mischief afoot, is not that Prospero is unable to cope with the threat but that unmet, the threat would be as lethal to him, he now realizes, as it would be to any other mortal. To repeat, for all his superior magic, he is not God; he is not even an Ariel.

The memorable speech in which Prospero reassures the young couple in this climax of his action constitutes an articulation of the epiphany that that action has provided, not only for Prospero but for all of us:

> Our revels now are ended. These our actors
> (As I foretold you) were all spirits, and
> Are melted into air, into thin air.
> And like the baseless fabric of this vision,
> The cloud-capp'd tow'rs, the gorgeous palaces,
> The solemn temples, the great globe itself,
> Yea, all which it inherit, shall dissolve,
> And like this insubstantial pageant faded
> Leave not a rack behind. We are such stuff
> As dreams are made on; and our little life
> Is rounded with a sleep.
>
> [IV.i.148-58]

Prospero's words here, if not his perceptions, completely transcend the situation in the play, encompassing masque, the island, Shakespeare's theater, the London of that theater, and the greater globe beyond in the same eternal flux. Whether we realize it or not at the moment of utterance, they proclaim the end of comedy for all the principals in the play, good and bad alike, and for the order that comedy has persuaded us to dream of and has seemed at times to present. That Prospero himself at last understands the end of the Renaissance world's most engaging fantasy is evidenced by his abrupt dismissal of the young people to such maturity and discretion as they may have already achieved. As we have already noted, here he no less abruptly abandons his master plan to rehabilitate the moral stature of his former enemies and quietly accepts the truth that Gonzalo will enunciate so beautifully nearer the end of the play:

> Was Milan thrust from Milan, that his issue
> Should become kings of Naples? O, rejoice
> Beyond a common joy, and set it down
> With gold on lasting pillars: in one voyage
> Did Claribel her husband find at Tunis,
> And Ferdinand, her brother, found a wife
> Where he himself was lost; Prospero, his dukedom
> In a poor isle; and all of us, ourselves,
> When no man was his own.
>
> [V.i.205-13]

To say that his play, or any image of the human action honestly portrayed, ends in comedy or tragedy is to say too little. To call it tragicomedy is an evasion. To say that it is divine comedy is more than we know and certainly more than Shakespeare allows. We can see clearly enough, however, that the action of a play like *The Tempest*, if it is to satisfy, must end in acceptances, of enemies as well as loved ones, not excluding any whom choice or circumstance has made one's neighbors. It is noble of Prospero to forgive his enemies, but it is especially to his credit that he can say finally of his neighbor Caliban, "This thing of darkness I acknowledge mine" (V.i.275-76). Above all, such a play must bring the key intelligence of the piece—again Prospero, the *senex*, the candidate for wisdom— to an acceptance of himself; and in the epilogue Prospero's last

words, appended to a bid for acceptance by the theater audience, make his self-knowledge and his acceptance explicit:

> Now I want
> Spirits to enforce, art to enchant,
> And my ending is despair,
> Unless I be relieved by prayer,
> Which pierces so, that it assaults
> Mercy itself, and frees all faults.
>> As you from crimes would pardon'd be,
>> Let your indulgence set me free.

This is all that can be said: the end of comedy and tragedy alike
is in the end a weariness of the flesh and complete hopelessness
unless there be grace beyond, the hope of which we seem
constitutionally unable to abandon but which lingers out of
reach if it is there at all.

Notes

1. Shakespeare's Exploration of the Human Comedy

1. The specific way in which this happened is irrelevant. Richard Hardin has taken to task recent critics, notably Northrop Frye and Francis Fergusson, who have written about the origin of Greek drama in primitive Greek ritual; see his article " 'Ritual' in Recent Criticism: The Elusive Sense of Community," *PMLA*, 98 (1983), 846-62. The value of these critics' work does not depend upon their accuracy about the precise path whereby the insights of primitive religion found their way into sophisticated literature. Both might well agree with the sentiment in Hardin's concluding sentence: "The prospects for a fuller understanding of ritual in relation to literature might be improved if we could agree that both these features of cultural life exist in an ecology . . . in which subject and object, worshiper and cult, reader (writer) and text acquire meaning only in the context of a community."

2. See especially Henri Bergson, *Creative Evolution*, trans. Arthur Mitchell (New York: Holt, 1911), pp. 1-39.

3. See especially Alfred North Whitehead, "The Order of Nature" and "God and the World," *Process and Reality*, ed. David Ray Griffin and Donald W. Sherburne (New York: Free Press, 1978), pp. 83-109, 342-51.

4. Susanne Langer, *Feeling and Form* (New York: Scribner's, 1953), pp. 327-28.

5. Henri Bergson, *Le Rire*, trans. Cloudsley Brereton and Ford Rothwell (New York: Macmillan, 1911), pp. 27-28.

6. J.L. Styan, *The Dramatic Experience: A Guide to the Reading of Plays* (Cambridge: Cambridge Univ. Press, 1965), p. 1.

7. Unless otherwise indicated, all quotations from Shakespeare in this study are taken from *The Riverside Shakespeare*, ed. G. Blakemore Evans (Boston: Houghton Mifflin, 1974).

8. According to Stevie Davies, however, Shakespeare was not alone in his awareness of woman's potential; see her recent study *The*

Feminine Reclaimed: The Idea of Woman in Spenser, Shakespeare, and Milton (Lexington: Univ. Press of Kentucky, 1985). The similarity between Shakespeare's idea of woman and that of Euripides has been set forth at length by Linda Lee Jacobs in her unpublished study, "Shakespeare and Euripides: The Androgynous Vision," Ph.D. Diss., University of Kentucky, 1985.

2. *The Comedy of Errors*

1. August Wilhelm Schlegel, *Lectures on Dramatic Art and Literature*, trans. John Black (London: George Bell, 1899), quoted by Harry Levin, ed., *The Comedy of Errors* (New York: New American Library, 1965), p. 160.
2. Samuel Taylor Coleridge, *Shakespearean Criticism*, ed. T.M. Raysor, 2nd ed. (New York: Dutton, 1960), II, 161.
3. William Hazlitt, *Characters of Shakespear's Plays* (London & Toronto: J.M. Dent & Sons; New York: E.P. Dutton & Co., 1906), pp. 253-55.
4. H.B. Charlton, *Shakespearian Comedy* (New York: Barnes & Noble, n.d.), pp. 47-72. (Charlton's book first appeared in London in 1938.)
5. Harold Brooks, "Themes and Structure in *The Comedy of Errors*," in *Early Shakespeare*, ed. J.R. Brown and B. Harris (London: Edward Arnold, 1961), pp. 55-71.
6. John Arthos, "Shakespeare's Transformation of Plautus," *Comparative Drama*, 1 (Winter 1967-68), 239-53.
7. Bertrand Evans, *Shakespeare's Comedies* (London: Oxford Univ. Press, 1960), p. 1.
8. Levin, ed., *The Comedy of Errors*, p. xxvii.
9. Unlike the Italians, Elizabethans apparently did not condone cuckoldry even when perpetrated in a good cause; and Shakespeare, though he had characters joke about it (Portia in *The Merchant of Venice*) and ridiculously attempt to accomplish it (*The Merry Wives of Windsor*), nowhere treated it sympathetically or seriously.
10. Evans, *Shakespeare's Comedies*, pp. 3-4.

3. *The Two Gentlemen of Verona*

1. T.W. Baldwin, *William Shakspere's Small Latine and Lesse Greeke* (Urbana: Univ. of Illinois Press, 1944), I, 641-42.
2. See O.J. Campbell, "*Two Gentlemen of Verona* and Italian Comedy," *Studies in Shakespeare, Milton, and Donne*, Univ. of Michigan Publications in Language and Literature, No. 1 (Ann Arbor: Univ. of Michigan Press, 1925), pp. 49-63.
3. All the principal sources for *The Two Gentlemen of Verona* are

presented and discussed in Geoffrey Bullough, *Narrative and Dramatic Sources of Shakespeare* (London: Routledge & Kegan Paul; New York: Columbia Univ. Press, 1957), I, 203-68.

4. Marianne Moore, "Poetry," in *Poems* (London: Egoist Press, 1921).

5. See Howard Nemerov, Introd., *The Two Gentlemen of Verona*, ed. Francis Fergusson (New York: Dell, 1965), pp. 24-25; and also Charlton, *Shakespearian Comedy*, pp. 41-43.

6. Sir Arthur Quiller-Couch, ed., *The Two Gentlemen of Verona* (Cambridge: Cambridge Univ. Press, 1921), p. xiv.

7. Ralph M. Sargent, "Sir Thomas Elyot and the Integrity of *The Two Gentlemen of Verona*," *PMLA*, 65 (1950), 1166-80.

8. II.i.172 and II.iv.26. The third reference appears in *3 Henry VI*; see below. The fourth is in *Hamlet*, III.ii.93.

9. Charlton, *Shakespearian Comedy*, p. 38.

4. *Love's Labor's Lost*

1. George L. Kittredge, ed., *The Complete Works of Shakespeare* (Boston: Ginn, 1936), p. 193.

2. Castiglione, *The Book of the Courtier*, trans. Thomas Hoby, in *Three Renaissance Classics*, ed. Burton A. Milligan (New York: Scribner's, 1953), p. 615.

3. See M.C. Bradbrook, *The School of Night: A Study in the Literary Relationships of Sir Walter Raleigh* (Cambridge: Cambridge Univ. Press, 1936); and Frances A. Yates, *A Study of "Love's Labour's Lost"* (Cambridge: Cambridge Univ. Press, 1936).

4. The term is, of course, Spenser's, *Amoretti*, Sonnet 1.

5. Following Berowne, who is not to be relied on at this point, V.ii.542.

6. This is a part of the conclusion that R.G. Hunter reaches in his illuminating article, "The Songs at the End of *Love's Labour's Lost*," *Shakespeare Studies*, Vol. 7, ed. J. Leeds Barroll (Columbia: Univ. of South Carolina Press, 1974), pp. 55-64.

5. *A Midsummer Night's Dream*

1. For examples, see E.K. Chambers, *William Shakespeare: A Study of Facts and Problems* (Oxford: Clarendon Press, 1930), I, 360.

2. Enid Welsford, *The Court Masque* (Cambridge: Cambridge Univ. Press, 1927), pp. 324-36.

3. Some would end the play with the conclusion of Theseus's last speech (V.i.370), arguing that the epithalamium of Oberon and Titania that follows is suitable for a wedding but inappropriate for a public performance. One should note, however, that their joint bless-

ing of the chamber and bed of Theseus and Hippolyta completes their action and is quite appropriate in any case as a mark of the reconciliation of that feuding pair. Robin's epilogue, which follows (it is actually his second one), is clearly a theatrical bid for applause.

4. Frank Kermode, "The Mature Comedies," in *Early Shakespeare*, ed. John Russell Brown and Bernard Harris, Stratford-upon-Avon Studies, No. 3 (London: Edward Arnold, 1961), p. 214.

5. John Palmer, in *Political and Comic Characters of Shakespeare* (London: Macmillan, 1965), pp. 440-57.

6. A useful study here is Minor White Latham, *The Elizabethan Fairies* (New York: Columbia Univ. Press, 1930); but more recently K.M. Briggs has brought additional material to bear on the subject and corrected the notion, proposed by Latham and others, that Shakespeare gave some of the fairies their diminutive size. See Briggs, *The Anatomy of Puck* (London: Routledge & Kegan Paul, 1959), pp. 12-16, 44-47.

7. Briggs, *Anatomy of Puck*, p. 15.

8. Ibid., p. 71. See also C.L. Barber, *Shakespeare's Festive Comedy: A Study of Dramatic Form and Its Relation to Social Custom* (Princeton, N.J.: Princeton Univ. Press, 1959), pp. 130-31.

9. Paul L. Olson, "*A Midsummer Night's Dream* and the Meaning of Court Marriage," *ELH*, 24 (1957), 112.

10. "If we have unearned luck / Now to scape the serpent's tongue, . . ." (V.i.432-33).

11. Northrop Frye, "The Argument of Comedy," in *English Institute Essays, 1948*, ed. D.A. Robertson, Jr. (New York: Columbia Univ. Press, 1949), pp. 67-68. Barber develops this insight, giving the woods special credit: "The woods are established as a region of metamorphosis, where in liquid moonlight or glimmering starlight, things can change, merge and melt into each other," *Shakespeare's Festive Comedy*, p. 133; the discussion continues, pp. 133-36.

12. Marjorie Garber has perceptive comments on this point with respect to a number of plays in the canon, including *A Midsummer Night's Dream*; see her *Coming of Age in Shakespeare* (London and New York: Methuen, 1981), especially pp. 116-43.

13. See S.B. Hemingway, "The Relation of *A Midsummer Night's Dream* to *Romeo and Juliet*," *Modern Language Notes*, 24 (1911), 78-80.

14. Barber aptly notes that Lysander here "describes in little the sort of tragedy presented in *Romeo and Juliet*," *Shakespeare's Festive Comedy*, p. 126.

15. Leo Salingar comments briefly but cogently on the role of chance in Shakespearean comedy, *Shakespeare and the Traditions of Comedy* (Cambridge: Cambridge Univ. Press, 1974), pp. 23, 227-28.

16. Barber makes a good case for taking it so (*Shakespeare's Festive Comedy*, pp. 120-21), but observes: "This Maying can be thought of as happening on a midsummer night, even on Midsummer Eve itself." David P. Young discusses the matter at some length and also seems to favor a linking of May Day and Midsummer Eve, *Something of Great*

Constancy: The Art of "A Midsummer Night's Dream" (New Haven, Conn.: Yale Univ. Press, 1966), pp. 18-21.

17. Barber concludes his account of the play with some interesting observations about the dreams in it and about the shadow-substance antithesis in Shakespeare generally, *Shakespeare's Festive Comedy*, pp. 157-62.

18. Latham, *The Elizabethan Fairies*, pp. 176-218.

19. Mark Van Doren, *Shakespeare* (Garden City, N.Y.: Anchor-Doubleday, 1953), p. xii.

20. Salingar, *Shakespeare and the Traditions of Comedy*, p. 228.

6. *The Merchant of Venice*

1. Elmer E. Stoll, "Shylock," *Journal of English and Germanic Philology*, 10 (1911), 236-79.

2. See Lawrence Danson's balanced account in *The Harmonies of "The Merchant of Venice"* (New Haven, Conn.: Yale Univ. Press, 1978), pp. 126-69.

3. Harley Granville-Barker, *Prefaces to Shakespeare* (Princeton, N.J.: Princeton Univ. Press, 1946), pp. 335-36.

4. The texts of all the sources of *The Merchant of Venice* are in Bullough, *Sources of Shakespeare*, I, 445-514.

5. Van Doren, *Shakespeare*, p. 81.

6. Thomas H. Fujimura, "Mode and Structure in *The Merchant of Venice*," *PMLA*, 81 (1966), 499-511.

7. *The Taming of the Shrew*

1. References to the text of *The Taming of a Shrew* are to the edition published in Bullough, *Sources of Shakespeare*, I, 69-108. The text of Gascoigne's *Supposes* is also in this volume.

2. The best discussion of what Shakespeare "does with the genre of farce" in this play is that by Robert B. Heilman, editor of the Signet Classic edition of the play (New York: New American Library, 1966), pp. xxxi-xlii.

3. The most influential piece in the development of our modern interpretation of Kate is probably that by H.C. Goddard in *The Meaning of Shakespeare* (Chicago: Univ. of Chicago Press, 1951), I, 68-73.

4. J. Dennis Huston in an interesting analysis of Petruchio finds in him the Shakespearean equivalent of the Aristophanic comic hero, *Shakespeare's Comedies of Play* (New York: Columbia Univ. Press, 1981), pp. 60-62.

5. Bullough, *Sources of Shakespeare*, I, 123.

6. Coppelia Kahn, *Man's Estate: Masculine Identity in Shakespeare* (Berkeley and Los Angeles: Univ. of California Press, 1981), pp. 114-18.

7. George Meredith, *An Essay on Comedy and the Uses of the Comic Spirit* (New York: Scribner's, 1897), pp. 54-55.

8. Though he does not deal with *The Taming of the Shrew*, R.G. Hunter might well have included Katherina in his *Shakespeare and the Comedy of Forgiveness* (New York: Columbia Univ. Press, 1965).

8. *The Merry Wives of Windsor*

1. See O.J. Campbell, "The Italianate Background of *The Merry Wives of Windsor*," Univ. of Michigan Publications in Language and Literature, No. 8 (Ann Arbor: Univ. of Michigan Press, 1932), pp. 81-117; and Salingar, *Shakespeare and the Traditions of Comedy*, pp. 228-38.

2. Few have challenged the assertions of John Dennis (1702) and Nicholas Rowe (1709) that Shakespeare wrote *The Merry Wives* in response to Queen Elizabeth's expressed wish to see Falstaff in love. Jeanne Addison Roberts, however, has argued convincingly for an earlier date than most critics, who have tended to assume that the play was written after *Henry V*. See her *Shakespeare's English Comedy: "The Merry Wives of Windsor" in Context* (Lincoln: Univ. of Nebraska Press, 1979), pp. 41-50. Roberts believes that Shakespeare received the Queen's expression of interest when halfway through composition of *2 Henry IV*, and interrupted work to write the unscheduled comedy. This argument has the great merit of putting the Falstaff of *The Merry Wives* where he belongs, in the line of a consistently developing character whom we last see in the concluding act of *2 Henry IV*.

3. See Roberts's survey of the shifts in critical judgment of the Windsor Falstaff, *Shakespeare's English Comedy*, pp. 84-118.

4. Frye, "Argument of Comedy," p. 69.

5. Sir James G. Frazer, *The Golden Bough*, 11 vols. (1911-15; rpt. London: Macmillan, 1955); F.M. Cornford, *The Origin of Attic Comedy* (London: Edward Arnold, 1914); Jane Harrison, *Prolegomena to the Study of Greek Religion*, 3rd ed. (Cambridge: Cambridge Univ. Press, 1922).

6. Frazer, *Golden Bough*, IV, 235.

7. Ibid., pp. 236-37.

8. Ibid., IX, 211-12.

9. Ibid., p. 212.

10. Ibid., pp. 227-28.

11. Barber, *Shakespeare's Festive Comedy*, pp. 206-9.

12. Langer, *Feeling and Form*, pp. 348-49.

9. *Much Ado about Nothing*

1. It is common among producers and critics to put the "merry war" between Beatrice and Benedick in focus and let the rest of the

action serve as background. See the discussion by Larry Champion, *The Evolution of Shakespeare's Comedy: A Study in Dramatic Perspective* (Cambridge, Mass.: Harvard Univ. Press, 1970), pp. 67-81, and his note (p. 203) on critics who implicitly acknowledge the priority of these lovers, "though they almost apologetically continue to speak of Hero and Claudio as the main plot."

2. One example is Franco Zeffirelli's movie version of the play (1966).

3. Salingar characterizes *Much Ado about Nothing, The Merchant of Venice, All's Well That Ends Well,* and *Measure for Measure* as plays in which "an interest in character and morality competes with, and threatens or overshadows, the festive mood," *Shakespeare and the Traditions of Comedy*, p. 18. All four plays have novella sources, and Salingar details the connections between them at some length (pp. 314-21).

4. At the beginnings of Acts I and II. There is no mention of her at the wedding.

5. Mark Twain, *Huckleberry Finn* (New York: Collier, n.d.), pp. 306-7.

6. The text is in Bullough, *Sources of Shakespeare*, II, 112-34.

7. Few critics defend Claudio absolutely, but fewer still take him seriously as a lover. One exception is Hunter, who writes, "Claudio's brutal denunciation of Hero is the result of his former love for her—a love that has been transformed into a hatred all the more intense because it was formerly love," *Comedy of Forgiveness*, p. 101. Hunter goes on to see in Claudio an anticipation of Posthumus, who also falls victim to false appearance and subsequently merits forgiveness by his contrition.

8. The phrase is Castiglione's, *The Book of the Courtier*, p. 604.

9. Ralph Berry finds Claudio's reliance here upon the sense of sight without reference to the controls of judgment and experience an error in "knowing" that is widespread in the play and is central to the action. His discussion of this point is very useful, *Shakespeare's Comedies: Explorations in Form* (Princeton, N.J.: Princeton Univ. Press, 1972), pp. 154-74.

10. David Lloyd Stevenson found the problem not in Claudio's love but in the incompatibility of that love with the world in which it had to operate: "Romantic sentiment had been disciplined by Berowne and by the ladies of *Love's Labour's Lost* and had been parodied by Touchstone, Jaques, and Rosalind, in *As You Like It*. In Shakespeare's final love-game comedy, *Much Ado About Nothing*, romance is shadowed for the first time by the threat that an attempt to adapt it to everyday reality could lead to an outcome not in the least comic. . . . Claudio's entanglement presents in a harsh and derisive manner the ironies and paradoxes involved when Elizabethan romantic sentiment sought fulfillment in the actual world of the sixteenth century." *The Love-Game Comedy* (New York: Columbia Univ. Press, 1946), pp. 208-15.

11. Walter N. King comments tellingly, "It is here that the social abnormality of aristocratic society in Messina is exposed once and for all for what it is—shallow and perverse application of a standard of behavior that is both automatic and uncharitable." "*Much Ado About Something,*" *Shakespeare Quarterly*, 15 (1964), 150.

12. John Russell Brown in *Shakespeare and His Comedies*, 2nd ed. (London: Methuen, 1962), p. 123, sees this as a happy course for Claudio and Hero: "In the end their love is justified by his imaginative recognition of the 'sweet idea' of Hero's true beauty." This view of the situation is interesting but highly speculative; nothing in Claudio's behavior before or after his reunion with Hero suggests it.

13. For example, Alexander Leggatt sees it as a signaling that must be achieved in the formal staging of the scene, "if it is well staged (as there is no excuse for it not to be)," *Shakespeare's Comedy of Love* (London: Methuen, 1974), p. 165.

14. Evans in his comment on the play finds the Claudio-Hero story dispiriting in almost every way, but he feels that the affair of Beatrice and Benedick redeems it. He notes their kiss in Act V but overlooks the fact that Benedick immediately thereafter makes peace with the "opposition." *Shakespeare's Comedies*, p. 87.

15. Francis Fergusson, *The Human Image in Dramatic Literature* (New York: Doubleday, 1957), p. 157.

16. Salingar, *Shakespeare and the Traditions of Comedy*, p. 312.

10. *As You Like It*

1. The 1590 text of *Rosalynde* is printed in full in Bullough, *Sources of Shakespeare*, II, 158-256.

2. Helen Gardner, "*As You Like It,*" in *More Talking of Shakespeare*, ed. John Garrett (London: Longmans, Green, 1959); rpt. in Kenneth Muir, ed., *Shakespeare: The Comedies: A Collection of Critical Essays* (Englewood Cliffs, N.J.: Prentice-Hall, 1965), p. 60.

3. On this point see the *Oxford English Dictionary*.

4. For example, see Harold Jenkins, "*As You Like It,*" *Shakespeare Survey 8*, ed. Allardyce Nicoll (London: Cambridge Univ. Press, 1955); rpt. in Jay Halio, ed., *Twentieth Century Interpretations of "As You Like It"* (Englewood Cliffs, N.J.: Prentice-Hall, 1968), pp. 38-40.

5. This is not to deny the validity of S.L. Bethell's perceptive comments on the artificiality of *As You Like It* in his chapter "Planes of Reality," *Shakespeare and the Popular Dramatic Tradition* (Durham, N.C.: Duke Univ. Press, 1944), pp. 34-38. This play throughout, more than almost any other, tends to support Bethell's thesis that the Elizabethan audience was accustomed "to respond spontaneously and unconsciously on more than one plane of attention at the same time" (p. 26).

6. Similar points have been made about all of Shakespeare's plays, most notably by T.W. Baldwin, *The Organization and Personnel*

of the Shakespearean Company (Princeton: Princeton Univ. Press, 1927).

7. See J. Dover Wilson, *Shakespeare's Happy Comedies* (Evanston, Ill.: Northwestern Univ. Press; London: Faber & Faber, 1962), p. 151; and the brief objection by David Young, *The Heart's Forest: A Study of Shakespeare's Pastoral Plays* (New Haven, Conn.: Yale Univ. Press, 1972), p. 43.

8. Young, *Heart's Forest*, p. 50.

9. Frye, "The Argument of Comedy," p. 67. See also Frye's *A Natural Perspective: The Development of Shakespearean Comedy and Romance* (New York: Columbia Univ. Press, 1965), especially pp. 118-59.

10. Anne Barton, "*As You Like It* and *Twelfth Night*: Shakespeare's Sense of an Ending," in *Shakespearian Comedy*, ed. David Palmer and Malcolm Bradbury, Stratford-upon-Avon Studies, No. 14 (London: Edward Arnold, 1972), p. 162.

11. *Selected Essays of Montaigne in the Translation of John Florio*, ed. Walter Kaiser (Boston: Houghton Mifflin, 1964), p. 72.

12. This is the implication of Charlton's remarks about romantic comedy in general and *As You Like It* in particular, *Shakespearian Comedy*, pp. 283ff.

13. Many critics make this point, but they vary widely in their interpretations of what the discordant notes mean. See Barton, "*As You Like It* and *Twelfth Night*," p. 166; and Barber, *Shakespeare's Festive Comedy*, pp. 228-29. Barber has a useful discussion of this and related points, but he sees Shakespeare as making fun of an evoked ideal life "because it does not square with life as it ordinarily is." The ideals that Jaques makes fun of, however, are those we often take to our bosom; and thus he satirizes all of us in a fundamental way. Contrary to Barber's view, the "infected body of the world" is very much in evidence in Shakespeare's Arden.

14. Barton, "*As You Like It* and *Twelfth Night*," p. 166. Barton, however, sees a Jaques of "sudden dignity" in the last scene of the play, and she applauds his comments there.

15. Anne Barton, Introduction to *As You Like It*, in *The Riverside Shakespeare*, p. 367.

16. Barton, *Riverside Shakespeare*, p. 367.

17. Barton, "*As You Like It* and *Twelfth Night*," p. 166.

18. See Gardner, "*As You Like It*," p. 69.

11. *Twelfth Night*

1. Leo Salingar, "The Design of *Twelfth Night*," *Shakespeare Quarterly*, 9 (1958), 117.

2. In Johnson's edition of *The Plays of William Shakespeare* (London, 1765); see *Johnson as Critic*, ed. John Wain (London & Boston: Routledge & Kegan Paul, 1973), pp. 188-89.

3. J. Dover Wilson, *Shakespeare's Happy Comedies*, p. 181.

4. Kenneth Muir, *The Sources of Shakespeare's Plays* (New Haven, Conn.: Yale Univ. Press, 1977), p. 132.

5. T.W. Baldwin, *William Shakespere's Five-Act Structure* (Urbana: Univ. of Illinois Press, 1947), p. 715.

6. Salingar, *Shakespeare and the Traditions of Comedy*, pp. 8-19; Barber, *Shakespeare's Festive Comedy*, pp. 248ff.

7. Carolyn G. Heilbrun, *Toward a Recognition of Androgyny* (New York: Knopf, 1973), pp. 36-37.

8. Walter N. King, ed., *Twentieth Century Interpretations of "Twelfth Night"* (Englewood Cliffs, N.J.: Prentice-Hall, 1968), pp. 5-12.

9. Joseph Summers, "The Masks of *Twelfth Night*," *The University of Kansas City Review*, 22 (Autumn 1955), 30-32.

10. Ibid., p. 24.

11. Some critics see in Sir Toby's advocacy of Sir Andrew Aguecheek merely a device to bilk the fool of his money; see Van Doren, *Shakespeare*, p. 139. This does not quite account, however, for Sir Toby's eagerness to press for a duel with Cesario-Viola once he has detected a hint of real rivalry in that quarter.

12. According to *The Riverside Shakespeare*, p. 364, the attribution of the speech to Benedick and the stage direction about kissing originated with Styan Thirlby and Lewis Theobald, respectively.

13. See John Vyvyan, *Shakespeare and Platonic Beauty* (London: Chatto & Windus, 1961), pp. 33-62.

14. See the text in Bullough, *Sources of Shakespeare*, II, 346.

15. See the essay by Milton Crane, "*Twelfth Night* and Shakespearian Comedy," *Shakespeare Quarterly*, 6 (1955), 1-8.

16. Charles Lamb, "On Some of the Old Actors," in *Elia. Essays which have appeared under the signature in The London Magazine* (London: Taylor & Hessey, 1823); quoted in Herschel Baker, ed., *Twelfth Night* (New York: New American Library, 1965), pp. 172-73.

17. Van Doren, *Shakespeare*, p. 143.

18. Bethell, *Shakespeare and the Popular Dramatic Tradition*, p. 178.

19. This was a summer production of 1966. Sir Andrew Aguecheek was given unusual prominence, with David Warner in the role.

12. *Troilus and Cressida*

1. R.A. Foakes, "*Troilus and Cressida* Reconsidered," *Univ. of Toronto Quarterly*, 32 (January 1963), 142.

2. See Harold Wilson, *On the Design of Shakespearean Tragedy* (Toronto: Univ. of Toronto Press, 1957); and Brian Morris, "The Tragic Structure of *Troilus and Cressida*," *Shakespeare Quarterly*, 10 (1959), 481-92.

3. See O.J. Campbell's two studies, *Comicall Satyre and Shakespeare's "Troilus and Cressida"* (San Marino, Calif.: Huntington Library, 1938) and *Shakespeare's Satire* (London and New York: Oxford Univ. Press, 1931). Among those who see in the play a serious reflection

on life are W.W. Lawrence. *Shakespeare's Problem Comedies* (New York and London: Macmillan, 1931) and L.C. Knights, "The Theme of Appearance and Reality in *Troilus and Cressida*," in *Some Shakespearean Themes* (Palo Alto, Calif.: Stanford Univ. Press, 1959), pp. 65-83.

4. *Henry V*, II.i.76, and *Twelfth Night*, III.i.55.

5. See Anne Barton's introductory essay to the play in *The Riverside Shakespeare*, pp. 443-47.

6. Bethell, *Shakespeare and the Popular Dramatic Tradition*, pp. 124-28.

7. See Barton, *Riverside Shakespeare*, p. 446.

13. *All's Well That Ends Well* and *Measure for Measure*

1. *The Book of Common Prayer, 1559: The Elizabethan Prayer Book*, ed. John E. Booty (Charlottesville: Univ. Press of Virginia, 1976), p. 290.

2. Salingar, *Shakespeare and the Traditions of Comedy*, p. 16.

3. Ibid., p. 17.

4. See Bullough's discussion, *Sources of Shakespeare*, II, 381-88.

5. See the discussions by W.W. Lawrence, "The Meaning of *All's Well That Ends Well*," *PMLA*, 37 (1922), 418-69; by Anne Barton in her introduction to the play in *The Riverside Shakespeare*, pp. 499-503; and by Bullough, *Sources of Shakespeare*, II, 375-80.

6. Barton, *Riverside Shakespeare*, p. 502.

7. M.C. Bradbrook, "Virtue Is the True Nobility: A Study of the Structure of *All's Well That Ends Well*," *Review of English Studies*, 26 (1950), 298-99.

8. G. Wilson Knight, *The Sovereign Flower* (London: Methuen, 1958), pp. 131-57.

9. Barton, *Riverside Shakespeare*, p. 500.

10. *Johnson as Critic*, ed. Wain, pp. 193-94.

11. See, for example, Nevill Coghill, "Comic Form in *Measure for Measure*," *Shakespeare Survey*, 8 (1955), 22-25.

12. See the treatment of the play by Hunter, *Comedy of Forgiveness*, pp. 204-26.

13. Bernard Knox, "*The Tempest* and the Ancient Comic Tradition," *English Institute Essays, 1954*, ed. W.K. Wimsatt (New York: Columbia Univ. Press, 1955), pp. 52-73.

14. *Cymbeline* and *The Winter's Tale*

1. *The Complete Plays and Poems of William Shakespeare*, ed. William Allan Neilson and Charles Jarvis Hill (Boston: Houghton Mifflin, 1942), p. 426.

2. Carol Gesner, *Shakespeare and the Greek Romance: A Study of Origins* (Lexington: Univ. Press of Kentucky, 1970), pp. 80ff.

3. See especially Joan Hartwig, *Shakespeare's Tragicomic Vision* (Baton Rouge: Louisiana State Univ. Press, 1972).

4. See Eugene M. Waith, *The Pattern of Tragicomedy in Beaumont and Fletcher* (New Haven, Conn.: Yale Univ. Press, 1952), pp. 36-42.

5. Gesner (*Shakespeare and the Greek Romance*, pp. 47-79) finds elements of Greek romance in a wide variety of plays, including *The Comedy of Errors, Twelfth Night, Romeo and Juliet, Much Ado about Nothing, Othello,* and *As You Like It.*

6. The sources of all three of these plays are presented and discussed in Bullough, *Sources of Shakespeare,* VIII.

7. Ibid., p. 44.

8. Ibid., p. 43.

9. Frye, "Argument of Comedy," p. 72.

10. G. Wilson Knight, *The Crown of Life: Essays in Interpretation of Shakespeare's Final Plays* (New York: Barnes & Noble, 1966), p. 129.

11. J.A. Bryant, Jr., *Hippolyta's View: Some Christian Aspects of Shakespeare's Plays* (Lexington: Univ. of Kentucky Press, 1961), pp. 207-225.

12. See Hallett Smith, *Shakespeare's Romances* (San Marino, Calif.: Huntington Library, 1972), p. 118. This sense of "allegory" is presented in some detail in Bryant, *Hippolyta's View,* pp. 4-9.

13. Francis Fergusson, *The Idea of a Theater* (Princeton, N.J.: Princeton Univ. Press, 1949), pp. 234-36.

14. St. Augustine, *The City of God,* XVI.37, trans. Marcus Dods (New York: Random House, 1950), p. 560.

15. *The Tempest*

1. Northrop Frye, Introduction to *The Tempest,* in *William Shakespeare: The Complete Works,* ed. Alfred Harbage (Baltimore: Penguin, 1969), p. 1371.

2. Hallett Smith, "*The Tempest* as Kaleidoscope," in *Twentieth-Century Interpretations of "The Tempest,"* (Englewood Cliffs, N.J.: Prentice-Hall, 1969), p. 6. In his introduction to the play in *The Riverside Shakespeare* (p. 1606), Smith calls the location of the island "ambiguous."

3. Frank Kermode, ed., *The Tempest,* in The Arden Shakespeare (Cambridge, Mass.: Harvard Univ. Press, 1958), pp. xxv-xxvi.

4. Bullough, *Sources of Shakespeare,* VIII, 275-99.

5. D.G. James, *The Dream of Prospero* (Oxford: Clarendon Press, 1967), pp. 72-123.

6. From the title of Silvester Jourdain's account of the Gates shipwreck.

7. Bernard Knox, "*The Tempest,*" pp. 52-73.

8. Ibid., p. 54.

9. Ibid., p. 53.

10. W.C. Curry, *Shakespeare's Philosophical Patterns* (Baton Rouge: Louisiana State Univ. Press, 1937).

11. Van Doren, *Shakespeare*, p. 282.

12. Ibid., p. 283.

13. Curry, *Shakespeare's Philosophical Patterns*, pp. 184-85.

14. For example, see J. Dover Wilson, *The Essential Shakespeare* (Cambridge: Cambridge Univ. Press, 1932), p. 143.

15. At the beginning of his conversation with Miranda in Act I, Scene 2, Prospero makes a point of putting aside his magic and dealing with the girl purely in his role as father (lines 23-25). He even asks her to help remove his mantle, which is presumably his badge and instrument of office. At line 169, however, sensing that Ariel is approaching to give his report, Prospero stands; and many editors here follow John Payne Collier in supplying the stage direction "Puts on his robe." Miranda's interest is now at its peak, and her mind is "beating" to hear a full account of Prospero's reasons for raising the tempest, but he tells her, "Here cease more questions. / Thou art inclin'd to sleep; 'tis a good dullness, / And give it way. I know thou canst not choose." Accordingly, editors here supply the stage direction "Miranda sleeps." The point should be made, however, that Prospero's magic never depended upon his mantle and that he could and did put Miranda to sleep without warning and when she was least ready for it. Only Collier's added stage direction at line 169 saves Prospero from this imputation.

16. Knox, "*The Tempest*," p. 62.

Index